IAN McKELLEN

Also by Garry O'Connor

BIOGRAPHY

The Pursuit of Perfection: A Life of Maggie Teyte
Ralph Richardson: An Actor's Life
Darlings of the Gods: One Year in the Lives of Laurence Olivier and Vivien Leigh
Sean O'Casey: A Life
The Mahabharata: Peter Brook's Epic in the Making
The Secret Woman: A Life of Peggy Ashcroft
William Shakespeare: A Popular Life
Paul Scofield: The Biography
Alec Guinness, the Unknown: A Life
Universal Father: A Life of John Paul II
The Darlings of Downing Street: The Psychosexual Drama of Power
The 1st Household Cavalry Regiment 1943–44: In the Shadow of Monte Amaro
Subdued Fires: An Intimate Portrait of Pope Benedict XVI
The Butcher of Poland: Hitler's Lawyer Hans Frank
The Vagabond Lover: A Father–Son Memoir

FICTION

Chaucer's Triumph
The Book That Kills
Death's Duel

DRAMA

Debussy Was My Grandfather / The Madness of Vivien Leigh: Two Plays
Semmelweis / De Raptu Meo: Two Plays

IAN McKELLEN

A BIOGRAPHY

Garry O'Connor

St. Martin's Press
New York

First published in the United States by
St. Martin's Press, an imprint of St. Martin's Publishing Group

IAN McKELLEN. Copyright © 2019 by Garry O'Connor.
All rights reserved. Printed in the United States of America.
For information, address St. Martin's Publishing Group,
120 Broadway, New York, NY 10271.

www.stmartins.com

Library of Congress Cataloging-in-Publication Data

Names: O'Connor, Garry, author.
Title: Ian McKellen : a biography / Garry O'Connor.
Description: First U.S. edition. | New York : St. Martin's Press, 2019.
Identifiers: LCCN 2019032544 | ISBN 9781250223883 (hardcover) |
    ISBN 9781250257550 (ebook)
Subjects: LCSH: McKellen, Ian. | Actors—Great Britain—Biography.
Classification: LCC PN2598.M478 O27 2019 | DDC 792.02/8092
    [B]—dc23
LC record available at https://lccn.loc.gov/2019032544

Our books may be purchased in bulk for promotional, educational,
or business use. Please contact your local bookseller or the
Macmillan Corporate and Premium Sales Department
at 1-800-221-7945, extension 5442, or by email
at MacmillanSpecialMarkets@macmillan.com.

Originally published in Great Britain by Weidenfeld & Nicolson, an
imprint of The Orion Publishing Group Ltd, an Hachette UK company

First U.S. Edition: November 2019

10 9 8 7 6 5 4 3 2 1

In memory of Winston Peter O'Connor,
born and died 20 September 2011

'Grief fills the room up of my absent child,
Lies in his bed, walks up and down with me'

William Shakespeare, *King John*

By the study of their biographies, we receive each man as a guest into our minds, and we seem to understand their character as the result of a personal acquaintance, because we have obtained from their acts the best and most important means of forming an opinion about them. 'What greater pleasure could'st thou gain than this?' What more valuable for the elevation of our own character?

Plutarch, Life of Timoleon

Contents

List of Illustrations   xi

PART ONE — Chance or Providence?

1   The Brown God   3
2   The Clatter of Clogs   11
3   Unfinished Business   24
4   The Mafia   34
5   Undeclared but Hidden Passion   48
6   Encounter with a Giant   53
7   We Can't Match Him   59
8   *Jeunesse Dorée* in Dour Edinburgh   65
9   Travels with My Peers   79
10 Wolfitting down Hamlet   83
11 Actors Seize Power!   91
12 One Step Forward, Two Back – or One Back, Two   101
     Forward?
13 The Matching of Equals   110

PART TWO — Atrocities and Absurdities

14 Enter Ganymede   123
15 Validation   130
16 The Robot Factory   137
17 Body and Soul   153
18 The Other Strong Yearning   164

19	Pay-off Performance	171
20	Not So Much in the Cupboard but in the Safe	177
21	Self-Awakening to Spirit	185
22	Who Was Olivier's True Heir?	189
23	Underneath All the Tolerance	202
24	Shining a Light through Celluloid	210
25	New Labour Interlude	218
26	Hollywood God Hubris	221

PART THREE — Casting Final Spells

27	Your Double Goes Before You	237
28	A Footfall of Memory Interlude	254
29	Saturnalia Time	257
30	Tergiversator	270
31	Double Standards	276
32	Interlude: The McKellen Banterland	286
33	It's a Mad, Mad World, My Masters	295
34	Small Men Locked in a Big Space	303
35	What Do We Do Now We're Happy? Vicious Old Queens	308
36	Corporate Caretaking	316
37	Gandalf Doesn't Do Weddings – Neither Does Lear	323
38	Finale	329
	Acknowledgements	339

List of Illustrations

FIRST PLATE SECTION

Birthplace in Burnley (Author's own)
Childhood home in Bolton (Author's own)
Docklands home (*The Times*/News Licensing)
With Sean Mathias in The Grapes (Eyevine/Adrian Lourie)
Peter Cook (John Bulmer)
In *Six Characters in Search of an Author* (John Bulmer)
In *Deutsches Haus* with Margaret Drabble (John Bulmer)
In *Richard II* (Don Smith/*Radio Times*/Getty)
In *Ruling the Roost* with Caroline Blakiston (Photostage/Donald Cooper)
In *Twelfth Night* with Roger Rees (ArenaPAL/Chris Davis)
In *Too True to Be Good* with Judi Dench (Photostage/Donald Cooper)
In *Romeo and Juliet* with Francesca Annis (Photostage/Donald Cooper)
In *'Tis Pity She's a Whore* with Paola Dionisotti (Photostage/Donald Cooper)
In *Dr Faustus* (Photostage/Donald Cooper)
In *Macbeth* with Judi Dench (Photostage/Donald Cooper)
In *Coriolanus* with Gregory Hicks (Alamy/Mirrorpix)
In *The Alchemist* with Paul Brooke (Photostage/Donald Cooper)
Meeting President Jimmy Carter while performing *Amadeus* in Washington (Shutterstock/Jeff Taylor/AP)
At Downing Street to meet Prime Minister John Major (*The Times*/News Licensing)

Protesting outside the Russian Embassy in London with Peter Tatchell (Alamy/Carol Moir)

In *Othello* (Photostage/Donald Cooper)

SECOND PLATE SECTION

In *Priest of Love* with Janet Suzman (Alamy/Everett Collection)

In *Walter* (Alamy/Moviestore)

In *Richard III* (Alamy/Allstar Picture Library)

In *Apt Pupil* (Alamy/Sportsphoto)

In *Gods and Monsters* (Alamy/Everett Collection)

In *X-Men 2* with Rebecca Romijn (Alamy/Moviestore Collection)

In *The Fellowship of the Ring* (Alamy/AF Archive)

In *The Return of the King* (Shutterstock/Pierre Vinet/New Line Cinema/Kobal)

At the royal film performance of *An Unexpected Journey* with Cate Blanchett (Getty/Dave M. Benett/Wire Image)

In *Uncle Vanya* with Antony Sher (Photostage/Donald Cooper)

In *Aladdin* with Roger Allam (Shutterstock/Alastair Muir)

In *Waiting for Godot* with Patrick Stewart (Getty/Walter McBride)

At the Empire Awards with Patrick Stewart (Getty/Ian Gavan)

In *Vicious* with Derek Jacobi (Shutterstock/Alastair Muir)

In *All Is True* (Alamy/Entertainment Pictures)

In *Mr. Holmes* (Alamy/Everett Collection)

In *King Lear* with Romola Garai, 2007 production (Alastair Muir/Shutterstock)

In *King Lear* with Danny Webb, 2018 production (ArenaPAL/Johan Persson)

ONE

Chance or Providence?

1

The Brown God

I knock on the front door. The docklands home of Ian Mc-Kellen is in a terrace, on a road with double yellow lines either side, and through which hardly more than one car can pass at a time. The blue door opens as if by itself onto a view of books on shelves. No sight of McK.

'Come in! I'll be with you in a moment,' a familiar voice calls out. At a glance the house is narrow, with a long room running its length to a full-width window with a step or two up to a riverside balcony and a bust of Shakespeare. It is on five floors, a lower floor, a ground floor and bedroom storeys. Elegant with stripped wood, the aura is Victorian. It resembles a cabin; reverse the house through ninety degrees, and I can well imagine it as the below-deck of a royal river-boat: like Cleopatra's barge, the burnished throne which burns on the water.

There's a clump, clump, clump behind me from heavy shoes descending a wooden staircase.

We hug. We are like family, friends from Cambridge, but haven't seen each other for a few years. I have written to him to request an interview. Although I have known McKellen since 1958, I am here for the first time on a mission, that of would-be chronicler or interviewer.

A moment of uncertainty. My eyes move to the window. The image I have is hardly that of 'a sweet Thames that runs softly while I end my song,' for there's a sight of dark water. I think

3

of the strong brown god – sullen, untamed and intractable – T. S. Eliot's Thames. The vibes are of Shakespeare and Eliot, not inappropriately given McKellen's lifelong love affair with W.S.

'I know,' McKellen says, as if picking up my sense of the view. On this cold grey March day this is something of an anti-climax. Gulls wheel in the air above. Downriver on one side is Greenwich, while on the other we just get a glimpse of Tower Bridge. We speak briefly of the sheer expanse of water and the industrial landscape on the opposite bank.

As if to grace the river with beauty he has since acquired an Antony Gormley sculpture of the human body similar to Gormley's Crosby Beach sculptures in Liverpool, which stands on the tidal beach below.

We are about the same height, five foot eleven, but he is more solidly built than me, so probably heavier, and strong in physique with a well-toned skin. He was very good-looking at Cambridge, where most of us never thought of him as gay, or didn't really think about it at all, but now his looks have a rugged authority, encrusting still a basic handsome and youthful presence. His shoes have iron heels. His jeans are well worn and have holes and glitter adorning them. He sports a heavy-studded metal belt, and an open-neck white shirt, which reveals his chest, a slight butch or Gothic feel to the image. He exudes an easy-going healthiness. It's a real power-dressing display, far from the duffel-coats of his younger self.

A dentist's chair, a favourite personal effect, a friend tells me, has accompanied him from his previous home in Camberwell. I look around. A not very pleasant but brief thought flashes through my mind – of Laurence Olivier playing the Nazi den-tist Szell in *Marathon Man* with Dustin Hoffman as his victim. I don't ask.

'I'll make coffee. How do you take it?'

'Black with a dash of cold milk. Thanks.' He departs to the mauve kitchen where there's a black marble counter. I am by the balcony and climb the steps, looking over at the low-tide pebbles. He once found stranded there an animal corpse, hairless, waterlogged and bloated. He asked himself if it was a calf or a sheep or a goat or a dog. He stared at it until the tide came in. And for the next twenty-four hours he was off his food. He could not face meat after this and became vegetarian.

Still, this is not the time to bring up an unidentifiable, decomposing body on the beach. But with Ian there is always a degree of darkness as well as light. 'Uncomfortable' is how a close friend has called him, but had they meant that he was uncomfortable in himself, or that this was how he made you feel?

We sit down to coffee. We would start with Cambridge. This was his first step on the ladder to professionalism. I am at once aware in him of a difference that I hadn't thought of before, a difference from so many of the leading lights there at the same time, among them Julian Pettifer, Clive Swift, David Rowe-Beddoe, John Drummond, Antony Arlidge, John Tusa, John Tydeman, to name but a few.

'If I may start with a leading question. Why did you feel so different from most others who were up at Cambridge?' I mention some of the names.

'Yes, you are right. I suppose it was my age. I was nineteen. Just at that age one year made a big difference.'

It was National Service. They were two years older. Drummond had been in the navy, learning Russian, John Tusa a Royal Artillery officer in Germany, Tydeman an Artillery officer in Malaya, Rowe-Beddoe a lieutenant in the navy, Tony Arlidge an RASC corporal in the Army Legal Service in Berkeley Square – me a sergeant in Brighton in the Education Corps.

'They'd seen the world. I was away from home for the first time, with a foolish accent. Rowe-Beddoe and Tydey – they were more mature, so much more mature . . .' Is this the characteristic self-put-down of the celebrity?

I look at the face, which is a narrative in itself. The eyes engage one with a quizzical and somewhat defensive look, but when I look back inquiringly, this is quickly replaced by a smile.

The eyes are surrounded by wrinkles that change with and emphasise each mood. One feels there is an enormous well behind, filled with ages of memory and long, slow, steady thinking, but their surface is sparkling with the present, like the outer leaves of a vast tree. Who is this now? Which from the gallery of characters he has been? Not hard to guess. Gandalf.

A moment later there is shadow, a queer look comes into the eyes, a kind of wash, as if the deep wells are covered over. This for a moment could be Ian McKellen at twenty, playing Justice Shallow in *Henry IV Part 2*, when I acted in the same production for the Marlowe Society at the Arts Theatre, Cambridge. The blue eyes are the same, or nearly the same, at forty, fifty, in the various roles on stage or on film, and will be the same at eighty on stage or in the dressing room, on screen or off, recorded by private individuals by phone, camera, by the press . . . There's the piercing power stare of Magneto, the envious certainty of Iago spinning his lies to make Othello jealous . . .

'I didn't really know who I was – a closeted gay. Cambridge was great for me . . . all the many parts I had played there, as I loved for the first time going out in public and displaying my emotions. I enjoyed disguising myself as a closeted gay boy.'

He relaxes to enumerate the virtues of being an actor at Cambridge among so many talented people, and to point out that 'it was not about being the best. The point is that the playwrights have written the best plays, and it was a great privilege to do them with your friends and colleagues.' Memories of performances and the virtues and strengths of that great period flow easily.

The face and person change all the time yet never change. It is no one and yet everyone. He may claim, as he has, that he feels on his own, a bit of an orphan. No partner, no family, living by himself.

'For a good reason,' I say to him, 'we have been called a mafia, a family.'

'Yes, I suppose we were a mafia, something like that. You could call it a mafia . . .'

Ian told me, 'I'm not going to get involved in any book.'

He expressed reluctance to be made the subject of a book when I broached the idea early in 2017. He had already told me five years before about Derek Jacobi's *As Luck Would Have It*. 'I can't understand why he wanted to do it.''I don't want to sound unkind, but it would be impossible. I couldn't work with you, I would interfere with everything you wrote. Look . . . I've only got a few years left, and I'm not going to get involved in interviews. When I was asked to write my autobiography, the publishers sent me a three-page letter listing the people they wanted me to talk to, and where they wanted me to agree to go around the world to be interviewed. I just couldn't do it. I just could not go around talking about myself.' Nevertheless, with the publishers Hodder and Stoughton, he had gone quite far down the road, accepting an advance, which he returned.

'If I did it with you, I'd be wasting your time, my time, correcting and disputing things, and changing things. I don't want to . . . I haven't got the time to write it myself . . . I can't of course stop you . . . Write it after I'm dead. Go and find someone else . . . It would be too painful, writing about myself.'

Later, he related to the *Sunday Times*, 'Edna O'Brien said to me –' he imitates the writer's soft Irish burr, does a kindly tilt of the head – '"Now, you write it for your mother," who died when I was twelve, "and you'll tell her what's been going on." But it was a big block, a big difficulty.'

I rather agree with him that he is not the right kind of person to do it himself, although I did not believe that he would be difficult to work with.

And so we ended, with him friendly but regretful: he reaffirmed he could not stop me doing this. The conversation might continue another time. He has not read the three books written about him. A previous subject of mine, Alec Guinness, the subject of my books *Master of Disguise* and *The Unknown*, liked to quote A. E. Housman's, 'Worse than the practice of writing books about living men is the conduct of living men supervising such books.' I take consolation from this. As for delay, there is Dr Johnson's famous exhortation in *The Rambler*: 'If a life be delayed till interest and envy are at an end, we may hope for impartiality, but must expect little intelligence; for the incidents which give rise to biography are of a volatile and evanescent kind, such as soon escape the memory.'

Ian has a very matter-of-fact, grounded documentary side of his mind. I am not surprised this had drawn him before he left school to consider becoming a journalist. Although repeatedly approached to write about himself, he says he failed to raise any enthusiasm, although he has penned many biographical articles and opinion pieces. He has always been curious about life and people, and about himself and his own reactions, and while sometimes narrow in his focus he stands up for, believes in truth, and the liberating value of truth. He has, too, the essential quality of a good journalist, of listening and trying to be fair, which is why he is so often on an excellent rapport with first-class journalists and critics such as Michael Billington, Michael Coveney, Bryan Appleyard, John Lahr and many others who have interviewed him at considerable length and more than once. As a good journalist does, he takes every question seriously.

In Stratford when playing less demanding roles in the late seventies, he wrote a couple of chapters, and observed at the time, 'I suppose I could take the weary old pages out and see what they are like. I wonder if it is worth spending two years on a book which disappears into the remainder sales within three months of publication.'

In the autumn of 2014, after his friend Derek Jacobi's *As Luck Would Have It* was published, Ian's agent started wooing publishers with a simple paragraph proposal. In June 2015

Richard Brooks reported in the *Sunday Times*: 'The actor Sir Ian McKellen has turned a one paragraph outline of his proposed memoirs into a payday worth close to £1m. After lengthy negotiations involving several publishers, McKellen, 76, had sold the as-yet-unwritten book to Hachette.'

As Ian explained to me, he actually did more than reject the offer straight away. He cleared his schedule to do the task, as he also told the unlikely-named Boudicca Fox-Leonard in the *Telegraph*, 'only to realise he didn't want to do it'. For after his lifetime of telling stories this was one role he did not fancy.

He gave back the £1.2m advance, as it had apparently become, rather than reflect on his life, telling Boudicca he could not remember most of it. 'It didn't seem very interesting to me. I didn't know who I was writing it for. I certainly wasn't writing it for myself. I don't want to go on a voyage of discovery.'

After our 2006 meeting I had found myself drawn into exploring and investigating McKellen's life, challenged to show this complicated and complex man in all shades and colours, yes, with drawbacks and faults, but also extraordinary virtues and strengths. The confrontation between Guildenstern and Hamlet in Act Three, Scene Two of *Hamlet* is the perfect pointer to the challenge. Hamlet presents Guildenstern with a pipe and asks him to play upon it. Guildenstern says he knows no touch of it, and Hamlet answers,

'It is as easy as lying . . . Look you, these are the stops.'

Guildenstern protests he cannot command these to any utterance of harmony, as he 'has not the skill'. Hamlet answers,

'. . . You would play upon me, you would seem to know my stops, you would pluck out the heart of my mystery, you would sound me from my lowest note to the top of my compass, and there is much music, excellent voice in this little organ yet cannot you make it speak . . .'

Forgive me, Ian, if I play on your stops! Here is the height, the presumption of my endeavour: to 'pluck out the heart'

9

of the Ian McKellen mystery – how any single being could create a monumental career of such depth and span; where the ever-recharging source of his energy comes from; and how his personality and character have continued to develop and change throughout his life. All in all to make it speak as it never has before, to 'sound him from his lowest note to the top of his compass'.

2

The Clatter of Clogs

'Thousands of Hobbit fans have the wrong address in the
Lancashire town, according to Sir Ian McKellen'

Burnley Evening Telegraph

Ian Murray McKellen was born into a family of professional
Northern stock in the Burnley General Hospital, East Lancashire, at 8.30 in the evening of 25 May 1939, just months before
the outbreak of the Second World War. His family ancestry was
Scottish, Northern Irish and English. The name McKellen goes
back a thousand years or more to the Celtic or Medieval English
Alan or Alain, meaning harmony or little rock, with McKellen,
or son of Allan, being the Scottish variant.

Denis Murray McKellen, his father, was a chartered civil
engineer. Photographs show a marked similarity to Ian: a direct,
challenging stare, similar height and dark hair. The strong,
longish face is unlined, the mouth turned up at each corner,
suggesting humour. A dimpled chin and a long jaw, but with
nothing sensual implied as in his son. The ears are long and
fleshy.

Ian's mother, Margery Lois Sutcliffe before she married, was
a traditional Lancashire housewife. In photographs she has a
warm and winning smile. They lived high above the centre of
Burnley in the leafy southern suburb of Rose Hill, on the road
to Manchester. Their house was right opposite Scott Park, a
spacious and wooded area donated by a nineteenth-century

philanthropic mayor, where Margery happily walked Ian's elder sister Jean as an infant.

Number 25 Scott Park Road suited McKellen senior and his family well. With a turreted third storey and four bedrooms, it stood at the end of a respectable, middle-class terrace. Up the road was Burnley Golf Club, and it led to rambles up in the impressive heights above the town, with marvellous and breathtaking views over the Pennines, at the peak of which now stands the tourist attraction of the Singing Ringing Tree, an abstract sculpture of metal tubes, erected in 2006 but with a distinct flavour of Lynn Chadwick and the 1951 Festival of Britain. Appropriate for Ian's early years, it sings when the wind is against it.

Denis, thirty-three years of age when Ian was born, was a socialist and a committed Nonconformist Christian. He had absorbed the family's tradition of public service, and worked as a council engineer in the palatial, pale greyish-yellow stone Town Hall. He and his wife were middle class and well-educated and not, as McKellen might sometimes imply, poor or working class. Their status was roughly midway between the Liverpool shipping magnate or cotton-mill owner and the lower-class factory workers, who weaved and spun in the smoky centre among the tall conical brick chimneys and lived in crowded terraces with cobbled streets.

Burnley's surviving monumental public buildings, such as the Town Hall, the Public Library and a former National Westminster and County Bank with its elaborate marbled walls and high ceilings (now an Italian restaurant), attest to an empire and financial power controlling nearly a quarter of the globe. This, as George Orwell – a writer especially relevant to Ian's Lancashire roots and outlook – recorded in his wartime essay 'England Your England', 'was peaceful as no area of comparable size has ever been. Throughout its vast extent, nearly a quarter of the earth, there were fewer armed men than would be found necessary by a minor Balkan state.'

By the time McKellen was born the Empire no longer held together so well. The aristocracy had declined, the solid hierarchy had faltered and the bureaucratic imperial civil service had imposed its constipated view of life with mounds of paper and red tape. Stagnation and a deterioration of morality had set in. As Orwell put it, 'The blimps and the half-pay colonel with bull-neck and diminutive brain, like a dinosaur – and the high brow with domed forehead and stalk-like neck, were both subject to the devastating impact of British foreign policy.' The ill-prepared country stumbled into war with Germany, the modern, more efficient and better-armed super-state. The McKellens, however, did not believe in war. Ian's father, grandfather and great-grandfather were for religious reasons strongly principled pacifists, and Ian staunchly followed them.

Denis was ambitious for himself and his new-born son, and for his five-year-old daughter, Ian's sister Jean. But as he took the bus down Manchester Road to his office his mind must have been in turmoil. Call-up and general mobilisation were imminent; the weak and temporising Prime Minister Chamberlain at last declared war on Hitler on 3 September 1939.

In the Second World War the view of conscientious objectors was often misunderstood and scorned, with the result their careers and families suffered. 'We were called names at school and people in our street wouldn't speak to us,' the daughter of one conscientious objector recalls, 'and the landlord said he wouldn't repair our house after it was bombed, because my father wouldn't fight. I'm afraid it always seemed to be my mother who suffered because of it.'

But Denis did not have to put his pacifism to the test, or to the danger of being arrested and imprisoned, because his employment was declared a 'reserved occupation' – essential in wartime, and therefore exempt from call-up. So he kept his job. In fact he could have been stopped from joining up even if he had wanted to.

Apart from the cruel arrests and imprisonments a new spirit of tolerance and awareness was coming into play, while Chamberlain introduced tribunals to test the sincerity of genuinely held beliefs. More conscientious objectors were coming forward not afraid to stand up for peace. But it is likely that Denis kept his unpopular pacifism hidden and quiet. We shall never know what would have happened if he had had to make his own stand against the war, just as we don't know what Margery's opinions were. There is no reason to believe he would not have stood up for his convictions; the deeper reason he never put on a uniform never became an issue, but it may well have brought some feelings of guilt. Presumably it was not known locally that the borough engineer would refuse to fight for his country. How deep pacifism went was also never to be tested in Ian's case: after he left school in 1958 he went straight up to Cambridge, electing to go there before his National Service. When he left three years later National Service had been abolished. He says he would have refused to do it. A streak of pacifist fundamentalism similar to his father's was injected into Ian's spirit, but possibly also well-guarded by the feeling that it was necessary to cover something up.

Ian's grandparents were actively proselytising Christians, his mother's father a Congregationalist minister in Romiley, a village near Stockport. Grandpa Sutcliffe was noted for his mild-mannered approach, while William Henry, Ian's paternal grandad of fearsome aspect, was a Baptist lay preacher also in Romiley, suggesting a strain of Ulster protestantism in the family. He made extravagant gestures 'from the shoulders', according to Ian in a contribution he made to an anthology of essays and poems, Susan Hill's *People*, which devotes a section to McKellen. Congregationalists asserted that the only head of the Church is Jesus Christ, implicitly denying the supremacy of the Crown, believing the only statute book was the Word of God. Baptists are closely allied to Congregationalists, holding the Scriptures as the sole standard of faith and practice, with the Holy Spirit the only source of regeneration. Baptists were traditionally anti-gay, and still are in some parts of the globe, for example in the American South.

Denis sought or was given a move to Wigan, for reasons unknown, but probably as a promotion with more responsibility, in the same post of borough engineer. The departure from Burnley was hasty. Only two months after Ian's birth the family made their move south-west into the Greater Manchester area, to a town-centre dwelling. McKellen's short-lived stay at 25 Scott Park Road provides something of a mystery. Burnley's Historical Society put up a blue Heritage plaque with the date of his birth next to the front door in 2003. But on a visit to Burnley McKellen said that though he did live there at one point, 'I am certain that's not where I was born.' This left the civic leaders red-faced.

But this address is on his birth certificate registered only two weeks after his birth, and on the electoral register. When challenged further by the local press, Ian did not reply. Usually such tributes do not get placed on houses until after the demise of the subject; there are no plaques on the homes where he spent the next eighteen years.

Elements or shades of Denis – the sense of responsibility, determined upward mobility, firm connections and honesty – can all be detected through Ian's life and work. Alice McKellen, née Murray, Ian's paternal grandmother – known in the family as 'Mother Mac' – whose memory and legend were revered, was 'a real star' and a 'wonderful star' according to her grandson Ian. She had lived just outside Stockport with her husband William McKellen. Both were members of the Christian Endeavour Church at Hatherley and she once sang a solo at its huge celebration at Manchester Free Trade Hall in 1902. Ian was baptised in the very same chapel dedicated to his devout grandmother two years after her death on 20 August 1939. An early family activist was his great-great grandfather on Alice's side who worked fifteen hours a day, six days a week.

He successfully campaigned for half-day Saturday working.

Denis, highly qualified as he was, was a man with wide cultur-al interests. He loved the theatre, as did Margery, and alongside his strong Christian beliefs was a socialist intellectual. In an England full of slums and unemployment, with every British statesman doing the wrong thing with unerring instinct, inevi-tably left-wing thinkers were polarised by the fixed attitudes and sham feudalism of the public-school-educated leaders. 'There was no intelligentsia that was not in a sense left . . . Perhaps the last right-wing intellectual', writes Orwell, 'was T. E. Lawrence.' Denis sowed the seeds of anti-privilege and anti-snobbery in Ian's character. 'Since about 1930 everyone describable as an "intellectual" has lived in a state of chronic discontent with the existing order,' Orwell observed.

Denis and Margery naturally voted Labour in the 1945 election, and when George VI and Elizabeth drove through the cobbled market place, Ian asked his father what the King's politics were. 'He's a good old Tory, I should think,' was the reply. When asked about his likes and dislikes in 1990, Ian said that his least favourite virtue was 'patriotism'. But Lancashire had begun again to prosper in the manufacture of munitions, while its young men and women of military- or factory-hand age flocked to the colours or the factories. The atmosphere became more egalitarian. The permanent legacy of this level-ling influence were the flat vowels shared by all.

The McKellens were to all appearances a reticent bunch, and certainly uncomfortable about disclosing personal details of their lives; they were broad-stroke Lancastrians, forthright but not ones for private revelations. Margery's mother had died giving birth to her younger sister Dorothy, and her father, Sut-cliffe, married again. One day Dorothy pointed to a photograph of her blood mother and asked her stepmother who it was. The answer was, 'Oh, that's a friend of your father's . . .'

No one knew there had ever been a professional actor in the

McKellen family until 2016, when Ian appeared in an episode
of the BBC genealogy documentary series *Who Do You Think
You Are?*. He discovered that Frank Lowe, a Victorian uncle of
his maternal grandmother, had been for a while quite famous
in melodramas with titles such as *The Two Orphans*, but then
had sunk to 'illegitimate' variety shows (as opposed to legiti-
mate theatre) in which he declaimed monologues without any
of the glitz and command of Ian's later one-man shows. He
died of tuberculosis in his mid-forties, abandoned by his wife in
the workhouse, so he fared rather worse than performing dogs.
The revelation that he had acting in his blood heartened Ian,
although he found Frank's demise very saddening.

Margery had the thread or spark of the performer in her
make-up. She acted in amateur theatricals, as did her daughter, Ian's older sister Jean, more frequently than her mother.
(Jean, who went on to be a schoolteacher, was an enthusiastic
amateur performer, and, like her brother, loved the theatre all
her life). In an interview in later life Ian recalled a glimpse of
Margery: during the once-weekly bath she gave her son, she
performed the story of the radio programme she had heard
the night before. Much loved by Ian, she remains a somewhat
shadowy, romantic figure for him. The impression is that she
was fulfilled in family life. She was thirty-three when he was
born, in the prime of life.

Number 17 Parson's Walk, the four-bedroomed house that
Denis and Margery bought in Wigan when Ian was still a baby,
was semi-detached, smaller and undeniably less smart than
Scott Park Road, on a noisy bus route and walking distance
from the industrial, coal-mining centre. Appropriately named
for scions of professional preachers, the fact that over the road it
faced Mesnes Park (pronounced 'mains'), with grandstand and
duck ponds, an even more spacious and ambling open space
than Scott Park, must have been important for Denis and Margery with their two small children. While the larger picture was
one of war and devastation, Wigan was spared, situated as it

was north of Manchester, beyond the reach of the Luftwaffe. Ian's early years in this red-brick semi backing onto the grounds of Wigan Cricket Club, to reach which he had to climb over a wall in his garden, would appear settled and serene

When Ian came back to Wigan in 2002 to film a documentary on his life for America's CBS, in anticipation of him winning a major award for *The Lord of the Rings*, the broadcaster filmed him in Mesnes Park as he touched the shiny right foot of the statue of the Wigan MP Sir Francis Sharp Powell, supposed to bring luck, and told of the Wigan Little Theatre where he first saw Shakespeare and 'the seeds of my life as an actor were put down'. Two years earlier he had restored and reopened the rose garden there, dedicating it to the memory of Denis. A concrete star with 'Ian McKellen' leading other stars for famous living notables of Wigan is embedded in the new civic centre pavement. But it strikes me as a significant deepening of the McKellen mystery why he is occasionally reticent or full of regret on the subject of Denis. I cannot see that the move and ten years spent in Wigan, much though Ian embraced it in retrospect with imagination and warm identification, could have greatly benefited Margery's health.

Two years before the McKellen move into Wigan, Orwell published his account of its 'lunar landscape of slag-heaps and to the north . . . you could see the factory chimneys sending out their plumes of smoke. The canal path was a mixture of cinder and frozen mud, criss-crossed by the imprints of innumerable clogs, and all round . . . stretched the "flashes" – pools of stagnant water.' Denis must have been tough, partaking in the existence in England of what Orwell calls the 'curious cult of Northernness, a sort of Norman snobbishness'. This trait is apparent sometimes in Ian, as when, much later in life, furious at London's theatre scene and Hollywood's rejection of him, he went off to act in Leeds.

Denis is hardly touched upon in accounts of McKellen's life. He was a typical Northerner, a man of 'grit', grim, dour, plucky, warm-hearted and democratic. In his deeply felt pacifism and sense of fair play he wanted to put the 'truth' of the Gospel message and Jesus's non-retaliatory mercy into action. Forgiveness was especially evident when the family entertained a German prisoner of war on Christmas Day. There was a kind of sackcloth and ashes fundamentalism about the move to Parson's Walk with its noise, and on some days its stench and bad air, in spite of Mesnes Park over the road. The family must have been aware, for instance, of the business of robbing the shale or dirt trains, the 'immense and systematic thieving of coal' by the unemployed as they lived near the railway line. Their own home must have been warm in winter with coal being as cheap to buy as it was.

We do hear Denis practised at the upright piano downstairs with his clumsy large hands (like Ian's), playing Chopin, Liszt and Tchaikovsky. The classlessness of the family which Ian underlines is perhaps a bit false, and here a further *aperçu* of Orwell again carries weight, when he points out that not only socialists but intellectuals in general claim to be outside the class racket and can see through the absurdity of wealth, ranks and titles. '"I'm not a snob",' he writes, 'is nowadays a kind of universal *credo*.'

From his earliest days onwards Ian embraced Wigan and identified with it. So when, much later, Ian was making his name, the *Express* headline 'The Olivier from Wigan' had a ring of truth about it. But it also gave a false impression, for the McKellens were not far from Orwell's description of his own family, 'lower-upper-middle class', with better education and a different outlook on life. Raised in this smoke-blackened Wigan 'amid the deprivations of war', every good, well-brought-up, middle-class boy who had a rigorous primary school education in a faith school, then free grammar school and university, might be tempted – with the hindsight of left-wing political leaning – to put a Dylan Thomas rags-to-riches spin on things when he became famous. In the 1970s, by then much feted and applauded, Ian was tempted, in his imitations of the comedian George Formby, to sing the working-class credential song of Wigan Grammar School:

> Oh Wigan is a grand old town;
> The Romans knew it well.
> It always had its Good King Coal
> As long as folks can tell.

But ironically, while he would go on to win a place there, he only briefly attended the school. The family moved out before he could settle down.

Ian, interviewed later, tells how 'smoke smutted Monday's wash on the clothes line and blackened the parish church like the faces of miners clogging home from the pits.' Still, in his pride in belonging to Wigan, McKellen remembers haircuts, 3d 'for a scalping back and sides, singeing with a wax paper taper and a rub-over with Bronco Lav. paper'. He recalls the Fattest Woman from the twice-yearly fair, glimpsed under her tent flap, and Anita, at 18 inches, 'Their majesties' smallest subject, together with showgirls and the Siamese twins pickled in a jar.'

Then there was the accent, not at all the received BBC English spoken in the soft south of London and Sussex. The diphtheria Ian caught when he was three must have been very worrying, for although vaccination against this killer disease was introduced in 1941, it hadn't yet reached Wigan. Of children who suffered the symptoms, which began with fever and sore throat, 90 to 95 per cent did not die – a good statistic for those years. Ian had to be isolated in hospital, but soon recovered. It created no serious lasting ill-effects. But some claim it did have a long-term effect on his voice, with the distinctive elongation of vowel sounds. Others say the flat Lancashire vowels he heard all around him had more influence.

Discipline ruled in the Wigan Wesleyan school in Dicconson Street, which he attended with its large classes, its free meals, a third of a pint of milk during breaks, and its emphasis on religious instruction and imperial values – just as it did at home, where he was made to work hard. He would walk across Mesnes Park to school every day. 'I have very fond memories of living in this house. I always regretted that my parents sent me to bed early. I used to kneel before the window and see the children playing in the park and feel really sad.'

The LMS railway lines at the back of Wigan's cricket club, for which he was the second eleven's scorer, link Blackpool (where he went only once, for the Illuminations) and London (five hours away by steam). On that line, he excitedly spotted the first diesel engine on its practice run. This was 1944, he was five, and on the train travelled a family called the Levicks (Mrs and two children), evacuated from Middlesex. They stayed with the McKellens, but before this Ian knew the war first-hand only through Mickey Mouse gas-masks, blackout at the windows, and nights under the iron shelter in the back room.

Margery's presence in his life, mainly undefined by episode or incident, was of a very loving and typical mother at home, provider and unconditional supporter of husband and children. At home there were no sweets, except the Horlicks tablets Denis obtained from his air-raid warden service. They had more than enough sugar from the rationing and swapped it for tea coupons, drinking water with their meals. On Saturdays they blended top-of-the-milk, margarine and some butter to make up for the lack of the real thing. Margery baked twice a week. Ian's favourite was ginger parkin.

In Wigan, aged nine-and-a-half, he had his first gay kiss. The memory of this must have made him feel different from others. Even so, it was part of the usual kind of playground investigations little boys and girls engage in. These fumbles, which happened after Sunday School, could be described as showing some kind of early defiance of the family religious conventionality. The other boy's name is entirely forgotten.

Ivor Novello, in those days a gay icon for an underground

minority, was a particular enthusiasm of Margery, so she must have innocently responded to the camp and flamboyant aspect of theatricality and shared it with Ian. She bought tickets for Novello playing in *King's Rhapsody* at the Manchester Opera House, where one evening Ian was on the edge of his seat watching Novello languorously leaning across a chaise longue with a glass of champagne. It brought on his first erection, nursing it and proud, as he recounted the event later. Ian knew he was gay from this very early age. He did admit to being very taken, when only six years old, with a girl in games of doctors and nurses during playtime. And he did later write love letters to a girlfriend, which she kept but destroyed when the time came for her to be married.

But when, aged twelve, he watched a love scene in the cinema between men and women he could feel, he says, 'the heat rising in the cinema, and I was getting cooler'. Much later he admitted that he loved being touched by women – and touching them – but not in any deep and lasting sense. At the schools he attended he says he knew no other boy with a similar inclination to love the same sex as he had, and he conveys in his website CV the impression he felt bullied and ashamed, and this kept him alienated from other boys. There is some equivocation about all these feelings, as if there was uncertainty. At puberty, so he told Andrew Billen of the *Evening Standard* in 1999, he wondered if he were changing sex and waited for breasts to sprout. 'I fumbled and flirted my way through puberty and no one helped me to understand myself.'

Always Margery was a real, hands-on mother who was there for him. His impression on others of being grounded in reality, his practicality and calm, owe much to her and are evident in the solidness of the older man.

In the early summer of 1949, with little forewarning or explanation, Margery was taken into Wigan Royal Albert Edward Infirmary. It is not in the nature of a ten-year-old to ask what the matter is, so Ian was kept in the dark.

*

Life went on. With stoic public-minded spirit, Denis had started up a committee to turn the Mesnes Park grass tennis courts site, dug over in the war to grow vegetables, into a rose garden, which opened that August.

After a time in hospital Margery returned home, but there was no mention of what was wrong with her. In the last year at his Wesleyan school, it was time for Ian to move and he took the eleven-plus exam for a place at Wigan Grammar. His report says he had 'made a good start' and won a 'residuary place', which was then converted into a free place. But now the family were ready to move out of Wigan to Bolton, for Denis had been appointed chief borough engineer there. Ian's free place was transferred to Bolton School without having to take another exam, but with the provision he took the extra Latin tuition required for entry.

3

Unfinished Business

Reticence and tight lips still ruled the household in their next home. As a better-off, middle-class family they had a television. In the limited prosperity of immediate post-war years, material circumstances had improved. Denis was now appointed borough engineer and town surveyor in Bolton, ten miles east of Wigan, an increase in responsibilities that showed his reliability and broad practical grasp.

Margery, who had been diagnosed with breast cancer, which Denis knew but kept to himself, was no longer the brave and feisty woman she had been in Ian's earlier years. She tired very easily and, barely remarked upon by Ian at the time, her condition worsened.

Denis clearly loved parks and open space, for 34 Barrow Bridge Road in Bolton, their new home, in much more propitious wooded surroundings, is on high ground well away from the dark Satanic mills and foul colliery air. A detached white pebble-dash mansion lies in extensive grounds that descend to a private estate. Over on the other side of Barrow Bridge Road, along which trotted equestrians from a local riding school when I visited in 2018, is open country. A monumental bleach works chimney stands sentinel at the end of Barrow Bridge Road, in homage to the past industrial era.

The family by now had enviable status, though people never used to talk about how much they earned for fear of envy. Denis's salary had risen to between one and two thousand a year, when the average working wage was £300; next door lived the director of Ebro Engineering works and his family.

Ian swapped the place won with ease at Wigan Grammar for the more elitist Bolton School, a direct-grant grammar school. Among its alumni was Irving Wardle, later the influential drama critic of *The Times*, who had played Hamlet at Bolton. Yet still Margery weakened as her cancer spread and she was more confined to bed. As she grew fatigued so easily she then moved downstairs into a living room and then was taken into the Royal Bolton Hospital.

Much that was going on engaged Ian and distracted his mind from this profoundly disturbing development. No school could have suited Ian more than Bolton. Everyone liked him here, and extra-curricular pursuits such as acting and debating were pushed as vigorously as academic achievement. Ian excelled at everything and looked forward to the Sixth Form Camp each year at Stratford-upon-Avon. Out of school we see his more reckless side. On days off or during holidays, lazily stretched out in Bolton's Central Park, he had a much stronger, wild and overwhelming urge to run off with the dark-eyed, greasy, long-haired, fair-hands from the Silcocks Brothers fairground campsite.

Like Denis's unacknowledged pacifism, Margery's illness was barely if ever discussed, only mentioned at the time of prayers in chapel or at bedtime. In August 1951, prior to his second year at Bolton School, Ian went with his form master to summer camp in Saundersfoot, West Wales. He had no prior warning of his mother's deterioration until other friends arrived to tell him gently that Margery had died – without him having had any further contact with her. She was forty-five and Ian was twelve. He must have been distraught, inwardly inconsolable. But he showed nothing.

Margery, he had hoped during the time she was in the bed downstairs, was getting better. How could God have let his mother die like this? It was little wonder that he turned almost at once, even if again he showed no sign of this, against the deeply practised religious ethos of his family. He was not by his father's and sister's and grandparents' side at the funeral in Bolton's Congregationalist Church. In spite of their pleading with him, he refused to attend. Ian had been close to Margery, but Denis had little rapport with his son and remained remote and unapproachable to him. The fault must be laid at Denis's door, for it should have been from the father that affection was forthcoming. Correspondingly, Ian may have felt some unconscious anger towards Denis over Margery's death: if God the Father had let Margery die, so could his own father have done the same. Ian had no place to channel his grief or anyone to share it with; mourning by himself in an unexpressed and even secret way, he became somewhat lonely, shy and introverted. The little orphan boy persona perhaps began here and stayed part of him.

Many years later he was to tell Lynda Lee-Potter of the *Daily Mail*, 'I thought she was recuperating.' He would confess that the only fortunate thing about her dying young 'is that I can remember that love. There was never any bad feeling, nothing to disrupt our relationship. The memory I have is of a person who felt fulfilled by her life, by looking after me and my sister, and running the home.' One feels, from the way he describes her now, that had she lived, she would have understood him in later life.

One day in the late 1990s, he returned to his first house in Barrow Bridge Road. He knocked on the front door. The current dwellers had bought the house from Denis after Margery died, and the lady, who had done all the dealings with Margery, told Ian that when she went to bed one night with her husband, she had seen the landing light on when she believed it had been put out. She went to turn it off. 'As I did that,' she said, 'I saw your mother standing on the landing.' Half-asleep the following morning, still in that same state, she heard the phone ring. The caller said that Ian's mother had died the night before.

She believed in this return of Margery's ghost to the house, adding that she always thought that his mother came back to the place where she'd been happy, just to say goodbye. 'She'd never told anyone, but she wanted me to know.' For Ian, learning this – and he clearly believed it was true – helped to lay his mother to rest.

But at the time of her death Ian repressed his love and grief. The bid for needed love, squashed and unfinished towards Margery, and denied expression, became a driver towards endless achievement and ambition.

With everything firmly if sometimes uncomfortably hidden, Ian, popular with classmates and teachers alike, progressed to the highest reaches of Bolton School. Mrs Parkinson, waitress in the school dining room, served him his dinner many times when he was on one of her tables. On one occasion he showed her a photo of a girl he was friendly with and she summed up, 'He was always a likeable lad.' Mr Poskitt, the headmaster, much admired as a Jehovah-like figure and a force for good, made McKellen head boy.

Like recognises like, and McKellen was to encounter many head boys in his future profession. They tended to retain the sense of entitlement that such a school position entails, relaxed and assured in the way they straddled the worlds of art and management.

I was at a similar kind of school as Bolton, then called a direct-grant public school. I cannot recall girls being talked of much – it was an age when private emotions and desires, of whatever complexion or tendency, were not discussed or shared. Those boys with the position Ian won for himself, who had rather grand roles at school to uphold, such as head boy, secretary or chairman of this or that school institution or society, were treated generally with awe and admiration. The leaders who emerged from those schools had impeccable records and standards to maintain, and as so many boys were late in sexual development, dating, courting and scoring was simply not an issue as it is today.

Excitement was confused with the terror of expressing what McKellen always knew from the start, that he was gay. In contrast to Stephen Fry, Ian experienced no sexual awakening which brought love, despair, pain and disgrace. Nor was there a simple, buoyant optimism and respectful disregard of women, without specific gay attachments but with silent acceptance of his orientation, such as Derek Jacobi experienced all through his growing-up. Ian's own awareness of good and evil, and his puritan Nonconformist roots that were steeped in John Milton and John Bunyan, probably stemmed from the time before he was able to understand them.

It was in Ian's ambition early on as a child to become an actor that his true soul was formed.

Grown-ups had laughed when they had asked him what he wanted to be when he grew up, and he answered, 'an actor'. Aged three, he was in the audience at the Manchester Opera House *Peter Pan*, where he pointed out you could see the crocodile wires. This was the start, and from then on, he saw a whole range of vivid performances at weekly repertory companies in Wigan and Bolton. His sister Jean appeared as Bottom in her all-girl cast of *A Midsummer Night's Dream*; John Gielgud's Japanese-style Lear entranced him in Manchester, too, just as Ivor Novello had.

His first experience of *Macbeth* was seeing Doris Speed (later Annie Walker in *Coronation Street*) as an amateur, murder-fuelled alpha female. Aged eight, beneficiary of a Father Christmas visit, back at home he mounted on his Pollock's toy stage a Laurence Olivier cut-out from the film of *Hamlet*, waggling and jiggling him at Jean Simmons' Ophelia. The figure of Olivier became a prime object of early hero worship.

He graduated to play numerous roles, both male and female, in the Bolton School plays, in the converted mansion playhouse known as Hopefield Miniature Theatre, as well as in the school's Great Hall. Among these in successive years were Prince Hal and Henry V. *The Boltonian*, the school magazine, found his 'originality in youthful majesty a breath of fresh air'. It was noted, presaging a concern of future critics, that the way he modulated some lines 'appeared rather odd'. He appeared in these plays in the sixth form, but earlier he had cross-dressed as one Rosie Meadows, and Margaret, the Fair Maid of Fressingfield, in the Elizabethan comedy *Friar Bacon and Friar Bungay*. He suffered, playing Malvolio, from being upstaged by Toby Belch, and had firmly instilled in him the principle that 'the actor furthest from the audience is the most dominant,' as he read in a stage manual. He was ticked off by his classics teacher for trying to get his own back on Belch by craning his neck, with the prophetic 'Of course McKellen has greasepaint flowing in his veins.' He was present on stage the whole of Fritz Hochwälder's *The Strong Are Lonely* as the Father Provincial of the Jesuits. This difficult assignment was applauded as demonstrating 'an astonishing degree of maturity'. Just as important, it was the very first of his old men: a study in failure and eventual despair.

With yearly visits to Stratford-upon-Avon to camp near the Memorial Theatre, queuing for a half-crown standing, he was overpowered by Peggy Ashcroft as Imogen in *Cymbeline*. He was sure her grace and beauty was targeting him alone. When he went round for her autograph, up close he could see she was old enough to be Imogen's mother. Yet on stage she was essential youth in voice and gesture, and this feeling of her divinity stayed with him. In Susan Hill's *People*, he was quoted as saying his emotion at this was akin to falling in love.

So there was plenty to exercise mind, body, voice (learning how to drop the Lancastrian accent when necessary, how to project his voice in the appalling acoustics of the Great Hall), and his emotions in public. It amused him to think how his parents once boasted to a friend that he had two accents, the one that he used at school and the one that he used at home.

Debating, too, was his forte, on one occasion on the controversial Shavian subject, 'This House considers that the

emancipation of women has led to the enslavement of men.'
He opposed this vehemently, so with Susan Parry his co-opposer
it was overwhelmingly defeated, 129 to 7, with no abstainers.
He delivered a paper on Samuel Beckett with a compelling
selection of quotations from Beckett's *Endgame*, showing early
on his confidence in public speaking and expressing his ideas.
He criticised Beckett for pessimism and a negative reflection of
life, which he showed to be facile and cynical, but praised him
for his accurate observation. Perhaps, deep down, the despond
struck a chord.

From 1957 onwards he drank deep of Peter Brook's production of *The Tempest* with Alec Clunes' Caliban, John Gielgud's
Prospero and his Lear (knocking the hat off a woman in front
when she giggled in the mad scene at the St James Theatre).
Olivier and Vivien Leigh performing *Twelfth Night* and *Macbeth*,
and Peggy Ashcroft as Rosalind. He saw Judi Dench as Juliet
with John Stride as Romeo at the Old Vic. Observing performances of the great actors of his teens was a pointer to the future.
Sometimes he went with friends, sometimes on school visits,
and further afield with Denis.

By contrast, he warmed instinctively to the rich music-hall
and variety stage, then at its height. He first saw Joseph Locke,
the tenor, famous for his signature tune 'Hear My Song, Violet-
ta', at a Thursday afternoon matinée in early 1953 at the Bolton
Grand Theatre. He obtained permission through his father's
contact with the manager to stand in the wings backstage. He
said he could see the 'theatricals' coming through the stage door
'reeking of Guinness and fairly drably dressed . . . then putting
on their shining suits, going out and doing something rather
smashing.' This was when he became irresistibly fascinated by
the lure of the theatre. The singer, having done his 'act' of Irish
songs and in between chatting to the audience, left the stage to
Sigmund Romberg's 'Goodbye' from *The Student Prince*. His rapt
audience would not let him go, and kept demanding an encore
until the stage manager, in white tie and tails, came on and

ushered a reluctant Locke into the wings. The contrast between
the glamour portrayed on stage and the dressing-room seedi-
ness of old troupers, a kind of *nostalgie de la boue* (nostalgia for
the seamy side) became a lasting thread in Ian's theatrical soul.
But from those early years, too, came the dark shadow that the
unfinished business with Margery cast over him, which remains
part of him to this day.

Visits to the cinemas were disenchanting. The half-dozen cinemas in Wigan were grubby, with threadbare carpets, smelly
toilets and rickety seats. Cigarette smoke floated up and along
the beam from the projectionist's lantern, and in the smoky
haze, courting couples necked in back-row double seats in the
dark, which faintly disgusted him. With the Big Feature, watery
ice-creams were on sale from the pinafored sales-girls saunter-
ing up and down the aisles, waving their flashlights. The fleapits
with dreams and fantasies bred among germs inspired Ian so
little it is hardly surprising he didn't get around, for a long time,
to making films. On leaving Bolton School in September 1958,
the young idealist McKellen wrote in the *Bolton Evening News*
that he longed for a community 'where a faultlessly complete library is at hand, where a cinema declines to show bad films and
a theatre presents new, good plays before they are old or have
gone bad. Utopias must be dull places, full of satisfied people
. . . perfection, like complete virtue, is fortunately inhuman. But
when will a local cinema and a professional theatre give what I
also may want?'

One day, out of the blue Denis asked Ian how he would feel
about him marrying a new girlfriend called Gladys. Margery
had been dead for two years and Ian was fourteen. Ian con-
curred, on the condition that he had a dog, which became part
of the marriage settlement – a corgi called Glyn. Gladys was
a devout Quaker, a religion closely allied to the Baptist and
Congregationalist Churches. As we see her in photographs, she

was tiny compared to the much taller Denis and unusually for that era, wears slacks. She and Denis took their vows informally at the Friends Meeting House in Liverpool. Over the following years, she and Ian were to grow close.

For a while his ambition on leaving school had been to become a journalist. He applied to the editor of his local newspaper who turned the sixteen-year-old McKellen down, and he says (again perhaps slightly underplaying himself in an offhand way) he 'drifted to university', and then to acting.

Gemini, the zodiac sign under which McKellen was born, is said to be a cold-blooded sign, and for those who are great believers in astrology it points to a calculated love and dedication that might be called 'driven' ambition. This now took over. Not only McKellen, but many of the post-war generation of grammar and direct-grant public school alumni who sat examinations or were interviewed for places and scholarships at Cambridge and Oxford showed an astonishing ambition. In the words of *Henry V*'s Chorus, after long years of war and toil:

> Now all the youth of England are on fire,
> And silken dalliance in the wardrobe lies –

Yet it was specifically the intelligent, well-educated children of upwardly mobile parents who never before had dreamed of their offspring entering those bastions of privilege and class, who now took on their more blasé and condescending rivals to show their mettle in every aspect of university life. This was especially true in the burgeoning media and performance arts.

Apart from the beauty and romance of Cambridge's architectural glories and, unlike Oxford, its idyllic atmosphere of academic seclusion, a new emancipation was unlacing and exposing itself everywhere in a generation of outsiders who wanted to claim the inside for themselves without the dead hand of the past upon them. As Glenys Roberts, a Girton girl undergraduate and friend of Ian who had escaped 'stifling suburbs' at the time McKellen applied to St Catharine's, says,

> It was a cusp of time and we were well aware of it ... You
> could feel the combustion in the air. Cambridge was the place
> to be. The philosopher Wittgenstein was a recent memory.
> E. M. Forster could still be glimpsed returning to his rooms by
> the Cam in King's College. F. R. Leavis was teaching in the
> English faculty and scientist Francis Crick, about to win the
> Nobel Prize for discovering DNA, was researching in the sci-
> ence labs and giving bohemian parties on the outskirts of town.

It was in the theatre that the most extraordinary explosion of
talent happened.

McKellen, as full of restless energy as anyone of his age, but
able to focus and single-mindedly direct his ambition better
than most, soon found it would be an unlooked-for plus to read
English at St Catharine's. He was head boy of Bolton School,
brimming with confidence, well versed in public debate, the
beneficiary of his headmaster's ambition to increase the
number of places won from his school to Cambridge. To crown
everything, he had not only played all those leads in school plays
but also significantly (and even perhaps ironically, given Denis's
pacifism), he knew the role of Shakespeare's Harry V by heart.
It was part of him even when aged eighteen on his first visit
to Cambridge and would forever be: king and commanding
officer.

4

The Mafia

'Tell me who influences you, and I will tell you who you are'

Jean-Louis Barrault

By the time he left school, McKellen had seen half of Shakespeare's plays and acted in a handful ('I must have been quite a sweet little boy,' he reflected in 2006). Now, in February 1958, he was venturing to St Catharine's College in Cambridge to take the scholarship exams. His interest in Shakespeare was picked up on by his Cambridge interviewer Tom Henn, a war veteran and a W. B. Yeats scholar. Having noted that at school Ian had played Henry V, Henn asked him to recite the speech before the walls of Harfleur:

Once more unto the breach, dear friends, once more;
Or close the wall up with our English dead.

'I climbed up on a table and gave a rousing rendition of the speech,' McKellen recalled. 'That was enough. I was awarded an Open Exhibition.'

McKellen was following in the footsteps of a talented director in taking up a scholarship to read English at St Catharine's: 'I had been advised, as it was Peter Hall's old college, to do this.' Hall had made his debut at the Shakespeare Memorial Theatre in 1956 with *Love's Labour's Lost* and went on to direct

34

Peggy Ashcroft in *Cymbeline*, the performance that had made such a strong impression on McKellen as a teenager. In 1961, Hall would formally establish the Royal Shakespeare Company before taking over from Laurence Olivier as the first of four Cambridge men to serve in succession as artistic director of the National Theatre.

Why were they all from Cambridge? There was no degree in drama at Cambridge, no certificates, no specialists, no qualified academics. All of it was amateur. Yet it could be claimed that Cambridge student theatre had a more profound influence on post-war theatre than any other formative institution. Hall was undoubtedly at the head of a 'glitter list' of Cambridge graduates who went on to become luminaries in British theatre, otherwise known as the 'Cambridge mafia'. This notion of a mafia, sometimes naughty and jokey, sometimes pervasive and intimidating, was especially applicable to the students who had acted and directed, and then went on to become professionals. The word 'mafia' is supposed to come from the Sicilian word for bragging. On Peter Hall's death in 2017, Richard Eyre, his successor at the National Theatre, unconsciously subscribed to the mafia idea by calling him the 'godfather' of British theatre.

John Barton, Hall's close friend and contemporary, could well be thought of as deputy godfather. After graduating in 1954, Barton became Lay Dean of King's and remained active in student drama until leaving academia to join Hall at the RSC. During Ian's first two years, John Barton, together with George 'Dadie' Rylands, head of English at King's, virtually ran undergraduate theatre as practised by its leading lights.

Heydays have only a short span, but this heyday was deep and explosive, and long-lasting in its impact. The most prestigious acting societies were the Amateur Dramatic Club or ADC, the Marlowe Society, which was run by Dadie Rylands and of which Ian was president in his final year, the Footlights Club, the Mummers and University Actors. The last was formed after the war to put on twentieth-century plays, often staging their English premieres.

In a 1993 article for the *Observer* Richard Eyre described how university drama was centred on the ADC Theatre, housed in a converted cinema. With the technical apparatus of a modest repertory theatre, he claimed that it tried to mimic the professional model to the point of extreme parody. 'Intrigues, jealousies, stars and careers were conceived on the lines of what were imagined to be the real thing,' he said, while actors if rejected started their own groups. Generally, in Eyre's somewhat splenetic hindsight, he saw himself and his fellow thespians as 'cocky, immodest, self-regarding, ostentatious, vain and self-important'.

Eyre came to believe that he suffered a 'contagious condition' that he didn't start to recognise until he had stopped being an actor himself. This was 'university acting', the kind of acting that is all architecture and no heart, assembled by an intelligent mind conscious of meanings, content, style and history. Over-conscious, in short, and saddled with an implicit editorial commentary 'that runs parallel to the performance, telling the audience what to think about the character and his predicament – and that the actor is more important, or more intelligent, than the character he is playing. It's like music written by computer.'

Richard Eyre arrived at Cambridge in 1961, the year in which Ian graduated. Though they did not overlap as students, Eyre was to have an important presence in McKellen's professional career, directing him in *Richard III*. As an undergraduate Eyre performed in a musical with naked Girton girls. During rehearsals the director, Stephen Frears, unhappy with what he was doing, had sent him to a hypnotist to unlock the rich seam of untapped talent and Promethean vigour that he was convinced lay within his 'unpromising shell'.

The 'contagious condition' was not present in earlier years. The generation of actors of which Ian was part (covering the years of John Bird, John Tydeman, both of whom directed brilliantly there, and Clive Swift) were shaped by six years of war and over a decade of post-war austerity; its powers of expression and aspiration were earthed in the struggle for survival and emerged in performances and concepts of an extraordinary precocious maturity, even wisdom. The competitive in-fighting identified by Eyre had not yet raised its ugly divisive head, and love ruled the hearts of those who participated.

Everyone, even if not positively involved, was touched by the theatrical bug in McKellen's Cambridge years. Mafia families, once they have gained control, have a tentacular spread into all areas of society. There was a host of Cambridge societies and clubs to supply the mafia's appetite for performance and excitement not only about the theatre, but also for literature, cinema, travelling to foreign lands, politics, and of course intimate relationships. This urge as well as capacity for freedom was everywhere, as recalled by Glenys Roberts, who went on to become a journalist. 'Today's well-travelled younger generation cannot imagine the joy I experienced on a hitch-hiking holiday when I came upon Byron's name carved by his own hand on Greek temples. Or saw Brigitte Bardot on screen openly enjoy her sexuality in a way previously open only to men.'

To begin his Cambridge acting career Ian had to perform two speeches, one by Shakespeare, one modern, in auditioning for the Amateur Dramatic Club. He chose Aaron's speech 'Now climbeth Tamora Olympus' top' from *Titus Andronicus*, as he had been impressed by Anthony Quayle performing it in the Peter Brook/Olivier production. His modern speech was from a role made famous by Olivier: that of Archie Rice in *The Entertainer*. Ian's emulation of Olivier, which had begun in childhood with his toy figurine of the actor, was set to become a motif through all he did.

Head of the selection committee was John Barton. Trevor Nunn, who went up to Cambridge in 1959 and followed Richard

Eyre as artistic director of the National Theatre, recalls his own first impression of Barton:

> My mental picture of my first sighting betrays some of the impressionable eighteen-year-old student I was and something of the need eighteen-year-old students have for legends and larger than life heroes and enemies . . . He chewed razor blades for fun, he knew every line of the First Folio by ear . . . was hilariously absentminded, obsessed with cricket, a chain-smoker, an expert on Napoleon and somebody who enjoyed working sixteen hours a day without a break.

Ian recounts that 'the panel was unimpressed' with both his audition pieces, 'but John insisted I be allowed into the ADC. So I was.' On the basis of Ian's audition, Barton picked him for the role of Justice Shallow in his Marlowe Society production of *Henry IV Part 2*. 'He must have detected enough of the character man in me, that he might use and develop.' This was to become an historic moment in Ian's life.

I have in front of me an ADC programme: 'Nursery Productions, Tuesday and Wednesday 28th & 29th October 1958 at 8.15.' These were one-act choices from *The Infernal Machine* (Cocteau), *The Voysey Inheritance* (Granville-Barker), *The Government Inspector* (Gogol), *The Good Woman of Setzuan* (Brecht), *Antony and Cleopatra* (Shakespeare) and *The Apple Cart* (Shaw). John Wood, who was to change his name to John Fortune and David Frost were respectively Sextus Pompeius and Second Servant in the *Antony and Cleopatra* scenes. Corin Redgrave played Edmund Voysey. Star of the night, in his first term already using that rather flat, gravelly, hesitant and yet unexpectedly emphatic voice as King Magnus in *The Apple Cart*, was – you might well guess – Ian McKellen. This was certainly an appropriate role for the scope of his talents, though perhaps he didn't yet have the technical skill to carry it off. 'It was all wrong,' commented Richard Cottrell who was to direct him later as Richard II: 'gangly, awkward, his voice whistling. But I thought, "He's special".'

He had no confidence, Ian said of his Cambridge perform-ances as a juvenile, and thought of these performances, such as the morose, angry son in Pirandello's *Six Characters in Search of an Author* or Posthumus in Dodie Rylands' production of *Cymbeline*, as self-conscious, embarrassed and embarrassing. As I directed him myself in the Pirandello play at the ADC I can vouchsafe that this was not so, and that his melancholy display of hurt was deeply real and affecting. I remember him as being very thoughtful to direct, easily accepting of comments, with the characteristic gesture of raising both arms above his head and folding them as he considered a point.

But then there were Ian's roles as old men. He acted in twenty-two plays at Cambridge and among these the old men were the most singled out for praise. Ian's mimicry of age was second nature to him. First the voice, with its cracked, slightly mumbled consonants, the sibilant 's' and elongated vowels, nat-urally sounded old. Second, he tended without effort to stretch and bend his limbs somewhat eccentrically. In *Love's Labours*, a musical adaptation of Shakespeare's play, 'McKellen and [Michael] Burrell, as Holofernes and the Rev. Nathaniel, are themselves worth a visit,' wrote the *Broadsheet* reviewer.

It was his Justice Shallow in *Henry IV Part 2* that critics called the very best performance they'd ever seen by a student actor. Michael Burrell asked Ian to do a talk with him some years later in Soham at the Brook Theatre. 'I know what,' says Ian, 'let's do the Shallow and Silence scenes from Henry the Fourth.' So there were these two men, seventy years old, now the right age, performing the characters with whom they had triumphed fifty years before when they were anonymous, as actors were in Marlowe productions, and had stolen the show. They both retained enormous affection for Shallow and Silence as crusty, warm-hearted old men recalling their early days.

London critics, agents, managers flocked during the Mc-Kellen Cambridge years to help that particular 'magic' gain a foothold in the professional theatre. Kenneth Tynan and Harold Hobson, the two most influential critics (and the most eloquent pen-pushers), were poles apart as competitors and in social attitudes but about Cambridge they sang from the same hymn-sheet. 'The A.D.C. Theatre has become a true gymnasium of talent, where plays are staged with lively professional assurance; and the flow of this talent from Cambridge to London (from the Fen to the Wen, so to speak) gets swifter every season,' wrote Tynan; 'the tradition of slapdash amateurism in university acting has been decisively smashed.'

Hobson visited frequently, and the Arts Theatre production of the *Henry IV* plays sent him into raptures: these Cambridge performances gave him more pleasure, more illumination, he said, than he received nine times out of ten when he went either to Stratford or to the Old Vic. He asked, 'Why should a group of Cambridge amateurs be able to put up not only a better show, but an infinitely better show, than companies that contain many of our best players directed by our leading producers?' His answer was their simple, unadorned belief in the words Shakespeare has written, without any exaggeration. He singled out Clive Swift's Falstaff, who did not supplement the words by 'hawking, slapping, pawing, and winking', and 'the first time in my life I understood why Falstaff is supposed to be one of the great comic characters in English fiction . . . The virtue . . . also, in the Prince [Jacobi], in the Chief Justice [John Fortune], in Hotspur [Simon Relph], in Justice Shallow [McKellen], and in the King [Terence Hardiman] was intelligent speaking . . . It was because the foundations of this rationality were precise-ly laid that a structure could be raised on them of surpassing loveliness.'

Ian was a year behind Derek Jacobi, who also hadn't done National Service, and two behind Clive Swift, who for him 'had gravitas and seemed middle-aged'. When Swift went up to take his entrance exam, 'hardly anyone went there to act', he says. He smoked because it was so cold and recalled his shaving water froze. 'Even if I get in I can't live here,' he wept, and could not write in the exam because of the cold.

Swift said Ian was hard to know, and if he talked about his family, 'I seem to remember it was in a jokey way.' He was perhaps the least complimentary of Ian's friends about his acting at Cambridge, viewing him only as a character actor, and saying he didn't show much distinction. John Tusa, in reviewing *Six Characters in Search of an Author*, did not in a complimentary review of other players even mention him, while Waris Hussein, who also directed him, thought his acting was full of mannerisms, although in time he learnt to tone them down. In *Saint's Day*, John Whiting's large-scale political allegory, Ian was commended with Jill Daltry by Ann Dowson for creating an atmosphere of tension and concealing 'the shiftedness of the writing by the conviction of their acting'.

Hugh Walters, the resident comic actor, who held the record of appearing in thirty-three productions at Cambridge, remembers Ian played seven old men, 'but could not play the lead, although his observation was wonderful. He had that swaying from the hips as the lead in *Cards of Identity*.' Walters also says no one bothered whether you were gay or not and was highly sceptical of Cambridge, which he called, like Eyre, 'a place of spurious fame'. He was not very flattering about Jacobi either: 'he had an old-fashioned voice . . . and acted with the mirror there in front of him.'

Derek Jacobi, who was at St John's College, was undoubtedly the reigning star of the Cambridge stage of McKellen's first year. Ian instantly fell headlong in love, not surprisingly given his passion for the theatre.

Clothes mattered at Cambridge, and sartorially the pair could not have offered a stronger contrast. As Cambridge men were predominantly drawn from single-sex public or grammar schools, they were not only snobbish but intensely aware of the attractions of appearance both to their own sex and the under-represented opposite. 'Cambridge was an extremely self-conscious society that perpetuated its own values and bred introverted cliques, while the clothes everyone wore were important not as social badges alone, but as symbols of a particular desired persona,' Colin Bell, an Open Scholar of King's, wrote in an article in the student paper *Broadsheet* in 1959. This was relevant to both Ian and Derek. Bell claimed that wealth, class, even nationality, although often revealed in dress, 'were not as elsewhere the sole conclusions to be drawn from any particular style; more important was the allegiance or ambition within Cambridge society that they were pre-designed to show.'

Derek Jacobi dressed undoubtedly as a 'particular desired persona' of his own design and creation, as he admitted to me once. McKellen recalls that Derek was very glamorous, and he was highly conscious of his appearance, wearing 'very tight trousers and his hair done up at the back. We were in duffel-coats and corduroys, and Derek was very differently dressed rather like his mates in Leytonstone, rather dandified.' Unsure how to express his hidden secret, in his duffel coat and tweed jacket, McKellen felt unattractive with his father's 'big hooter', as he called it, and his 'jug ears'. Adding to the abject sense of shortcoming was, perhaps, a touch of the heroic victim mentality from the early loss of his mother. Sometimes there were cracks (if only slight) in the North Country reserve, such as an evening Ian recalled from his first year: 'After the *Three Sisters* party [in which he played Baron Tuzenbach], I was drunk and carried down from the Gibbs building [where Barton had his rooms] on the second floor.'

In contrast to Ian, Derek was at once aware of social rank, class, and radiated an instinctive sense of hierarchy. Derek, in spite of his apparently humble origins, could assume princes and nobility from the word go: 'rather aloof with an aristocratic bearing, he trailed success and achievement – he was glamorous', said Ian, who in his ecstatic hero-worship called him the 'bees knees, and easily the most accomplished actor in Cambridge, and with a wonderful ability in verse'.

Ian joined the debating society, the Cambridge Union, and attended college meals, but Derek, apart from the theatre, was an outsider and never seemed to work. 'He was never in college, he never had any connection with college, and he was always going to become a professional,' says Ian. Compared to Derek, Ian believed himself a novice, having to learn painfully from John Barton and Dadie Rylands. Derek knew instinctively: 'Derek was a born actor, whereas I was a plodder.' While not exactly this, Ian certainly laboured very hard at every role. I directed him twice during his first two years, and while he said of himself his acting was all gesture and no heart, in the two juvenile roles he played he was very moving. The first was as the Son in *Six Characters in Search of an Author*. The second was a role in *Deutsches Haus*, the first play by fellow student Richard Cottrell, who had served two years of National Service prior to university. Ian played Harry, an army private who makes Anna, a German girl, pregnant. 'Mr McKellen's exploration of the emotion of disgrace when he recognises his moral inability to stand up to the responsibilities he has incurred is a poignant climax to the second scene,' wrote Harold Hobson in the *Sunday Times*. Anna was acted brilliantly by Margaret Drabble. After playing at the ADC it enjoyed a run at the Arts Theatre in London, so may be counted as McKellen's very precocious first West End performance. Terry Hardiman, also in the cast, recalls it being so real that one performance when they played with trepidation to an audience of servicemen in uniform, one squaddie shouted out, 'Watch it, mate, he's going for his knife!'

Ian and Derek performed together in Richard Cottrell and Clive Swift's musical *Love's Labours*, which transferred from Cambridge to the Lyric, Hammersmith. One Saturday night after the show Hardiman and McKellen ended up staying at Derek's house (Ian could not recall why), and it was a long haul from Hammersmith to Leytonstone. He claimed he must have missed the bus 'or something' but insisted 'there was no hanky-panky'. Next morning Hobson reviewed the show in the *Sunday*

Times. Seeing the review, and that he, as Holofernes, was the only actor mentioned, Ian quickly hid the paper away in case Derek read it.

Another time during this run when he had nowhere to stay, he put up with Hardiman's family in Billericay. Terry remembers how well Ian got on with his warm-hearted mother. Terry, who had taught for a year in a rough comprehensive before Cambridge, and whose father was a policeman, believed being in a play was a cocoon 'against a very worrying world'. Ian, he observed, had 'riveting mannerisms and a strange sibilant voice, almost a whistle in it'.

Love's Labours became something of a cult for those who'd been in it and they went on celebrating it with reunions until its fiftieth anniversary, at which they sang the catchiest numbers with Swift at the piano.

Ian's confession that for a while he was desperately in love with Derek was much repeated in later years but it was nothing that was explicit at the time. The passion McKellen felt for Derek continued throughout Cambridge. In 1959 Derek had his twenty-first birthday and his devoted mum and dad gave him a Ford Cortina. Cambridge and local Leytonstone friends were invited to the bash in a local hall, McKellen and I among them. No such celebration or present happened for McKellen. There was also from the start a difference between them sexually: Derek has always adored women and gets on famously with them, while love and affection towards women took some time with Ian: he appeared friendly but with an inner reserve, even uninterest. The reticence may have been related in some way to the early loss of Margery. Elizabeth Proud, who became a successful actress with the BBC Sound Rep, and who acted with Ian at Cambridge, says that in playing a love scene opposite him he would never look at you. This could also of course have been shyness. But another Cambridge friend, preferring not to be named, recalls Ian sticking his bum out when he had to kiss one girl in a scene.

*

It was at Cambridge that McKellen, aged twenty-two, supposedly lost his virginity, with Brian Taylor, known as Brodie. The novelist Margaret Drabble, who attended Newnham College, remembers Brodie well at Cambridge as a personable, very handsome young teacher. Keen McKellen watchers, of which there are legion, believe the love affair with Brodie started as far back as May 1958, when Ian was eighteen and acting at the Bolton Little Theatre, situated near the gasworks. Here, amateurs, mostly boys and masters from Ian's school, had joined to put on plays in this venue reeking of gas burners. During *Twelfth Night*, in which Ian played Sebastian, piercing the Olivia with his powerful blue eyes so she went weak at the knees, he had encountered the 'God-like figure' of Brodie, two years older than him, studying to qualify as a schoolteacher. He was 'a golden boy – golden-haired and very tanned, and so forth. Very long lashes,' according to Geoffrey Banks, who played Feste. Banks, interviewed by Mark Barratt, an earlier biographer of McKellen, had taught in the sixth form and spotting his talent had put Ian on the path of his big Shakespeare roles with Prince Hal, Henry V, Malvolio, when he had impressed audiences with his commanding voice. Banks's instinctive stage sense picked up Brodie's matinee-idol appeal to Ian. Ian also, according to his oldest friend Michael Burrell, had an occasional fling.

While Brodie and Ian were clearly an 'item' at Cambridge, to those who knew Ian it was not at all public. As Ian says, he was a closeted gay boy who enjoyed disguising himself, though no such disguise was evident to his friends. He made a point about how ex-public schoolboys made fun of his Northern accent, though as he said, as a child he always had more than one accent. Again, this flexibility showed shrewd ambition. He had joined the Union when he first arrived, and far from being excluded from parties, where he claims he suffered agonies of self-consciousness, this was not an observation that most of his contemporaries would have made about him. Why he should have gone around with the idea that he had a dark and shameful secret, namely that he was gay, while everyone of the same age was not at all bothered by such a realisation and proclaimed that tolerance was universal, is something about which he has remained uncomfortable and reluctant to explain.

Awareness of the illegality of homosexuality in the greater world outside Cambridge had been reinforced during the 1950s by repressive home secretaries, an example of which was the arrest and imprisonment of Lord Montagu of Beaulieu for 'consensual homosexual offences' in 1953 and '54. This provoked a backlash and led in 1957 to the Wolfenden Committee recommending the decriminalisation of homosexual acts in private between adults. In 1967 Parliament enacted the recommendation. It may not be too far-fetched to suggest Ian's susceptibility to fear of discovery had something to do with the way Denis the pacifist had gone through the war with his secret, not openly proclaiming his deeply held religious conviction and the McKellens' need to keep their secrets.

To have problems with one's sexuality was not unusual (either at that time or later) whether you were gay or straight. Noel Annan, Ian's contemporary Provost of King's, made the observation that it was hardly any easier for heterosexual men, especially at Cambridge where there were few women, and most could be described as bluestockings uninterested in sex.

Jacobi's perception of being gay at Cambridge is different and at odds with McKellen's. He felt there was no stigma about being gay, and it was never a shameful secret. Cambridge and his unreciprocated love for Richard Kay, another leading Cambridge actor, helped him to accept his sexuality 'without making a song and dance about it'. For Ian, it remained the opposite and he found 'he could only be confident when acting, because it's a wilful escape from life,' as he told the *Sunday Times* in 1999.

Ungainly as Ian considered himself, refusing to think, as most thought, he was good-looking, especially aware of and unhappy with his physical shortcomings, the size of his left ear for one, and his knees, he had already had opportunities to try his hand at many parts.

This is what Cambridge had done for him. He was already set on the course of converting himself to any size, shape, voice or condition to further his passion to act. To this he would become as constant as the Northern star, so that many years later, he could truthfully tell an *Observer* journalist, 'My body, my face – they're only interesting in terms of my work. Every haircut I've ever had has been for a role.'

5

Undeclared but Hidden Passion

'You're never so famous again as you were at Cambridge'

Michael Frayn

During his Cambridge years, or at least the latter part of them, Ian had a loving and intimate partnership with Brodie. It was to be as stable and secure as any relationship Ian has ever had, and if same-sex marriage had existed in those days, they would probably have tied the knot. Brodie has remained deeply loyal to him over the years, and they are still close friends.

But to his immediate and intimate family circle – sister Jean, father Denis and stepmother Gladys – Brodie was just a good friend, and in the tight-lipped way the family conducted itself, no one mentioned any other possibility even if they had thought of it. Jean most probably knew or if not suspected, while Gladys, who later admitted to Ian she knew all along, would no doubt have kept the McKellen senior silence, whatever she might have thought, given Denis's deep biblical convictions about the sin of homosexuality.

Brodie had impeccable manners, was handsome and charming and no one said, or has ever said, a word against him. This was someone who, clean-limbed and with the received Cambridge image, comes over as a Rupert Brooke Grantchester figure in tennis whites, a racket in one hand, but with a bottle of Lucozade rather than champagne in the other. Perhaps too, there was rather a High Church Anglican aura about him, for he associated with members of St Augustine's Church, with which Doris, his mother, with whom Ian got on famously, was strongly involved. Brodie was the perfect partner for Ian, one might well have judged, a secure, emotional anchor as well as secure home port, for one setting out on the perilous seas of an acting career. He was the dependable, faithful other half, or so commented John Tydeman, one who was always there.

With his Cambridge background Ian could count his blessings. This was England. Cambridge authenticated him in his father's eyes. Overriding probably all else was the confidence that Ian never put to one side, expressed by Stephen Fry, who found that the one clear advantage – probably the only real advantage – in having gone to Cambridge, was that he never had to deal with the problem of not having gone to Cambridge, 'which a lot of people regard as a problem and feel that somehow if only they had, their life would have been better and easier'. Fry also knew that having been there was not an automatic route to fulfilment and happiness.

Fry and many other Cambridge alumni he spoke for who became famous, tended to feel that instantly, from the start, they had superiority conferred upon them – as if when they walked around a corner everyone hopped into their orbit and behaved as if they were the only live person around. 'It is not an uncommon adolescent vision. Everyone else is a kind of extra . . .'

Yet as with Peter Hall, they sometimes had the haunting feeling that they never did anything really worthwhile.

Provincial repertory companies with their weekly or fortnightly change of repertoire, selected from West End hits, well-made plays from the 1930s and classics, gave rich training and experience to their mainly young members. Ian applied to, and chose from, three companies who offered him work. He started at the Belgrade Theatre, Coventry, on £18 10s a week, just over half the working man's average wage. This was a step above Derby

Playhouse and Hornchurch Repertory, which had also offered him jobs, but hardly up to the prestigious level of Derek Jacobi, who, narrowly missing Peter Hall's new Stratford company with a bungled audition, had gone straight into the pedigree classical fold of Birmingham Rep, quickly rising to leading roles. As Ian put it, 'he went off in glory again as expected, joined the prime company in the regions, Birmingham Rep.' There is again a touch of the disingenuous self-putdown in the aged McKellen who says this.

Ian, a slow-progress stickler, learnt and improved through a series of modest roles, starting with William Roper, Sir Thomas More's son-in-law, thoughtful and loyal, in Robert Bolt's *A Man for All Seasons*. Ian lived parsimoniously on Co-op food discounted for actors, and in digs in Corporation Street. His theatrical fare was humdrum, and among a hefty ration of potboilers Ian kept in his hand with old men, with grey hair, wrinkles and wigs as Tredwell, the butler in Agatha Christie's *Black Coffee*. He played Mr Snodgrass in *Mr Pickwick*, and a viperous old First Weasel in *Toad of Toad Hall*. His Konstantin in *The Seagull* hardly knocked anyone for six.

But he struck up an acting partnership with Bridget Turner, an ambitious rising performer like himself. Bridget, who died in 2014, was an ebullient and witty all-rounder. Ian gathered acclaim with audiences and critics until Bridget one day noticed something. Suddenly he got all the juvenile leads. And plays were chosen to show off his talent. She had been slogging away for two years 'without the same thing happening to me' and she baulked at the way the season was being shaped round him. Yet when she saw him as Simon Mason, an army officer, in an all-male cast, in *End of Conflict*, and notably revealing bare knees, 'I couldn't take my eyes off Ian . . . Fascination, charisma, call it what you like, he had it even then.'

After McKellen's fifteen wide-ranging roles in nine months in Coventry, even learning how to raise laughs in drawing-room comedy, Elspeth Cochrane, in her early days as a West End agent, twenty years older than Ian and with an acting and writing background, was seeking up-and-coming talent and snapped him up after seeing him in *End of Conflict*. She proposed him to Robert Chetwyn who had made a reputation running the Arts Theatre, Ipswich. Chetwyn upped his wage to twelve pounds, and offered adventurous parts over the next thirteen months at the Arts Theatre. Twenty-one plays, opening every other week, saw Ian playing mainly leading roles, which in the first months included David Copperfield and Henry V (which he had already done at school). Ian's unconventional approach, agreed between him and Chetwyn, involved the army entering through the small auditorium. He imagined it was in the audience and knelt down at the front of the stage to whisper the lines 'Once more unto the breach, dear friends, once more / Or close the wall up with our English dead.' He felt, he told John Barton, 'I got more because it was more real.' Not only was this production acclaimed locally, but it became the 'most notable of Ian's parts in Ipswich, together with the eponymous role in John Osborne's *Luther*,' Chetwyn said to Barratt, claiming that Ian was more straightforward in his emotional intensity, and 'rather better than Albert [Finney] who created the role two years before; tricky stuff, and not a crowd-pleaser.'

Ian listened carefully to comment and criticism, querying everything, which some could find irritating: John Tydeman says he always asked what you thought as his director, but then contradicted it. His curiosity was endless, the strong curiosity of a child that he was to keep all his life. His recall later of the roles he played was phenomenal. Yet while his consistency of memory was a fairly constant trait, he could be very contradictory at the same time. He had a tendency to be showy, dishing up to journalists, friends or fellow actors, exactly, even cunningly, what they wanted to hear. Like Jacobi, who was even more emphatic on the subject, Ian was dismissive of drama school and specialist training. He could voice equally the opposite opinion. To newcomer Nickolas Grace, with whom he acted at the time, who was just out of the Central School of Speech and Drama, Ian one day said that he himself really regretted not having been to drama school. Grace tells me in 2019 how Ian had 'seen me doing my Litz Pisk and Cicely Berry movement and voice warm-ups alone on stage and how important they were to me.' Yet Ian *had* had specialist voice training, admittedly less formal, and intense fight coaching with Barton, who was as Nunn says of him, 'an extremely dangerous sword-fighter', probably one of the best fight directors the theatre ever had. He had had three years' leading roles, which no drama school could ever offer or match (for there is no star system at drama schools, where roles must be shared). Off-stage Ian was already delivering the self-humbling chameleon, contradicting himself sometimes as a result.

For the moment, with a steady partner who visited him frequently, and spending the occasional weekend with family and friends while in stable employment, he enjoyed a fruitful life, apparently only feeling disrupted and prone to frustration when he had to play small roles, especially in Shakespeare.

At twenty-four, Ian's prospects could not fail to be expanding rapidly as he went from strength to strength. His agent fixed him to leave Chetwyn and join the Nottingham Playhouse company in its newly built theatre under the aegis of John Neville, who was tipped to become prestigious in theatre annals as the new Richard Burton or Peter O'Toole. But as the sharply ambitious and precocious Ian must in time have noted, he could be quickly forgotten over a longer time-span as a stage actor without any serious screen fame to count on.

6

Encounter with a Giant

Tyrone Guthrie, known universally as Tony, the director Ian worked with first at Nottingham in December 1963, was to have a lasting impact. He had an unusual appearance for one who worked in the theatre. He was extraordinarily tall with pronounced aquiline features, penetrating eyes and a military moustache – he had an army officer's bearing, yet one who wore shabby suits and sandshoes. In his old mackintosh he might easily have been mistaken for a farmer.

Angela Fox, mother of Edward, James and Robert, grandmother of Emilia and Laurence, and matriarch of one of the country's most luminous acting dynasties, called him the closest and perhaps the most understanding friend she ever had, with a philosophy of 'Rise above it' in any trouble, and a capacity to keep everyone on their toes. His formative power over great actors' development was legendary. Unusually for a director at that time, given a knighthood for his service to the theatre, Guthrie was a revered giant, as well as a highly eccentric individual who had a unique vision of the drama. He made pronouncements such as:

> It is only theoretically impossible to separate the actor's skill from his personality. Theoretically, then, the most skilful actor is the most protean, the actor with the widest range. It so happens, however, that the actors with the widest range do not usually go very deep . . . their performances [are] apt to be superficial. Some of the greatest actors have no protean quality at all. In

every part, though the make-up and costume may vary, the performance is almost exactly the same.

Ian, aged twenty-four, was not too young to have this test applied to him.

Guthrie cast a lasting spell over mid-twentieth-century performers, and so much was owed by so many to him. Not least of these was Laurence Olivier, who experienced his epiphany as an actor when performing Sergius in *Arms and the Man* with Ralph Richardson in the legendary Old Vic season of 1944. Olivier said he owed everything to Guthrie when hating the role of Sergius in *Arms and the Man*, considering Sergius 'a boring little prick'. Guthrie seized on this and pointed out, 'No, Larry, you've got to love him, celebrate and identify utterly with this.' Here was the challenge or gauntlet that Guthrie threw down to every actor aspiring to rise to greatness, not least McKellen.

Guthrie directed Ian's debut performance as Aufidius in *Coriolanus* in 1963, the company's first play at the newly built Nottingham Playhouse. John Neville had the title role. The director's approach was that consequent to Coriolanus's mother fixation he saw Aufidius as a figure whom Coriolanus, in same-sex attraction, 'worshipped in combat', in the words Guthrie used in an introduction he wrote to the play, 'and lusted after in his dreams'. As a result, a marvellous private hate exists between the rival commanders, which ranges through jealous possessiveness to open love before Aufidius turns against Coriolanus's ingratitude and treachery.

Here, for the twenty-four-year-old actor, was the first instance of being drawn into a psycho-sexual drama of homoerotic dimension which Shakespeare clearly underlines. Guthrie was intent on bringing out this bond between Aufidius and Coriolanus and was repeating the motif of homosexual desire that he, having consulted Freud's biographer Dr Ernest Jones, thought was inescapable between Othello and Iago when directing Ralph Richardson and Olivier in the roles in 1938 at the Old

Vic. Given Ian's aspiration to be like Laurence Olivier, there is an interesting similarity to be found here: in that production, Guthrie had wanted a climax of the Iago–Othello relationship to be fed with explicit intent, for example with, 'I'm your own for ever,' as a declaration of love. This 'inescapable' idea fell on stony ground with Richardson, 'when I', as Olivier said, 'flung my arms round Ralph's neck and kissed him, whereat Ralph sort of patted me and said, "Dear fellow, dear boy" for having lost control of myself and despising me for being a very bad actor.'

In *Coriolanus* the expression of explicit intent presented Ian with no problem at all, especially as Guthrie took him aside, conscious of his youth and relative inexperience, and rehearsed him privately. Extending such attention to such a relatively unknown figure was a typical Guthrie gesture; he cut away protocol at every turn and instinctively countered as much as he could the star system and leading man/leading lady axis on which the English theatre pirouetted.

Elspeth Cochrane, Ian's agent, recalled over lunch several years after he played Aufidius, how she found Guthrie at a first night at the Bristol Old Vic in 1946, alone under just a working light before the curtain went up, sweeping the stage, whereupon Ian and she responded together, 'He's God.' The hero worship by Ian – built up during rehearsals – reached the sky: 'It's the excitement he brings to everything. And his energy. He runs a jam factory in Ireland just to provide employment. The jam's called Irish Orchard!' At the Mayor's reception for the Nottingham Playhouse's Civic Opening, no food and drink was set aside for the cast. By the time they arrived everything had gone. Storming at this, Guthrie, ignoring royalty and the hoi polloi, entered the enclosure reserved for actors and before leaving seized a tray of gin and tonics for the company.

Ian panicked about the role at first and found difficult Guthrie's request for him at the end of the play to utter a cry of extreme grief at having killed Coriolanus. This is before he says the lines, 'My rage is gone, And I am struck with sorrow.' A heartfelt lover's cry, no less, was what Guthrie wanted. Ian was stuck trying to achieve this, even at the dress rehearsal. As Michael Crawford, playing the Second Serviceman, records, Guthrie took him downstage away from the others, quickly but loud enough for them to hear, and told him they were at the climax of a masterpiece. Guthrie's words were, 'Aufidius is a man but he can grow, as we all can, to behave like a god. His rage *can* turn to sorrow. Fill your mind, your imagination with your feelings and let your heart wail. If you can't do it, it's all a waste. You can.'

He tried and did it. The huge, wailing threnody, which he reached in the end, became a turning point for Ian, and he says it was then that he realised what acting was really about: 'to reveal yourself to your audience and make them empathise with you.' Playing Aufidius, sexually circling Coriolanus through the play, uttering threats like caresses, became the most exciting dynamic of the production, showing, as *The Times* said, 'a prodigious range of hysterical passion' and those who saw it remember it to this day. It freed Ian, gave him at an acceptable public level, possibly, for the very first time, the release physically and emotionally for his repressed homosexual passion. It gave him permission to be himself.

Ian continued to add to his experience through his Nottingham season and came up against some other rich and resplendent figures. In Peter Ustinov's *The Life in my Hands*, Ian played the young man who has raped a fifteen-year-old girl with mental illness. Ustinov used this as a springboard for a discussion of capital punishment. It exposed Ian, Ustinov told Ann Leslie, to show a raw, rough quality, employing his Northern accent, which Ustinov found impressive and exciting. 'I found him putting inflections into speeches which I, as the playwright, had not even thought of . . . [it was] an illuminating experience.'

McKellen was 'terrifically in love with Brodie, then,'

commented Richard Digby Day, interviewed by Barratt, who was part of his Nottingham company, 'always looking forward to him coming for the weekend. At the weekend they would disappear into a sort of home milieu.' It seemed Ian was instinctively fashioning himself into a unique character, both offstage and on, even in his mid-twenties.

Sombre violence and hysterical haughtiness followed in Pedro Calderón de la Barca's *The Mayor of Zalamea*, then 'racy and rough' Arthur Seaton in Adam Sillitoe's *Saturday Night and Sunday Morning*, perhaps underlining Ian's difference from the famous Albert Finney performance in its distillation and thought but missing none of the comedy. All these and more saw him through the winter of 1963 until his final appearance at the Playhouse in May 1964, when he was called upon to impersonate Sir Thomas More, now a sprightly greybeard, in an inferior script attributed to Shakespeare and his contemporaries Dekker and Heywood. Benedict Nightingale, then theatre critic of the *Guardian*, praised Ian's More, with his 'cleverly awkward movement [which] suggests a kind of self-mocking saintliness. [. . .] a performance of dignity without a trace of mawkishness.'

'The play was a ghastly mishmash of nothing,' commented a very miserable member of the same Nottingham company who had found them a most unfriendly lot. At the first reading Steven Berkoff had been amazed that this very young man with 'busy hair, wearing blue jeans and a jeans top' was cast as More. 'He looks far too young.' But when Ian started to read, 'he had an authority which belied his years.'

One day Berkoff, who had studied mime at the École Jacques Lecoq in Paris, was showing off some of Lecoq's technique. Ian, waiting and standing in his cloak, suddenly exclaimed, '"Where did you get that?" as if you buy it in the supermarket.' Berkoff, who thought Nottingham was an awful dump and felt that he was 'tripping around like a damp squib . . . with a few lines', was desperate for the slightest degree of attention. He struck up a friendship with Ian, lasting into the 1990s when they ended up as London neighbours in Limehouse.

Quarrels had broken out in this divided, contentious company between the two directors, John Neville and Frank Dunlop. Ian steered a diplomatic path and did not take sides, leading from the front in the very image of Thomas More. The cry the Volscian soldier, Aufidius, made at the climax of *Coriolanus* typified the impact McKellen made at Nottingham, showing, as Tyrone Guthrie declared, 'You cannot hide the actor in the part' – or certainly not when McKellen was playing it.

He had risen to the height Guthrie demanded of him and shown his protean power. McKellen was ready to move on and the next call came from London.

7

We Can't Match Him

In 1964, Michael Codron, innovative young London impresario of the day, had almost finished casting James Saunders' *A Scent of Flowers*, composed heavily in the Samuel Beckett mode, with the well-known Phyllis Calvert as a cruel, cold-blooded step-mother and Jennifer Hilary as the heroine Zoë, who is driven to suicide. Codron sought a young actor for Zoë's brother, 'Gogo' or Godfrey. Elspeth Cochrane and Calvert sent him to Nottingham to see McKellen as Aufidius, and with Calvert's insistence, Ian now had his first big break. All the action of the play takes place in a somewhat rambling, or back and forth, flashback, with Zoë's coffin in full view throughout. The good citizens of Golders Green, traditional pre-West End play-goers, gave up in incomprehension quickly, while the buzz of an offensive and necrophiliac piece all about sex and coffins turned people away.

Harold Hobson, writing in the *Sunday Times*, put everyone right when the play opened at the Duke of York's Theatre, saying the 'conclusion apparently prevalent in the suburbs is as unjust and stupid as to assert that Maupassant was indecently interested in indecent exposure'. The first West End night received fifteen curtain calls. Hobson's long review, mainly on Jennifer Hilary's performance, omitted mention of McKellen, although he was much praised by *The Times* for his fine display of controlled hysteria. Hysteria again!

Denis, with Ian's stepmother Gladys, was at the opening night of *A Scent of Flowers* on 30 September 1964, sharing the occasion. The following Saturday they made a trip to Kendal in the Lake District. Returning to Saviour Bridge, Bolton, they took a short cut to avoid heavy traffic on the A6. On a narrow lane a local farmer spotted a car coming the opposite way and braked his Land Rover to a halt. Denis did not stop, and in the head-on collision Denis received fatal chest injuries. In the interview with Lynda Lee-Potter thirty-four years later Ian said how he still felt the pain. 'I think he probably had a stroke because he was on the wrong side of the road. His insides were all bashed and he never regained consciousness. He lasted three days.' Gladys survived, although she was also in hospital with injuries.

Ian did not visit Denis those four days he lay in a coma, perhaps not quite wanting to believe his father was dying. He was still playing in *A Scent of Flowers*, which every night must have been quite macabre for him with the presence of Zoë's coffin on stage. One might speculate that his feelings were frozen by this event, just as they had been by Margery's death thirteen years earlier, so he did not fully pay his last respects.

So now, in a double turn of the fate with his mother, here was another traumatic family wound, as he admitted in that same interview. Just when he was feeling confident that 'perhaps we'd have been able to have an adult relationship, my father died. So there was a lot of unfinished business.' His self-image had been badly bruised because of the lack of communication with Denis, but his ambition would seem to have been even more deeply fuelled, and that would last. Unspoken grief 'cathected' him even more, in the word used by M. Scott Peck in *The Road Less Traveled*, to bond with the theatre and theatre people every bit as strongly as others do with their families. It was hardly a wonder he would continue with what became something of a preoccupation, if not an obsession, to emulate Olivier.

The funeral took place in the Chorley Old Road Congregational Church the following week, and Gladys, now over her injuries from the crash, served family mourners and friends, while a host of local dignitaries attested to Denis's distinguished service as Bolton's borough engineer. Gladys was to go on living until she was a hundred, and Ian till the end was a faithful visitor.

After the funeral he was back on stage the next Monday, with the ever-present coffin and with that deep and critical wound unhealed: 'To my dying day,' he told Michael Parkinson in 2004, 'I shall regret that I never completed my relationship with my parents by never telling them such a central thing about myself.'

As 'Gogo' he won his first acting prize, the Clarence Derwent Award for best supporting actor, for his display of controlled hysteria. One night, he announced in 2018 to the *Sunday Times*, Noël Coward came to see the show with Derek Jacobi. 'Derek was in his production at the National, and Noël Coward took him out, and I wasn't asked to join them afterwards.' The interviewer, Louis Wise, wanted to know why. 'They went off together to the Savoy [where Coward was staying] and if you want to know why you'll have to ask Derek Jacobi.' He then gave a naughty laugh. Derek avoided the advances and left straight after dinner.

The performance led straight to Ian's next job, when the National Theatre tried to snap him up for three years, to join the stable of rising contenders to become the next Olivier: Jacobi, Jeremy Brett, Edward Petherbridge, John Stride, Ronald Pickup and Anthony Hopkins. It was Maggie Smith, who had seen *A Scent of Flowers*, who put him forward to play Count Claudio in Zeffirelli's production of *Much Ado About Nothing*. He spent eight months at the National but did not settle down. Apart from minor roles for stars-in-waiting, Claudio was his biggest part, a young nobleman who falls in love with Hero, and is deceived into believing on the eve of their wedding that Hero has taken a lover. It was his first stage contact with Maggie Smith and Robert Stephens, who played the principals, and Albert Finney, as Don Pedro, who in the sub-plot woos Hero for Claudio. McKellen was not much enamoured of his role, as wooing a member of the opposite sex did not come naturally to him, and it foreshadowed an awkwardness with his future Romeo and Hamlet.

Zeffirelli and McKellen did not exactly hit it off either. He found the director's meticulous control over-the-top when, before a dress rehearsal, he accosted Ian in the dressing room, eyed him in his blond wig and moustache, and settling on his lap applied rouge and lipstick to his face while holding forth about Maria Callas, opera and other gossip. While Harold Hobson called this a memorable production Ian remained disenchanted, and according to Elspeth Cochrane, 'hated working with Zeffirelli, so much so he wanted to leave the company'. But he kept his feelings to himself, and it did not affect his acting, as attested by the anonymous *Times* reviewer, who reported that his flaxen-haired, hanger-on Claudio, vacillating between arrogance and ineffectiveness, made better sense than Albert Finney's commanding Don Pedro.

He had an eye for his rivalry with the other young Olivier contenders, too. He had at once a strong awareness of the more enviable impact Jacobi was making in roles such as Michael Cassio with Olivier as Othello, and while watching him from a distance, felt Derek had the kind of career that every actor might want, although as he put it much later, as 'Jeune Premier for Olivier, mind you, there were an awful lot of them!'

He did appear briefly with Jacobi at this time. When they went to Chichester to do John Arden's *Armstrong's Last Goodnight*, he and Derek were both covered in hair as hirsute Scotsmen. Ian described it to me once, back in 1965 (years before he and Derek were on television together): 'He was just in the first scene. He and David Ryall, Ted Petherbridge and I, had seen John Stride with such complexity speaking this Lowlands dialect of John Arden, which made us all laugh behind our beards – and then Derek, having played his scene, went off to watch the tennis. He was in *Black Comedy* (in which he made a hit), and I was in *Trelawny of the Wells*, which I don't think he was in. So that was the last and only time we worked together.'

Ian decided to leave the National. He got out because he could see there was no future for himself with the formidable competition. 'You just had to wait your turn to get the parts.' He was never one of Olivier's 'our gang'. He wrote to Olivier on 22 April 1965 declining his offer of a three-year contract and said that while he was enjoying *Much Ado* as much as the part allows (clearly not much), there was more chance of establishing his ability elsewhere. Even though, he said, 'my temperament is generally ambitious', now was the time to be on his own and 'explore a little'. Olivier wrote to Elspeth Cochrane to say that he was very unhappy at this decision, and was haunted at the 'spectre of lost opportunity'. Ian's main regret on leaving was that he never had the chance then, or in the future, to act with Olivier on stage. Many years later, in 1992, when McKellen was back at the National with Antony Sher, they had a dinner during which Ian sank into a gloomy reverie, declaring, 'We can't match him, none of us ever can.' Ian was fifty-three, and Sher looked at him in surprise because he had by now come to regard Ian as a better actor than Olivier. 'More truthful, more dangerous, and with his psychological studies of Shakespeare's dark characters – Iago, Richard III and Macbeth among the most remarkable – but he says nothing in reply – as we sit in silence.'

Ian shrugged at this, and aggressively refused to say more. Sher understood something from this: not the value and excellence of the roles Olivier had played (and he had been dead for eight years), but that he had simply lived his life on a different scale, and that neither he nor McKellen were on the same planet. Olivier was far, far above it, a restless soul forever howling, 'I'll show you!' 'An adoring mother,' says Sher, 'a cold father . . . his mother dies when he's very young, abandoning him to the stern rule of the clergyman father.'

Was there an echo here of Ian's own personal shades as he struggled to rise? He was still very much in this shadow, or rather the double shadow both of his father, and the secret of his sexuality.

8

Jeunesse Dorée in Dour Edinburgh

'Enter Ego from the wings, pursued by fiends. Exit Ego.'
Alec Guinness, *Blessings in Disguise*

Ian's early and brief big-company days were over; he'd had enough of that for the moment. He was now chancing his luck as a freelance actor in London. He and Brodie found a love nest in Earl's Terrace, a large ground-floor flat in Number 25, a quiet, secluded, tree-lined turning set back from the western end of Kensington High Street. The house was owned by the playwright Peter Shaffer. It was quite an enclave of theatre people, among them Peter Wyngarde. According to legend, Gerald du Maurier had been conceived at Number 25, which had belonged to his parents. It was a story that McKellen relished recounting.

Answer-phones had just been introduced, and much fun was had among this actor confraternity leaving each other messages with grand voices, pretending to be Olivier, Gielgud or Rex Harrison. Ian and Brodie's relationship of domestic intimacy was now quite open within their circle, if not in the wider world, while Brodie had stopped teaching – a profession, Ian observed, in which it would be impossible for you to declare you were gay. 'If I became a teacher, it would have to be hidden,' he pointed out, again in that 1998 interview. Brodie was to remain very loyal to Ian, with good memories of their shared closeness.

In 1966, Ian and Brodie entertained Wigan friends, Geoffrey

Banks and his wife Liz, before going to the Fortune Theatre to see him performing in *The Promise*. Ian, Banks told Mark Barratt, showed how nervous he was by worrying about if there were 'enough forks . . . Brodie just stood with his back to the fire and held forth. But once we were on our way to the theatre, Ian was back to his old self, chattering away.' It may be that Mc-Kellen was just being his awkwardly uncomfortable self, unable in private life to make decisions but always clicking in with the certainty of having a definite part to play. Performing expanded him into an utter carefreeness, but in social situations people would find him restless, unfocused, jerky, awkward.

Prior to this, Ian had opened in Donald Howarth's *A Lily in Little India*, seeing for the first time his name in lights over the theatre entrance in St Martin's Lane – third billing after Jill Bennett and Jesse Watson. The production had already run a few weeks at the Hampstead Theatre Club before its transfer, but, as McKellen said on the afternoon of the first night in late January 1966, they 'haven't got the photographs up yet'.

McKellen played the luckless juvenile lead as he had in *A Scent of Flowers*, this time escaping from a draconian mother: it is comic at first as his solution is to raise a prize Dragon's Fang Lily, a plant he is ready to defend with his life. When his mother makes her felonious assault on it through the bedroom window he hurls her to the ground and decamps with the cherished object to the home of a sympathetic girl.

Before the West End opening, Ian showed extraordinary nerve by inviting Lawrence Doble, a writer from the *Observer*, to spend the whole day with him. The ensuing article gives an insight into 'a day in the life of' his existence at that time:

This day's end is the evening on which the whole of his future life and career depends. To begin, here he is at 10.30, singing very loudly in his bath, letting into 25 Earl's Terrace some-one he has never met before, chatting away merrily when he emerges in sweater and jeans, serves coffee as the visitor eyes his books: Michael Foot's life of Aneurin Bevan very left-wing, politically correct even in 1965: a good choice for the *Observer* where Kenneth Tynan rules the critical roost. It is joined by Keats' letters, a biography of Ivor Novello. A touch of childhood is thrown in over coffee, the usual quiet teasing, testing of his visitor's sexuality as he asserts gently that it is not camp to be interested in music hall, it is being part of a tradition. 'I used to go backstage at the Bolton Grand while I was still at school . . . When we did a play at school I ran home for tea to get back quickly, or maybe I wouldn't go home at all. Doing a play was exciting. It was like having a secret.

Elspeth Cochrane may or may not join them for lunch, then it's the bank, petty purchases in Kensington High Street, and after a *piccata*, he confesses, going into the tube, that he has not slept much this week. His usual method of combating insomnia is to think of parts of his body, starting with his toes, but this hasn't worked. After a host of worries on arrival at the theatre, for instance whether his shoes need spraying to make them darker and inspecting sight lines in the gallery ('I couldn't see their eyes at the dress circle') they call on Jill Bennett in her dressing room. The privileged watcher is still in attendance, included in this intimacy and privacy, which at the same time is fake.

He and Bennett sit opposite in chairs only a foot apart and run through lines. 'I don't know why people make such a fuss about first nights,' [Bennett] says, digging her nails into the arm of the chair. 'My housekeeper's burning candles to St Anthony.' 'I wasn't a bit nervous until I got to the theatre,' says McKellen. Someone starts to do various exercises on another floor. 'I wish they wouldn't,' Bennett says, 'it makes me feel I ought to be doing them.' 'Olivier does weight-lifting,' says McKellen [again the Olivier obsession!], then adding, 'Maggie Smith plays records of the Beatles . . . She says they're soothing.'

They send up the lily which appears in the play:

McKELLEN: It's the star now.

BENNETT: It's very strong and big.

McKELLEN: A real Dragon's Fang.

Astonishingly, this carefreeness about the first night carries on until the first call: 'Fifteen minutes, ladies and gentlemen, to curtain up' with messages, good luck and a whole *Roi de Soleil* levee court unfolding around this actor, only twenty-seven years old, completely at ease, utterly unfazed while the impresario and playwright drop in with champagne and flowers.

McKellen won rapturous accolades in this role: 'a perfect mirror' for adolescent torments. *Plays and Players* described how his face, 'whether darkly framed by a Balaclava helmet or active with pride at the sight of the fast-growing lily, becomes a peaceful mirror for the amusements and ecstasies within'. He was now already established as a star on that rarefied plane of status and observance with its own rules remote from everyday life.

McKellen, still the humble Bolton boy at heart, with his Vespa parked outside the theatre, had begun to be surrounded by his court, as yet a small one, and it was to continue thus. He had this capacity at a precocious age to open himself up to almost complete scrutiny, making a nearly open book of his life, while at the same time keeping something deeply hidden. The media, which never stopped making him the subject of interviews, photo-shoots, speculation, conspired with him to keep the secret of his sexuality. Why? To hint or suggest he was gay might still lead to a libel case – unless of course he was prepared to come out and admit it himself. What was to stop him? Fear of public opinion, the general prejudice against gay people? From 1967 sex in private between two men who had both reached the age of twenty-one was no longer illegal. Yet concern that it could adversely affect his career was still very strong and probably justified. Maybe, he thought, he wouldn't have been playing

David Copperfield in the TV serial he recorded during the St Martin's run of *A Lily in Little India*.

Among other productions, there was also the successful long run of Alexis Arbuzov's *The Promise* at the Fortune Theatre. In this he played one of two secondary leads, the other being Ian McShane, to Judi Dench. Ian with his usual critical perspicacity had spotted Judi Dench long before: pure acting personality and a rich, warm being on which he could draw to learn and develop his craft. She was five years older than him, too, so there was no doubt who was the senior, both in status and stardom. Yes, she was a woman, so there was no danger here for him in terms of sexual attraction, although maybe in competitiveness.

'Where have you been? We're all waiting to start!' The thirty-two-year-old leading lady, quite peremptory, short (only 5ft ½in) had barked at her leading man at the first Playhouse rehearsal. He was twenty minutes late, and suitably and charmingly abashed at keeping her waiting. He was highly excited at seeing the Juliet he had admired at the Old Vic in the flesh with John Stride in the 1957 production, and even more at the prospect of learning from her example. She was much more than 'a bit' of a role model for him because he had seen her as Juliet. 'The idea that if you were going to act seriously you would not be too careful about where you did it, but you'd be careful about the company you did it in, seemed to me was what Judi was doing, and that was what I decided to do myself, so she was a bit of a special person.'

This sense of seniority held during rehearsals and performance. She was streaks ahead of him. His image of her rehearsing was of her tapping her toe, finishing off the *Telegraph* crossword, just waiting for everyone to catch up. 'Come on, what's the problem?' Ian said of her. 'She has a facility for acting which is bewildering, with a blazing sincerity and honesty; it wasn't a series of tricks she pulled out of the bag, it was all freshly minted in front of your eyes.' Like that mesmerising effect Peggy Ashcroft had on him as an adolescent, here was the woman *anima* incarnate. There must have been an echo also of that unfinished business with Margery Lois McKellen, which he always carried forward inside him as part of his unsolved mystery. Yet, on the first night, as Judi confessed to Ian, even she was very nervous and told him, 'I'm just going to concentrate on the front row – focus on the three seats in the centre of the row and think that the Father, the Son and the Holy Ghost are sitting there.' Ian countered, 'They'd be sitting in one seat, surely?'

The Promise was a surprising hit and Judi Dench stayed with it well into the Fortune Theatre transfer, until the three-and-a-half hours of fur hats and coats began to pall.

After an unfortunate ten-day run for *The Promise* at Henry Miller's Theatre in New York, where it was picketed by American actors protesting against English actors appearing in the US, Ian returned to the Old Vic in a revival of Peter Shaffer's *Black Comedy*. Jacobi had rocketed to stardom in the original National Theatre production as Brindsley Miller, the lead. Ian did not play this but took over Albert Finney's limp-wristed dealer Gorringe – the 'antique-fancying pouf' in the phrase of the *Mail*'s Peter Lewis.

McKellen's first TV job had been in *The Tomb of his Ancestor*, the BBC Rudyard Kipling series in 1964, with two lines to say sitting up a tree in the rain on Hampstead Common. He told his agent, 'If that's your TV you can keep it!' He failed screen tests for *Barbarella!*. He failed to land the Australian outback outlaw Ned Kelly, when not only did he 'work out' for three months prior to the test, but also played a scene several times over in Bushey Park with others. Tony Richardson cast Mick Jagger.

A film he made with Gregory Peck with the unlikely title of *The Bells of Hell Go Ting-a-Ling-a-Ling* went the way of its title and closed down owing to early snow in Switzerland. McKellen received a welcome £4,000, although he was to feel sometimes he never earned enough, spent little or nothing on clothes, and took frugal holidays. Two films in 1969, *A Touch of Love* and an adaptation of *The Promise*, did little to expand his hopes.

In *Alfred the Great*, his first big-budget film, McKellen played Roger the Bandit opposite two stars hardly older than him, Michael York, acting the Norse King Guthrum, and David Hemmings as King Arthur. York and Hemmings, not only enemies in the film, rented rival castles, York Gergana Castle near Galway, Hemings the much grander Oranmore Castle. Hemmings kept a court, threw lavish parties, inviting over and feasting his friends, among them iconic models Penelope Tree and Cheryl Tiegs, and photographer David Bailey. Ian coveted their film stardom and profitably observed their behaviour for his next stage roles.

The play of *Richard II* deals with the events of 1398–1399, when Richard, at the end of his twenty-two-year-reign, aroused huge discontent by instituting forced loans, and by his cronyism and arbitrary rule. It is a chronicle of catastrophe which the king brings on himself. When Jacobi played the role in 1988 for Prospect, the same company as Ian in 1968, he was nearer the well-seasoned, mature king showing the wear-and-tear of history. The self-defeating arrogance and narcissism was to the fore, as traits unusual in a man of his age, the self-realisation of what he had done to himself as a mature ruler, movingly poignant.

Prospect was essentially a touring company, based at the Arts Theatre, Cambridge, since 1961 under the sway of the formidable and substantially built Elizabeth Sweeting; its manager. Toby Robertson, the same age as John Barton and a contemporary of his at Cambridge, became Prospect's artistic director, with Richard Cottrell as his second-in-command. Cottrell, who also had a close history at Cambridge with Ian, asked him if he would do a modest nine-week tour playing the impetuous, self-regarding, kingly narcissist with 'the face that like the sun did make beholders wink'.

McKellen, whose method was to seek contemporary figures to tie his view of a Shakespearean part to today's world (implementing the theory developed by Jan Kott, at the time the all-pervasive, fashionable Shakespeare guru), claims that he drew first for this part on the Dalai Lama, someone to present to modern audiences a clear idea of divinity and belief in the Divine Right of Kings. But the modest, self-effacing Dalai Lama had little in common with Richard except that he is worshipped as a god in his religion. The saintliness of this modest self-effacing figure, who is known worldwide and worshipped not primarily as a god (which he is to his own people), but as a prophet of peace and love, is never an aspect of Shakespeare's character. It is a paradox that while Ian (and Cottrell) made Richard 'Our Contemporary', they underlined and played for everything it was worth the medieval notion upon which Shakespeare shows Richard fixated – the Divine Right of Kings.

When it came to performance the Dalai Lama, who made a good headline, was dropped for the 'true contemporary', the pop idol. The appeal of McKellen as Richard became that of the self-destructive pop star whose hubris was that he was above everyone else, and that he was 'God', in other words a man-made ego-god. So Cottrell and McKellen found the modern as well as eternal appeal in the Plantagenet court, and with a slant of ageism made Shakespeare's 'goodies' its baddies. John of Gaunt, who when Alec Guinness played the king and Ralph Richardson Gaunt, was the true exponent of what Shakespeare was demonstrating about the corruption of power, became, as Paul Hardman played him, the evil antagonist.

The highly commendable result, then, was that McKellen, decked out in exotic finery, exaggerated toylike splendour, and with a seductive, youthful, pouting appearance, wowed young audiences with the production's defiance of age and the traditional established order. The contemporary parallels of David Bowie and Mick Jagger were now only too evident. This approach was applied throughout the play until Richard's sheer incompetence as a ruler showed up the falseness of his fame and attention, which fell away until he was left trapped and pacing the perimeter of his cell, harking back to lost glory: 'Oh world, thy slippery turn! Friends now fast sworn,/Whose double bosoms seem to wear one heart . . .'

While Alec Guinness had foundered in this role by confusing the insecurity of his own personal identity with Richard, McKellen triumphantly, in Guthrie's words, 'rose above', bringing great clarity to Richard's self-pity as his protective shell of majesty cracks and crumbles into pieces. He was exceptionally good in this latter part of the play. Sometimes the pathos of particular lines was over-egged, as Irving Wardle complained in *The Times*, but most memorable and revealing in its heartfelt power to move, was Ian's cry as Richard – 'Taste grief, need friends.'

Toby Robertson, Prospect's artistic director, did not wholly approve of Ian's reading of this line, and while admitting this story was against himself, said he felt Ian exaggerated the part. In the 'need friends' scene, he thought that 'he wailed those last words and I found it embarrassing. I told Cottrell that I thought they should be toned down. But neither he nor Ian agreed and so he went on saying them like that. Of course, that was the one speech that the critics commended!' Michael Billington was one: 'I have never heard the line . . . come across with such poignant urgency.'

Richard Cottrell reflected later, in 1981, that he and Ian saw Richard clearly in terms of his spiritual journey, 'shallow and heartless at the beginning, then the pivot coming at the "needs friends" speech – that suddenly came out as a great cry at a rehearsal . . . That was the turning-point.' Tydeman says he could in 2017 still hear the heart-rending tone in Ian's voice as he cried out 'I need friends,' then repeated it with the emphasis on need: 'I *NEED* friends!'

After they opened, McKellen, with his wide eclectic range of other influences – rather like rival playwright Robert Greene's attack on Shakespeare as the 'upstart crow dependent on our feathers' – was accused of stealing bits of his interpretation from, *inter alias*, Gielgud, John Neville, Paul Scofield and Alec Guinness. Audrey Williamson, journalist and author of *Old Vic Drama*, pointed out that his ceremonial entrance came from Gielgud, his rhythmic pacing in prison from Guinness.

While he had most likely seen the productions, McKellen, touchy and intellectual in self-defence as he could sometimes become, refuted these claims some fourteen years later ('My commitment is to the audience and not the critics'). There was no need for this. There was no doubt, in these first weeks of touring the role, that he had pulled off a towering *coup de théâtre*. Also paradoxically, the Dalai Lama idea they began with had an effect for Cottrell and McKellen, as Harold Hobson, a committed believer in God, attested; which perhaps shows that it does not much matter how you get there, as long as you do. 'From the moment of his entry,' he wrote, 'we see that this Richard regards himself not, as we have always thought, as divinely God-protected, but as actually divine himself.' According to Hobson, Mr McKellen had on stage 'more than human smoothness . . . his arms are upraised from the elbows, framing the godhead and the crown, and fixed like the many arms of an Eastern Deity. His Richard is a god, but neither Christian nor Hebrew. He knows no compassion for his creatures nor at first revenge. His serenity is celestial and appalling . . . And yet, this god, this Deity, when he is with his boon companions, his Bushey, Bagot, Greene is not a god at all but only an educated potboy . . .'

Young audiences, not surprisingly, were drawn like moths to this blinding illumination of youth and the underlining of student-age preoccupations, especially vulnerability, self-distrust and the painful journey towards self-knowledge. Maybe, too, the cry for friends was prophetic, a turning-point for youth, ready for expansion. *Richard II* opened the following year's Edinburgh Festival followed by a long continental tour.

*

When Prospect was asked to furnish a second play along with *Richard II* for the Assembly Hall in the 1969 Edinburgh Festival, Toby Robertson thought, first, of the film star Gary Bond as Henry V, then of Jacobi as Edward II, with Ian as his first choice for the part of Gaveston. When Jacobi, who was filming *I, Claudius*, could not appear, Robertson asked Bond again, who agreed. But Bond then dropped out, so there seemed no one else and the part of Edward II fell into Ian's lap. The task of playing both Richard II and Edward II in the same repertoire was monumental. Robertson, a charismatic convincer, took Ian to lunch and persuaded him.

So who *was* Toby Robertson? Six foot four tall, gangling limbed, warm-hearted, with a twinkling, mischievous look in his eye, and always protective and paternal towards his cast, he perhaps never had the attention and acclaim he deserved. Perhaps by being self-effacing he lacked the dictatorial streak that rocketed other directors into celebrity. He did not, as Peter Hall described it, see directing as an ego-fuelled, entrepreneurial profession, but rather more as a midwifery calling. When Robertson had directed Jacobi as Edward II for the Marlowe Society at Cambridge earlier, Jacobi said Toby helped him to feel 'as if Marlowe had written this part specifically just for me, with its amazing combination of vulnerability, doubt, passion, confusion and power – and, I have to add, specifically many and varied rhythms and musical notes'.

When Ian opened in Edward II in the dour Assembly Hall, with the innovatory staging in the round established by Tyrone Guthrie, the audience rose to its feet in tumultuous acclaim. Timothy West, who previously had played Bolingbroke, and now was the antagonist Mortimer, could not believe that, acted as it was 'in a gothic vault', a play that began with two men kissing on the mouth, could receive such a rapturous reception.

But there were dissenting voices, weighty with disapproval, for this must-see production. 'It is shocking and it is filthy,' John Kidd, a City Father, fulminated at the on-stage kissing between

Edward and Gaveston in that hallowed ground where the elders of the Kirk of Scotland meet. The police were called. Ian Mackintosh, the company general manager, managed to persuade them not to call off the production by saying he himself did not object, and his father and grandfather were moderators of the Church of Scotland.

The shock, as ever, generated welcome publicity, but it was the difference between the two kings he alternated playing that McKellen was most determined to emphasise, at the cost, perhaps, of some of the quality of the work. Both directors, Cottrell and Robertson, had the same approach to Ian, namely they had no overall mission to fulfil, and did not want in any way to impose their reading on the text. This was in the hallowed tradition, still, of Dadie Rylands' approach of letting the plays speak for themselves as their enabler and allowing their timeless appeal to come over. *Edward* was much more of an operatic and musical play with Marlowe's mighty lines.

Ian's portrayal underlined the coarser side of Edward's sensuality, which was not to everyone's taste. Robertson's ultimate trust in leaving it to McKellen to impose his own stamp on Edward did not at all please Harold Hobson, although he praised the 'bold and hypocritical production', proclaiming Marlowe 'as pro-sodomy and anti-snob'. While conceding Ian was an actor of great spiritual grace, 'he is not graceful to look at', and all these smacking kisses before his angry nobles suggested to Hobson little more than that Edward was tiresomely addicted to showing off. Finally, he believed the great ovation raised by McKellen 'was not really deserved' as his performance descended into 'monotonously exhibitionist reiteration . . . This is worse than disappointing: it is positively boring . . .'

Yet taking on this double yoke became 'the making of Ian'. Irving Wardle in *The Times* did not find the play to be boring at all, pointing out that Ian's Edward did not follow a linear development but a 'series of bold leaps involving startling physical transformations – the infantile lover, with no interest whatever in Kingship ... hardly able to lift a sword, changing into the blood-drunken warlord and finally the emaciated wreck in the sewers of Berkeley.' It was an extraordinary quirk of fate that by Jacobi's default, it was these two roles that established Ian's pre-eminence as the classic stage actor.

When Robertson had directed Derek Jacobi in *Edward II* at Cambridge, the production, in which I played a small part, owed much to the beautiful scoring, modulation and above all the pace of verse-speaking Jacobi and Richard Marquand as Gaveston brought into play. Behind Toby's production, together with Rylands' influence on the verse-speaking, had been the *éminence grise* of Barton's dictatorial hand. Reflecting on the contrast between the two productions nearly twenty years afterwards, Robertson told Joy Leslie Gibson: 'The production ... with Jacobi was quite different. It was a *political* play, I felt Ian brandished, *flaunted* the homosexuality ... I had had a fruitful and happy time with Derek exploring the play ... Ian was too actorish, too much "we're in the theatre."' Robertson missed the interaction of power and suffering that Jacobi brought to the part, claiming McKellen was too narcissistic and lost people's sympathy. 'My lasting memory is of his brandishing a sword over his head as the lights went down at the end of the first act. A typical, theatrical, McKellen gesture.'

This was not the first and last time Ian succumbed to what Hobson called 'the destructive tide of homosexual infatuation', although he was to become more subtle and discerning in his expression of it. The difference was that in *Richard II*, McKellen captured or showed the inner qualities of genius, the quicksilver brain (his own, that is), the need for secrecy that Richard possessed in common with Shakespeare. In *Edward II*, Marlowe, a writer of much broader pen strokes, did not possess this.

And curiously enough, too, the two sides of McKellen's amatory personality appeared to be emerging to the fore with these regal overreachers. With Richard there was the intense need and desire for worship and friendship, and with Edward the powerful urge towards expression of sexuality. Away from the theatre, on the one hand, there was still Brodie, ever faithful and dependable; on the other there was now to be someone else of a very different calibre.

9

Travels with My Peers

At this juncture Ian fell in love with a glamorous film star. Peter Shaffer once called the stage actor, vis-à-vis the takeover of professional evaluation of reputation by film and television, the endangered species. Yet the stage provides the only proof, believed Shaffer, of whether an actor can act greatly. Ian was now a star of stage but not of screen.

This must have been about the *Little India* time or shortly after: it is not exactly clear when. No admission was forthcoming, or has ever been made. McKellen could be very tight-lipped, and there was quite a strict limit to his self-admissions or public confessions, although he could appear disarmingly indiscreet when it suited him.

A case in point is that kiss in *Edward II* in Edinburgh, when the stuffy city elders' complaint sent the police to the Assembly Hall to see if it broke the law as an indecent act. It did not, and the police left the hall. But it is hard not to feel there was a deliberate teasing in the whole episode on McKellen's part, for years later, on his website, McKellen proclaimed with a certain waggish provocativeness, not to be taken too seriously, that at the auditions at the Hampstead Theatre Club to cast potential Gavestons he had to kiss them. James Laurenson, an actor a few years younger than him from New Zealand, got the part. 'I still recall the softness of his lips . . . It was a bonus throughout the run.'

Ian's sexual drive, as witness his acting in *Edward II*, was never in doubt, and it sometimes dominated, as and when he allowed it to. It flooded his work over the next years. A particular peak of this was to come; to give an example, when he acted Giovanni in *'Tis Pity She's a Whore* in London, on tour and in New York for the Actors' Company. About this Michael Billington wrote, 'his body quivering with a restless nervous energy, he suggests a man whose bottled sexual passion might explode like a mechanical retort.'

Yet the devoted monogamous partnership with Brodie Taylor had lasted eight years; both faithful in their Kensington High Street love nest, or so it seemed, until someone else came into view. Ian was feeling restricted in this relationship, that Brodie was tying him down too much, and he wanted to spread his wings. This was the moment when the film star Gary Bond, a year younger than McKellen, entered his life.

One of the 'most enduringly handsome actors' of his generation, Bond 'was also a resourceful and sensitive performer of wide range and polished technique'. Robertson and Cottrell had approached him in 1969 to play Edward II before McKellen took the role. He was the star from *Anne of the Thousand Days* and *Zulu*. He wanted to advance his career in classical roles so joined Prospect as Sebastian in *Twelfth Night*, Major Sergius Saranoff (the Olivier role) in George Bernard Shaw's comedy *Arms and the Man*, and a highly personable and lively Benedick in *Much Ado About Nothing*. To cap all these youthful, handsome appearances, he played the passionate and youthful Byron in Prospect's *The Byron Show*. He was, if you talk to people of that era, a highly desirable man who was openly gay, quite promiscuous, and therefore an enormous centre of attention for the gay community, while ostensibly having Jeremy Brett, another handsome and desirable actor, as his long-term lover. Brett at fifty would become a romantic icon with his unnerving attachment to playing the 'voluptuous baroque' Sherlock Holmes on television and in the press has been dubbed a 'misogynistic butthead' and 'a total sweetheart'.

Everywhere he went Bond turned female and male heads,

but it was the latter he responded to, and not just one or two. He was, one might say, the Rudolf Nureyev of the theatre scene, with something of the 'availability' streak sometimes common to both great female and male actors (Peggy Ashcroft was an example of the other side of the coin). After his time with Prospect his fame became legendary, with long runs dominating the musical theatre from 1972 on, as the lead in *Joseph and the Amazing Technicolor Dreamcoat*, and then the narrator and character Che Guevara in *Evita*. A former lover of Bond tells me, 'He was part of one of the first relatively out [gay] couples with Jeremy Brett, but theirs was an on–off liaison which lasted for years . . . Bond was irresistible, with an easy warmth of manner, wonderful humour and sometimes a wicked sense of fun. He was divine, lovely, and wonderful in bed.' But, my confidant adds sadly, 'Died early, ended up with an American artist.'

McKellen has kept silent about this sexual fling with Bond. At the time, when he was in the throes of his passion for Bond, he must have known the relationship with Brodie would not last. It could be that he was becoming restless and tired of the settled domestic life, and that this had already begun to decline. McKellen does say the relationship 'changed' in 1972, the date Bond opened in *Joseph*. He moved out of Earl's Terrace, and bought a terraced house in Camberwell, south of the river.

It devastated Brodie, who screamed and shouted outside the house until McKellen had to threaten calling the police to make the break final. It brought to an end the settled years they had been together. Brodie remained tight-lipped about what had happened and who the other man was: 'There really isn't anything I want to get off my chest,' he informed an earlier biographer of McKellen and today is quite reconciled and forgiving.

Bond brought about the final break-up with Brodie, to which McKellen referred obliquely with some self-denigration and understatement in 1971 to Michael Owen, that in his private life he was ineffectual. 'I can't make decisions. I used to be sure of myself and saw a distinct pattern for the future but now I am confused.' Bond died aged fifty-five, from an AIDS-related disease in October 1995. Brett died exactly one month before Bond.

So now Ian found himself single, living alone in Camberwell, and an established star of the stage, if not yet the screen. And he worried about one issue in particular that had never bothered Bond. Would audiences take his acting seriously, as Romeo for instance, if they knew that in real life he fancied Mercutio rather than Juliet?

10

Wolfitting down Hamlet

'The unconscious mind has only a few characters to play with'

Iris Murdoch, *The Black Prince*

Hamlet is a good person, and he is, although clouded by doubt, confusion and revengeful feeling, a very sane and rational being. To distort him otherwise or see him as a vehicle for an actor's personal feelings, or a vehicle for theatrical braggadocio, is beset with dangers, although often attempted, and sometimes achieved. Just as Jacobi, on balance and over a long classical career, could not usually convey violent evil consistently, so Ian did not – or not yet anyway – excel at goodness and balanced normality.

One plausible theory is that *Hamlet* is a play about Shakespeare's lost son, Hamnet, who died aged eleven-and-a-half. There is embedded in the play a very deep sense of grief, and of what might have been, frequently expressed by other characters: Gertrude, Polonius, Ophelia and Fortinbras. This interpretation is not mine alone, and it holds together a difficult conception of what is in many ways a flawed masterpiece, challenging to any aspiring actor.

The choice of the director is of paramount importance with this play as no other. One good example is Peter Hall's *Hamlet* with David Warner as an outstanding, soulful Prince. Voicing his ambition, after *Richard II* and *Edward II*, McKellen broadcast his desire to play *Hamlet* at Stratford, with Trevor Nunn directing. But while the Royal Shakespeare Company offered him a three-year contract, Nunn's participation was not forthcoming – though he repeatedly affirmed 'Ian is a brilliant, brilliant actor' – and so Ian declined the offer. Prospect, where his standing was high, said yes to the idea. But Toby Robertson, who had always in mind to direct Jacobi in the role, and did so later, did not, as he had in *Edward II*, want to direct Ian. Instead McKellen called on Robert Chetwyn, who had been Ian's director at Ipswich and, according to his agent, was determined that *Hamlet* should be seen in the West End.

Chetwyn, eight years older than Ian, a tall, bespectacled and mild-mannered man, who could 'turn the screws in rehearsal', came into the production on the crest of popular success, having directed since Ipswich a six-and-a-half-year run with *There's a Girl in My Soup* and then, just prior to *Hamlet, No Sex Please, We're British*; he had also done Joe Orton's posthumous *What the Butler Saw* at the Queen's Theatre, an unfortunate choice for Ralph Richardson to star in, which gave rise to the following, as far as I know, unrecorded incident.

This was when conventional West End theatre was turning to the challenge of making lunacy fashionable and subtle. Binkie Beaumont had taken the script to John Gielgud and Ralph Richardson on Joe Orton's specific request (one that most believed was a dark joke of his), while his agent Peggy Ramsay and Oscar Lewenstein respected his wishes because of his horrific murder by his partner Kenneth Halliwell. Gielgud said no, but Richardson was attracted by it and said he'd do it, provided certain cuts were made. He would not, for instance, discuss the size of Winston Churchill's genitals: reluctantly Peggy Ramsay agreed – and they substituted a cigar for the phallus! When they showed the script to Sylvia Watson, head of the board at the Haymarket Theatre, where Orton's play was to be performed, she asked to have some words explained – the first was 'homosexual'. After quiet previews the first night dissolved in fracas as members of the audience shouted 'Filth' and 'Get off the stage' and 'Give back your knighthood'. One headline next day said, 'Dead Playwright Booed by Gallery'.

Richardson, who put money into the production, had been tempted by such lines as 'Lunatics are melodramatic. The subtleties of drama are wasted on them.' But throughout the run he betrayed his classic symptoms of non-identification with the role, with the purpose of the play, and with Orton's stated intention, which was to shock the audience and be obscene. His main stricture on Orton's work, in spite of a conscious effort to overcome it, came from deep within him: it was, as Peggy Ramsay said, that he could not enjoy himself. He was unable to find anything of himself in the role that would enable him to relax.

What the Butler Saw signified there was now a seismic change in the cultural perception of madness, and also of homosexuality. In Orton's perception, these factors placing people outside society were strongly linked. His interest may have had something to do with helping mentally ill people, but was likely more to do with effecting a revolutionary change in society's consciousness. Richardson dipped his toe in Orton, and then believed he had made a terrible mistake. Neither he nor Gielgud, Olivier, nor later Scofield and Jacobi, would go near Beckett and Orton, and were circumspect about Pinter.

This new perception of madness was crucial background colour to Ian's *Hamlet*. Ian and Chetwyn had shared a grouse in common because it galled Chetwyn that he had never been asked to direct at the National Theatre, which he ascribed to his working-class background and (according to Michael Coveney, his obituarist) his lack of standing with the directorial mafia. Now they could get their own back. Chetwyn had some quite fanciful ideas about how they would do *Hamlet*, which they discussed at length, and to which Ian agreed. To begin with, the set would be all mirrors, justified as being a recurring image in the play. Instead of one they would have three ghosts, to which

Chetwyn added the unconventional notion that the stage would be 'covered with ghosts and Fortinbras's army, which in reality was only about five people, looked [*sic*] like thousands'.

Chetwyn convinced Ian with his concept that the ghost was not real, but all in Hamlet's mind, in other words a hallucination, so later it fitted to have him put in a straitjacket when he is sent to England (where everyone is as mad as he). Patrick Wymark, cast as Claudius, was quite circumspect about this, even confused: 'McKellen says they have no fancy interpretation to offer; the play is quite difficult enough . . . But this is broadly how they are seeing it: Hamlet is first shown as an extremely depressed little boy finding everything possible wrong with his world. Then he sees the ghost of his father which, Mr McKellen says, is a "mind-blowing experience . . ."'

When they rehearsed at the London Welsh Club on the Gray's Inn Road, McKellen had another Cambridge mafia figure, Julian Curry, as Horatio, and some other good friends, Susan Fleetwood (Ophelia), James Cairncross (Polonius/First Grave-digger), Nickolas Grace (Second Gravedigger/Player Queen) and Faith Brook, who portrayed Gertrude as increasingly weepy and alcoholic. Somehow rehearsals, once under way, did not reflect the comfortable set-up, for Grace observed how Ian and Chetwyn just focused on Hamlet himself and the immediate scenes affecting him, while the cast did not understand the concept of mirrors. Ian grew isolated and cut himself off. While a 'wonderful leader when he was happy,' says Grace, when he wasn't, this made for a 'production with bumpy gear changes'. When it opened in Nottingham, Toby Robertson did not like the production at all, while again in the Second Gravedigger's view the vibes on the first night were pretty awful, with everyone trying to say, 'Well done,' but finding themselves unable to. Ian himself was frustrated and grumbled to his friends such as Cottrell, 'What's wrong with it, what can we do?' No one was brave enough to tell him, prompting him to feel even more depressed, for as he said, when questioned many years later in

1990, what made him depressed was, 'When I act badly and no one seems to notice.'

Toby Robertson did not want the production to be seen in London, in spite of having the same 'youth' appeal as *Richard II* and *Edward II*. The *Nottingham Post* described McKellen's Prince Hamlet as a 'seventeenth-century loner on a mental LSD trip . . . you'd almost take him as a modern youth'. Yet Ian and Elspeth, his agent, were determined in spite of tepid management and poor reviews to bring it to the West End. They persuaded Eddie Kulukundis, the generous impresario and Greek shipping magnate, to back it, as a springboard, and then send it on a continental tour to recoup big financial rewards. Opposition was strong, voiced by Peter Ansorge, editor of *Plays and Players*: 'McKellen gives a sudden, shuddering emphasis to lines which seem to bear little or no relationship to his or any other interpretation of the play.' 'Self-intoxicated febrile juvenile,' fumed another critic, with diction of 'incredible eccentricity'. 'The best thing about Ian McKellen's Hamlet is his curtain call,' wrote Harold Hobson. The lamentable list went on and on. Yet defiantly McKellen told Wymark it was the best thing he had done so far – whatever the critics might say. He was suspicious 'that a lot of people hate me as an actor'.

There were continental raves and applause on tour, especially in Rome, where Faith Brook, with her 'befuddled doll' Gertrude, said all the audience was on drugs and Ian took fifteen curtain calls, exclaiming, 'I feel like Donald Wolfit' – referring to the great actor-manager of the mid-twentieth century, now out of fashion but famed at the time for his barnstorming Lear and Hamlet. Now on top form, basking in the adulation and enjoying *la dolce vita* off-stage, Ian, Grace tells me, in the fight scene with Laertes stabbed his own eyes with two fingers to bring tears to them. Yet still, with his psychotic approach, Ian apparently had made a fundamental misconception about who and what Hamlet was. Indeed, Hobson had said Ian lacked any compulsive conception in his performance, and that the 'whole evening created an impression of a Wolfit production without Wolfit'.

McKellen remained ambivalent about Hamlet. Many years later he turned against the role and in 1989 vented his anger in the *Independent*, exclaiming that 'Peter O'Toole was right when he said it was just one long wank from beginning to end – pure self-indulgence. So much of the play encourages you to be self-obsessed and neurotic . . . any actor more than thirty is dreary – Hamlet should be eighteen, a kid – otherwise his behaviour is inexcusable.'

He might have consoled himself that he did not come off as badly as Alec Guinness who had, twenty years before, among other eccentricities and lapses, cast Kenneth Tynan as his Player King. Tynan called Guinness's performance '*Hamlet* with the pilot dropped'. Guinness took on himself the full responsibility: 'It was my fault, don't blame yourselves,' he told his cast after the first-night curtain came down. 'I gave up in the first act.' *Hamlet* takes its toll on good actors.

Ian's constant revisionist spirit chipped in later with the claim that when Hamlet meets the ghost, it was immaterial whether the audience believes in ghosts or not. Much later, in 1980, McKellen was to say, 'The play is not about ghosts, it is about Hamlet's inner life, about his meeting with his own conscience, about his settlement with his friends, with his family and with himself. It is about a young person's search and that is why this play has always fascinated young people. And Hamlet is no dreamer, he is a person who thinks.' Ian was yet again reflecting on a very different view of the actor, himself, not quite knowing who or what he was when he played the Prince.

Hamlet is at heart a father-son play and implicit in it and in every aspect of Hamlet's character was Shakespeare's own grief over his son Hamnet's death. It may be stretching a point but perhaps Ian's difficulty with the part connected with his father. Ian and Denis had been affected by non-communication before Denis died. There had been no row, no anger expressed, no clearing of the air before the terrible accident happened, but only reticence and cover-up. It would have been better if both had been forthright.

The role is such a stumbling-block for ambitious actors. The play is a complex work, in which the main character fails to find a reassuring simplicity in himself. 'Hamlet is only interesting,' Peter Brook observed, 'because he is not like anyone else, he is unique.' He rages through every kind of style: obscene, cynical, choric, sublime; he passes from scorn and ironic incongruity to soul-searching meditation with effortless ease. For an actor, the best way to approach him is as a creative writer building a character. Interpretive ideas and critical analysis do not work. 'The gaps,' says Brook, 'the delays in action Hamlet causes himself through his own primary need to find himself, not only to be tragically reflective, but he is a genius in a crisis.' This summed up perfectly the problem Ian had, for it was he himself who was the genius in a crisis.

He had been along the right lines making Hamlet, or trying to make him, an image of modern youth, 'shaggy hair, stark jersey, dirty boots, medallion chain, fringed jerkin', but he fell short, as an actor, of showing the search and the need to find himself, or rather only showed this in impassioned fits and starts. The compensation was, as ever, his great gift of being magnetic on stage, and commanding and reassuring to the audience. Shakespeare made audiences secure in their contemplation of Hamlet with generosity and underlying stability; ultimately the effect of the tragedy affirmed life instead of denying it.

From poor reviews and an uncertain start he improved considerably, as certain of the best critics who saw it more than once (Irving Wardle, Benedict Nightingale, among others) faithfully recorded. As ever McKellen kept doggedly at it. J. C. Trewin wrote up Ian's performance as one of the five-and-eighty Hamlets he chronicled in a book, and saw it when it returned to the Cambridge Theatre in Covent Garden. He said that 'it was a little too soon for some hyperbole' but that it had emotional certainty and naturalism, which sometimes could go too far (in his delivery of, to Ophelia, 'You shouldn't have believed me'). He applauded McKellen, especially during the Play Scene, for his splendid sustained fury and decision. 'With, as ever, magnetism, theatricality and sheer energy to the fore.' Thus McKellen finally fulfilled Shakespeare's depiction of the melancholy prince.

The saint-like critic Trewin in his classic account was politely wary when old Hamlet's voice rose 'from the midst of a multiplicity of reflected ghosts', while the device 'which did not help Hamlet at all was his confinement in a straitjacket at "How all occasions." Once, I understand, a modern director, doubtless looking forward to "Denmark's a prison" (II.2), a phrase much quoted, made Hamlet act his early scenes wearing manacles.'

So much for 'modern directors', in other words directors with their own concept of Shakespeare. But, as McKellen got into his stride on tour and barnstorming took over, there were, after all, shades of Donald Wolfit.

11

Actors Seize Power!

'You learn through a theatre company that mutual dependence leads to a faith in the human spirit which is very sure'

Trevor Nunn

Kenneth Branagh remembers a joke he'd heard in relation to McKellen and the Actors' Company.

'Isn't it marvellous about Ian McKellen and the Actors' Company. This week he's playing Hamlet, and last week he was in something where he just played the footman.'

'What was the play called?'

'*The Footman.*'

Edward Petherbridge, the new visitor to McKellen's dressing room in the Cambridge Theatre after a *Hamlet* performance in September 1971, had much in common with Ian. Both were socialist pacifists with a belief in equality, while the visitor, when aged nineteen, had served three months in Wormwood Scrubs for his refusal to join up for National Service. Both had lost mothers at early ages, both were Northerners from industrial towns who shed their accents; both had been in Olivier's National Theatre company in the early days, although McKellen, after a short spell, had left. Petherbridge had stayed on at the National and played Guildenstern in Tom Stoppard's first successful stage play, *Rosencrantz and Guildenstern Are Dead,* but in spite of this had grown tired of it for the same reasons that Ian had left, namely there were too many young contenders for leading roles.

Ian told Edward he was going to Sheffield to help inaugurate the new Crucible Theatre, where he would play the old actor in Chekhov's virtual monologue, *Swansong*, with David William to direct. Later the same night, at 1 a.m., Edward telephoned Ian to ask if he could join him to play the tiny supporting part of Nikita, the old prompter. This flattered Ian no end: the actor who created Guildenstern in Stoppard's play at the National offering to walk-on at Sheffield? It was like, thought Ian, a champion golfer offering to caddy.

This was how McKellen's next venture, forming the Actors' Company jointly with Petherbridge, came into being. Two months later the potential founding members, including Petherbridge, Eileen Atkins and Robert Eddison, met at Ian's house in Camberwell. The principle behind it was a company of equals with equal pay and billing for all, sharing leading roles as well as smaller ones. Richard Cottrell outlined the concept: each member should have a leading part, a supporting part and a small part, while anybody had the right to drop out if they had an outside project they wanted to do instead, and with no bad feeling. Later, when they were under way, they printed a manifesto in their programmes with these principles: 'The Actors' Company is a group of experienced actors and actresses who have combined to play both leading and support-ing roles in their own Company. Through mutual discussion they have made all artistic decisions concerning plays, direc-tors and casts. Their aim has been to produce a company of equals.'

At this first meeting of the twelve, Eileen Atkins had to drop out because she was committed to plays in London and New York. Ian felt they were all rather proud and surprised at their own daring. The meeting swung between seriousness and hil-arity with Ian 'vaguely' and 'apprehensively' in the chair. The democratic first aim was that while actors are usually the last to be considered or employed, they would now take control of planning up to the time of starting rehearsals, they would choose the plays and invite the directors they wanted to direct. The second aim was 'equality' as 'all commercial theatre in Britain and, whatever their intentions, subsidised companies, rely on a pyramidal hierarchy with the star at the top.'

The auspices were good, and it was to be a testing enterprise to show how the principles would work. According to Ian in the company manifesto, to be chosen 'by other actors whose talent and ability one admires, is about the greatest compliment one can be paid. It is an inspiration – and a responsibility – which rarely comes the way of an actor in Britain. I feel that out of this something exciting *should* be produced for the audience to enjoy.' So here we have an early taste of Ian the proselytiser, the politician with a cause. For McKellen the Actors' Company would be first and foremost a test of how much he could live up to, and observe the principles of, equality – living and sharing roles and wages of £50 a week, as well as the billing. Finally, they needed sixteen founding members, to finalise the plays: Caroline Blakiston, Richard Cottrell, Marian Diamond, Robert Eddison, Robin Ellis, Tenniel Evans, Felicity Kendal, Matthew Long, Edward Petherbridge, Moira Redmond, Sheila Reid, Jack Shepherd, Ronnie Stevens and John Tordoff.

At first they had a great run of luck because Richard Cottrell, who had left Prospect to run the Cambridge Theatre Company based in the Arts Theatre, wholeheartedly supported the venture and suggested twenty-four possible plays. They dutifully read these and whittled them down to three. Ian kept a diary, recording that everything Cottrell had promised went on to happen. They accepted the £50 salary, much less than any of them could expect were they working in London or on television. The three plays they decided on were all on Cottrell's list of suggestions. 'No: it wasn't that he pushed us around, then or later; rather that he sympathised with what we wanted to do and then worked out how he might provide it,' said Margery Mason.

At Cottrell's flat in Soho they agreed to rehearse two plays concurrently, the third at Edinburgh during the day and during a three-week tour before joining it to the others in a six-week repertoire at Cambridge. '. . . We are poaching Royal and National territory.' Ah well! Ian's formidable competitive juices were roused. Democracies with workers' control 'are always more exhausting', said Cottrell. Everything took time to decide. 'I was touched when I was asked to join the company,' said Robert Eddison. 'I was *so* much older than all the others. But it was all the greatest fun, huge fun, though I did find the meetings endless and ghastly. I never knew what to say.'

Meantime, in a rather lean year for Ian's earnings – 1972 was one of the few times he visited the Labour Exchange – he took on, funded generously by Eddie Kulukundis, a musical based on *Henry V* with the appalling title of *Hank Cinq*. In the absence of him singing in it, he would direct. But this came to naught and directing two other West End revivals did nothing to entice him to follow the directorial paths of Gielgud and Olivier. Yet again these displays, although not especially rewarded critically, attest to the superhuman energy of the man, sometimes bordering on monomania: at the time he was one hundred per cent involved in three contemporary plays in the provinces, formulating and executing plans for the Actors' Company, as well, in typical Ian style, as proselytising the press on the company's behalf. The enemy in the good old Quaker, non-conformist family tradition, was 'them' – in this case the out-of-touch RSC and National, the star system of the West End, and so on. But how much actual equality was there between him and the rest of the Actors' Company, and was it an illusion?

They had their first three plays. First Richard Cottrell's adaptation of Feydeau's farce *Le Dindon* with the English title of *Ruling the Roost*; they coupled this with Ford's *'Tis Pity She's a Whore*, irresistibly combining infidelity, bourgeois French farce, and chiaroscuro Italian passion. The third choice was Iris Murdoch's new play *The Three Arrows*, set in medieval Japan. Petherbridge, who had been due to play Hamlet at The Mermaid, dropped this, and was free to take part; Felicity Kendal was voted to play Annabella the Whore. Ian valiantly went on propounding the equality.

> I was 'offered' Giovanni, Ford's hero, and Victor, Feydeau's pageboy. After a year playing yet another Jacobean neurotic (i.e. Hamlet) I should have preferred my bigger part in the farce; but by now I was really convinced that the idea of the company means as much to me (and indeed to my career) as the parts I should play. Petherbridge felt the same and abandoned his initial indifference to Soranzo in *'Tis Pity*. Robert Eddison accepted two parts with an impressive but limited impact, with the 'pious hope' of an equally good part in the third play – whatever that would be.

Stars in disguise surely!

Some members of the company, almost at once, noticed the head-boy leadership quality of McKellen becoming indispensable, in spite of his wishing otherwise. Quite a lot of psychologists, historians and commentators of all kinds, from Aristotle ('The worst form of inequality is to try to make unequal things equal') to George Orwell, have said equality is something of a mirage. Ian had to act equal the best he could, and naturally treated everyone as his peer. With his natural kindness and easy disposition this was not a problem. As everyone struggled to meet their commitments outside and within the company, and personal clashes sometimes arose as they battled to keep it democratic, Ian was determined not to be seen as the star, and would never, as Margery Mason, a former Communist Party member, reported, monopolise the meetings.

When it came to casting the Murdoch play, the chosen director, Noël Willman, gave the committee his opinion that there were three actors up to the demands of the lead role of Yoremitsu. These dominated more than in any other play in the repertoire. They left the choice to those 'who don't already have a smashing part'. In a roundabout way Ian was saying that he should get the part, and as Mason commented, 'Though no one was supposed to have more than one leading part, Ian managed to get the lead in two of them! He has great powers of leadership!'

In terms of the company the 'star' of this first season was understandably John Ford's *'Tis Pity She's a Whore*. I was at the Edinburgh opening. The revelation for me was that before seeing it, I had thought the incestuous passion of Giovanni and Annabella hardly rose above purely sensual infatuation. This production showed that there was far more scope in their passion, far more possibility for ambiguity and affinity of temperament between the pair, than I had supposed.

The company had set out to make it a splendid and psychologically complex work, taut in plot, entirely gripping from the first moment to the last of its three-and-a-half hours. David Giles, the director, set it in a Mazzinian Parma, and Kenneth Mellor's two-level set provided an inner chamber for the incestuous love scenes, while a murky colonnaded walk allowed for the action to flow over with ease. The accompanying business was for the most part concerned with refreshment of one kind or another and was an ideal match for the often acid, often very sharp, quality of Ford's verse. For instance, Giovanni clutched a half-filled bottle of claret from which he took a defiant swig during Annabella's marriage to Soranzo. The absorbing use of hats and a host of other excellent small touches, like Bergetto's return to retrieve his glove, aided the natural progress of each scene. There was one small excess when Bergetto carelessly stuffed an ice cream in his uncle Ronaldo's face.

The first of the stunning climaxes was Hippolita's death, engineered by the fascinating Vasques. T. S. Eliot wrote of this that Hippolita's sub-plot was 'tedious', her death 'superfluous'.

If he had seen this production he would have changed his mind, especially in the way that Ian's Giovanni used the moment to foreshadow his own end. In the space where Hippolita has died, heaping her curses on the fatal marriage, at the end of the act alone he curls up, aping her demise.

The grisly end, when Giovanni appears with Annabella's heart on the point of his dagger, could have been laughable, or could have been obscene. As played by Ian, it was purely horrifying, leaving a haunting and terrible image. His performance rose to triumphant self-extinction, showing he found its main drive not so much in lust, but a dreadful deformed kind of narcissism which lay at the very heart of Giovanni's incest. But he succeeded also in showing the purity and innocence of the passion.

'Repugnant!' cries Vasques, who Jack Shepherd played with a seedy, alienated honesty, while as Annabella, Felicity Kendal defiantly emphasised the genuineness of her repentance, overheard by as good and sensitive a friar (Robert Eddison) as one might hope for. Edward Petherbridge's Soranzo was an impeccably exact study of nobility excited to revenge: it afforded a fine contrast to Giovanni.

Unmistakably Ian was again back on course to being, as Hobson pronounced magisterially, 'the most exciting as well as the greatest of our young actors'. A definitive production, then, but paradoxically hardly vindicating the principle of equality.

The director Ronald Eyre (not to be confused with Richard) reminisces about the company's next production, the Feydeau play. It took him back to when he was working for the RSC, and they thought that they should make their leading players play walk-ons as well. They asked Judi Dench to play a maid in *Much Ado About Nothing* and she went to great lengths to disguise herself, found a dark wig, put freckles on. She did not want people to recognise her and say, 'That's Judi Dench', and so upset the balance of the scene. 'Now,' said Eyre, 'you'd never get Ian to do anything like that. He would always want to be recognised.

You were only too aware that it was McKellen playing the footman.' Not again, please!

If McKellen had revealed something deep about his character and ego in this first Actors' Company season, it was undeniable that he was established as the great actor. This was never to change. But he himself was constantly seeking to improve, seeking to become the best of what he could be. Equality with others could never wholly satisfy him. McKellen would never tire, never give up; and his command of the stage and audience, which was his great gift and the thing that drew audiences, backers and fans, would never fade or diminish over time. He created, even in the most evil and despicable characters such as Giovanni, an absolute reassurance and tranquillity.

The second season of the Actors' Company in 1972–3 in Edinburgh, London and the Brooklyn Academy, New York, with much of the same high-plateau performance, received similar kinds of rapturous appreciation and critical stricture. Ian made a big hit in the New York plays as Michael, the lead in Chekhov's *The Wood Demon*, exploiting rather than indulging his emotionalism, but never allowing the fits of the doctor's petulance to get out of control: 'heady, lyrical acting', wrote John Peter from New York, while his Footman (!) in Congreve's *The Way of the World* won raptures for his comic inventiveness in delivering just four lines.

He shocked everyone when playing Edgar, with Robert Eddison playing Lear, by taking off his clothes in the 'Mad Tom' scenes. The legendary critic Clive Barnes wrote of this New York appearance, while admitting the sensational unity of the company (their costumes had not arrived so they had to perform in modern dress), that the production was stuffed with good, unobtrusive performances – *but* for Ian McKellen: '. . . admittedly playing Edgar as if it were a star role, but this is the special genius of Mr McKellen's acting. He has a natural blaze to him that no amount of democracy can douse. His Edgar is deeply felt and beautifully presented. He is that rare bird, an intellectual actor with incandescence, so not only does he know what to do, he also seems to know why he is doing it.'

This review sums up the whole paradox of the Actors' Company's excellent two years of life. Inevitably Ian gravitated back to playing leading roles, in which he won the plaudits. McKellen's Prince Yoremitsu in *The Three Arrows* was described by Billington as 'some jet-black stallion beating against the sides of a corral and his voice sings agony out of the least expected phrases.'

Those who believe passionately in equality are often loath to admit the paradoxical nature of human life and art. Ian refused to rejoin the National in 1972 to play leads in *The Bacchae* and Molière's *The Misanthrope*, the latter being, I believe, a sad omission for his public. It is impossible to imagine a greater potential exponent of Molière's great comic hypocrites – Alceste, Harpagon, Tartuffe – with the opportunities to act out and enlarge their often monstrous demonstration of double standards and folly.

But now Trevor Nunn, with yet again the Cambridge connection clicking in, was offering a whole raft of glittering roles to take Ian through right to the end of the 1970s. He had wanted him in the company ever since seeing him and Judi Dench together in *The Promise* and Ian alone in *The Wood Demon*. 'There isn't a whiff of experimental theatre or radicalism about the idea,' Ian had said at the beginning of this new venture, 'and as all those involved are experienced, even well-established performers, it isn't at all conceived along the lines of a political co-operative . . . I always feel that in every field of entertainment, the actor knows best – perhaps about everything except his own performance.' Yet McKellen, inevitably monarch of all he surveyed, even a company of 'equal actors', was, according to Frank Middlemass as he told Mark Barratt, 'the only one who really knew what he was doing. He's got the sort of brain that can cope. I think most actors are too volatile. They're creatures of emotion. And you needed a business brain as well for the Actors' Company.'

Not only, then, was it a question, in Orwellian terms, of all animals being equal, and some animals more equal than others, it was also the eternal reality, perhaps, that nature abhors a vacuum. What greater challenge was there ever likely to be than a company of actors who had joined for their passionate belief in equality? What better microcosm could there be of today's political macrocosm than paying lip service to a fair and idealistic equality being a possible choice, that you could put to the vote, while actually this was impractical in reality? If Ian had pursued equality, then perhaps he should have ruled himself out of the voting that chose him to play Prince Yoremitsu.

But it was not to go on – for there was the question of funding, and who would back the venture? For the confidence of the Arts Council, they had to have stars. As the Actors' Company manager William MacDonald summed up, there were too many egos in the cauldron. Everyone talked about abandoning the star system, but everyone was a star or a potential star. People came to see the stars – McKellen and Petherbridge – so 'in a way we were obliged to pander to the star system.' Yet the 'excitement, the acclaim, the queues – it was marvellous'.

Later Peter Hall was to comment to *Vanity Fair*, and after there had been some talk of Ian taking over the National Theatre, for which he had declined to put himself forward: 'He loves to hide behind the will of the group, when in fact it is his will . . . I don't think he enjoys the inevitable unpopularity that comes with leadership.'

12

One Step Forward, Two Back – or One Back, Two Forward?

Barton had now left academia and King's, Cambridge, for a fully blown, if slightly tempestuous and wayward, professional career. He had collaborated magnificently as director and adapter with Peter Hall and Frank Evans in the landmark *Wars of the Roses* of 1961–3. Under Hall's wing he had begun directing at Stratford, notably with Peter O'Toole and Peggy Ashcroft in *The Taming of the Shrew*. For conflicting, temperamental reasons he and O'Toole had fallen out and this had been a disaster. Other productions had followed and the general opinion in the profession was that you either liked and got on with Barton and his way – a somewhat dictatorial and academic one – of controlling his cast, or you did not.

McKellen after his one-man dominance and exercise of responsibility in the Actors' Company, in 1974 joined the RSC, his former bête noir. Chastened perhaps, as if returning to university, he adopted the formal actor-formative methods using movement and voice coaches, that Nunn had implemented in turning the RSC into something of a theatrical academy to bring continuity, trust, stability and development to his hand-chosen few. The company was half the size of the one Peter Hall had run. McKellen was ready and eager for such transformation – to submit to tutelage and to renounce leadership in the administrative sense, as long as he had the big roles. He responded to this almost puritanical, Leavisite takeover of his life, concentrating on a close and meticulous attention to the meaning of text and its moral value (Nunn had been a student of F. R. Leavis at Downing College).

The directors at the top included Terry Hands with Barton and Nunn, and Cecily Berry, the outstanding voice coach, who with healing as well as inspirational guidance, directed a complete restringing and retuning of Ian's vocal propensity. Trevor worked in a very intimate way, working out relationships between characters, looking for the truth. Terry was interested in the epic scale of plays. John Barton was into the form of the language. 'Head boys direct,' Barton once told me, and he had been head boy at Eton, while Ian filled the same role at Bolton Grammar. What would happen now? Would Ian submit, or would he seek control, to take over the levers, and want to inject and fill each production with every new idea or intuition he had, with razor-blade chewing Barton in the chair?

Surrender and acceptance was the new model. Glenda Jackson was also in this company. Submission was the name of the game, for 'we all lie out on our backs with our eyes closed and do Cecily's breathing techniques, starting by breathing on a vowel and building up. She then comes around and when she lifts up one of your arms, totally limp, suddenly you know all about relaxation. It's all about conserving breath and energy.' Submission was not a game Glenda could play for long.

Ian was now a yogi on a new learning curve. He declared that this was a limited company 'in which a group of people all worked . . . It's hierarchical, that's its structure.' Sexual anxiety and adventure, in the form of the highly romantic affair with Gary Bond, was over; the inseparable-couple-bond with Brodie broken for ever, and here now, without the responsibility of leading the company, Ian felt himself back in the place he loved as his home, the theatre, in an inclusive family. Trevor (who had something of a reputation as an elusive Pimpernel) was surprisingly present in the green room talking to people. Gone for the time being was that complaint that you could never find him; as Kenneth Branagh said in his autobiography, he would throw his arms round you and hug you – 'I had been enveloped in Trevor's hair and beard and deafeningly loud in my right ear was an enormous vowel sound' (this was called 'being Trev'ed') – and then disappear.

Caryl Brahms, Ned Sherrin's collaborator and an incisive commentator, wrote an extraordinary foreshadowing of Ian's future role of Gandalf: 'His face, in no way arrestingly handsome, is indeed his fortune, in that the blob nose and the un-arresting features are splendid for disguise and are not forever pulling one back from his characterisations to his own personality. His voice is strange, a little disturbing. It seems to come from a cranny high in the back of his throat.'

But it was also a slightly eerie premonition of the future that he was to make his RSC debut with Marlowe's master magician.

McKellen now humbly admitted that he felt it was very difficult to be objective about his own work. Perhaps the prestige of the RSC, once held at arm's length, now seemed more hospitable and on a scale he could respond to. He looked to Barton's restraining hand in *Doctor Faustus*. He claimed he often asked directors, lest they should feel inhibited as some did, not to hesitate to be very basic in their criticism. He wanted to work with Barton and Ron Eyre (for the next RSC production) as they were both very gentle and sympathetic people, but at the same time they were tough enough, and cared enough about their own work and the plays they were doing, to say, 'That won't do'. They would always be pushing him further.

It is hard to recognise the more dictatorial John Barton in this. The result in *Doctor Faustus* was not altogether successful, because in this combination of both great Cambridge minds, something of the sexual, sensual side of the text was lost. Gone was that rapid sensual quality McKellen had shown in *'Tis Pity She's a Whore*, while somehow the whole production took place in the head, and the play remained as much an enigma as before. The text, much of it not written by Marlowe, is 'calculatedly ambivalent', as the Cambridge literary academic Anne Barton, then John's wife, wrote in the programme, in addition to Marlowe's atheistic, homosexual and political contradictions. In fact, one seemed confronted with two enigmas, first the play itself, with all its complexities, and its episodic and largely irrelevant comic scenes, which Barton omitted. Then there was the enigma of what Barton did with it in performance, not primarily in the way he reshaped it, but more in his view of the play as it came through in McKellen's interpretation.

Barton used life-size Japanese Bunraku puppets for the parade of Deadly Sins, Helen of Troy, and the miniature Good and Bad Angels. He tinkered with the text to make *Doctor Faustus* more uniform and give it the single setting of Faustus's study. He added lines from the English Faust-Book to chronicle missing links in the narrative. He provided one long, lively scene of his own from a few lines in the original, when the Duchess of Vanholt indulges in bawdy horseplay with Faustus under her husband's nose. As the Duchess was exuberantly played by an actual actress (Jean Gilpin) not a puppet, the relief and titillation was considerable!

The character of Faustus, like Edward II, is not a very individual creation. Perhaps his incompleteness, deliberate in Marlowe's version, instead of tantalising the audience, in Barton's version made it confront inadequacies that might otherwise have passed unnoticed. The result was that by putting all the attention on to Faustus, and in not allowing his audience to be distracted from him, Barton gave McKellen an impossible task.

He acquitted himself badly. In the early part when Faustus's curiosity is seen to consume him, he leapt about the set in a highly unrealistic manner, contorting his frame, introducing strange throbbing inflections into his voice. It was highly mannered work, absolutely running counter to the meticulous set detail, the dozen or so different kinds of chairs assembled on every level in every alcove of the vaulted study; it also, more importantly, ran counter to Emrys James's measured and demurely precise Mephistopheles.

Although his delivery of some of the finer verse was cunningly modulated, McKellen's performance became full of tormented mannerism, summoned possibly to sustain him through the exacting task Barton had set him. The slower sections, when Faust is ageing, registered more convincingly than the rest, but this was far from being one of McKellen's best performances. Hobson compared McKellen unfavourably with Emrys James's quiet Mephistopheles. The introspective attitude the puppets established did not help McKellen either.

And no less beaten backwards and forwards from two sides of the critical court were the other main roles Ian played in this London RSC season at the Aldwych, all of which were bursting with restless energy and sometimes untempered enthusiasm. His Marquis in Frank Wedekind's *The Marquis of Keith* was, for instance, imbued for B. A. Young 'with something of Hitler', which may be going a bit too far, while his Bastard in Barton's production of *King John* again evoked split critical views: for Michael Coveney it was 'strikingly heroic' while for Irving Wardle he was just a 'Pistol-like bumpkin' whose weird reading of the part 'one must ascribe to the director'.

Equally the lead role of Colin in David Rudkin's *Ashes*, a nakedly personal account of an infertile couple, had for Hobson an unacceptably muddled accent (of Belfast, Birmingham and Lancashire) and a 'fearful complacency' to a character's sexual discontent, 'determined to be disappointed'. Might there have been here something personal in this projection of the role in McKellen's apparently chaste and self-imposed continence during this period?

Ian's enthusiasm about sticking with the RSC extended into 1975 when he wrote to Nunn, strongly desiring to continue at Stratford in the 1976–7 season. His condition was, Nunn told me in 2019, that he should play Macbeth. It did not augur well for his first assignment, that of Romeo (and then Leontes in *The Winter's Tale*), but the perk here, and the excitement, was that he was to be working directly with Trevor, who perhaps had something of a desire to straighten out and redeem some aspects of those previous performances. After Romeo, but only after it, would he scale the greatest height he had reached so far.

'How do you manage to look so young?' a fan asked Ian, aged thirty-four, about to embark on Romeo, the star-crossed lover. 'It's the magic of theatre,' he replied, 'something always takes over.' This was disingenuous because McKellen worked hard at everything, and in Romeo's case it was youth he sought to capture. He told Benedict Nightingale, who met him walking one day on the Embankment below St George's, Pimlico, that you needed to be a mature age to play Romeo properly (in contrast to, 'You needed to be young to play Hamlet'). Nightingale noticed how disconsolate his mood seemed, as if very lonely. Back with Trevor, as at Cambridge, he re-awoke the influence of Dadie Rylands, who had instilled in him the most scrupulous attention to the classic texts, releasing them from the straitjackets of habit and convention. Perhaps also closer to the mind and being of Shakespeare than any other academic or literary figure of the day, 'Dadie' remained for Ian an inner driver of the essence of Shakespeare. In the plays about great lovers, *Antony and Cleopatra* and *Romeo and Juliet*, there are few opportunities for the actual physical and sexual demonstration of love. Romeo is a part of sexual longing, conveyed aurally, and clearly this was going to be a big plus in McKellen's performance, as equally his sense of grief over Juliet's death. As Ian put it, 'Romeo's mad – he's a suicide case – he can't reconcile the enormity of love with the business of having breakfast and being nice to people.'

Some felt he over-egged the teenage rapture, the puny and

cadaverous figure he cuts in Verona's brawling society, but underneath the fever and uncertainty he projected in the role, the commanding actor would always be there, as attested by Francesca Annis, who as Juliet felt that the marvellous quality he had was his enormous confidence, and that on stage you 'would feel you are not alone. He would be in control if anything went wrong.' At the end he gathered Juliet when believing she is dead and did a controlled dance with her body round the stage until he slowly collapsed.

One night something did go seriously wrong, during the balcony scene, for after the farewell words of behaving like the winged messenger of Heaven, sailing 'upon the bosom of the air', as he left Juliet he slipped on a wooden rung and dived fifteen feet to the stage floor. Ian took the fall in good spirits, and, not so badly hurt, appeared smiling at the curtain call holding up the offending ladder rung. But later he did express a wish to abolish the balcony altogether, although priding himself that he and Francesca planned and achieved twenty-seven laughs in the scene. One came from an explicit orgasmic gesture in 'Thus with a kiss I die!' – they cut this as it caused embarrassed laughter. Later he dismissed his whole performance as a failure saying, 'I came to it too late.' Perhaps Sheridan Morley's comment had stuck: 'the two lovers [are] not only star-crossed but visibly into their thirties which makes me wonder during their duller moments why they aren't looking forward or worrying about their children's education.'

But once again it gripped audiences everywhere when so often this play can be dull. Nunn loved his exuberance and youthfulness. While Tyrone Guthrie had commented, 'You cannot act what is not in your physical nature,' this is not entirely accurate. The capacity to love was there, but he did not trust it, and was frightened to show it, while otherwise in acting he showed his true feelings.

He, Nunn and Annis, in spite of the barbed criticism, brought off *Romeo and Juliet* and prolonged its life in London at the Aldwych. Not so Ian's Leontes in *The Winter's Tale*, who was a victim of directional confusion, with Nunn doing the opening part of Leontes' torture and jealousy at court, Barton in control of the rustic Bohemia, and Barry Kyle tying up the loose ends at the close of play. It simply did not work. Ian remained, it was said, 'unmutilated' by the internal laceration of the play's abdomen, bowels and groin. *The Winter's Tale* did not stay the course and was dropped from the repertoire. Ian had no great fondness either for playing in Stratford's large auditorium.

He loved the subsequent tour of the next season as Andrei in *Three Sisters* with Ted Petherbridge as Vershinin, and Sir Toby in *Twelfth Night*, and joined with huge relish in every side of Nunn's innovative small RSC touring company, pitching in with building and bolting a portable high-raised platform, and then drumming up support for student workshops. Nunn had rejected the idea of the grander, non-stop tours in different places with little contact with audiences. This company was nearer the Actors' Company formula and Ian masterminded it as they worked more as a collective (Timothy Spall took over as Andrei). Trevor called the venture one of the best experiences of his life. 'Ian's always with us at the get-in,' explained the tour's lighting designer. 'He co-opted a three-boy team of help-ers who followed him up and down the portable scaffolding of the lighting towers, carrying cables, connecting point sockets, and becoming totally involved in the production.'

Here another side of the indefatigable loner emerged in Sheffield, playing for the first time the off-stage role of roving ambassador for his live theatre family, gathering plaudits for his flawless and untiring connection with every aspect of the work. The perfectionist at heart, he still had that fire and commitment shown at Cambridge, when amateur casts would stay up all night lighting and staging the plays. Indubitably it was in the work where he had found his soul and if he had stolen fire from heaven like the mythical Prometheus, it was to keep theatre alive and aflame. At the heart of it, too, was the roving gift he had so admired as a boy in the gypsies of the Bolton fairground, always moving on, always travelling life's highway with a song and a smile.

13

The Matching of Equals

'A book where men may read strange things'

Lady Macbeth

September 1976

Nine years after their success together in *The Promise* in 1967, Ian and Judi Dench had teamed up again in a revival of *Too True to be Good*, George Bernard Shaw's political extravaganza. Dench played Sweety Simkins, the cockney nurse who masquerades as a French countess, although she held the view (not very popular at this time) that Shaw's plays were more fun to be in than to watch. Ian, who played Popsy, the burglar who preaches social change, which came easy, defended Judi's fully rounded performance against some criticisms. Trevor had wanted to do *Macbeth* with them and that was their condition of joining.

When Judi and Ian found themselves matched up as the Macbeths, as they started rehearsals at Stratford-upon-Avon in the summer of 1976, both had very different preconceptions of the approach they would make to the murderous duo. 'I am always against those Lady Macbeths,' said Judi, 'who are strong and evil at the beginning. If they can do it on their own, why do they invoke the spirits to help them?' and, 'We try and tell a psychological story about people.'

Trevor saw the play as showing how the Macbeths were

110

unfulfilled in marriage and the thought that this was the cause of her breakdown. Her cold ambition is what drives Macbeth and finally turns him against her. As Ian explained to John Barton:

> I must believe in what I'm doing . . . I don't believe in witches and I don't believe in God, and Macbeth clearly believed in both these concepts. I've never killed a man . . . and I've never murdered . . . I've never been married, and so I have to imagine my way into all those aspects of his life by thinking of people I know, or it may be by thinking of a modern man, a contemporary whom I don't know personally but who's vaguely in Macbeth's position.

So who would be the modern parallel this time? He tried to think of generals who had gone into politics. Then he thought it was something more because 'Macbeth is the glory of the world, he's the golden boy.'

Ian started again on his exercise of trying to match modern political figures to parts. Fortunately the need to explain, to tell rather than to show, often vanishes in the result as the acting instincts take over. This time his parallel was Muhammad Ali, the greatest athlete in the world. He asked himself what it would be like if Ali decided that he wanted to be President of the United States. John McEnroe also figured in this modern match-up game of Ian's. The next idea, that of Nixon, was firmly flattened by Trevor Nunn: 'No, no, he's not Nixon, he's Kennedy. It's the golden couple, everyone loves the Macbeths.' So the Kennedys it was. I am not sure if they or the American public would be flattered.

The RSC was in financial crisis, but Nunn managed, as he says, 'to shoehorn [the production] past the board' as a no-cash Other Place studio production with a nil budget. *Macbeth* is a decidedly difficult play to stage successfully. 'The writing is superbly dangerous, fast, lean, urgent, beautiful, it cuts like the sharpest, subtlest blade, it gets under your skin: it's truly disturbing,' says Antony Sher, and he, a later Macbeth, was to take much on board from Ian's performance.

There had been many disastrous Macbeths. Derek Jacobi had fallen into the decidedly treacherous trap of attempting it for the RSC on a huge cumbersome set with cantilevered platforms unsuited for its twelve-week tour. This production, directed by Adrian Noble, had Jacobi wearing a sleep-suit costume which made him look like a moon astronaut. Peter O'Toole's sounded the death knell of the prestigious Prospect Company, which was such a high point both in McKellen and Derek's classic careers. After seventeen years' absence from the stage, O'Toole had returned for the 'Scottish play' at the Old Vic, directed by Bryan Forbes. O'Toole called the play 'Harry Lauder'. Before the curtain rose on the first night, Forbes found O'Toole in his dressing room naked except for the Gauloise between his lips: 'Can't wear them darling, they're hopeless,' he said of his costume, and went on in jogging bottoms and gym shoes.

Denis Quilley, when he played Macbeth, sensed the sexual arousal awoken at the thought of Banquo's murder, which prompted him to put his hand down the front of Diana Rigg's dress and fondle her nipple while saying, 'Good things of day begin to droop and drowse.'

None of these Macbeths had quite matched the most famous mid-twentieth-century Macbeth disaster when Ralph Richardson, directed by his close friend John Gielgud, and playing opposite his passion, Margaret Leighton, was on the receiving end of Kenneth Tynan's poisonous tongue. Tynan dismissed him as 'a sad facsimile of the Cowardly Lion in *The Wizard of Oz*'. 'Give me five pounds,' Richardson had gone backstage saying to his colleagues: 'If you don't give me five pounds I'll have it put about that you were in my *Macbeth*.'

Undaunted by these failures, Ian was not even fazed. Trevor Nunn was not tempting providence when he opted to present his showpiece *Macbeth* on the miniature scale of the 160-seater Other Place at Stratford rather than in the cavernous main auditorium. Within whispering distance of the furthest-away audience, the 'Poor Theatre' approach had a chalk circle defining the playing area with a barrier of beer crates, outside of which the cast sat on stools ready to move inside and participate. At the back of the stage a wall of two sections of rustic wood had a narrow slit through which Macbeth left to murder Duncan, and later to charge after Macduff over whom he'd seemed to triumph. Then, as Benedict Nightingale described it, through it the 'observing, calculating, remorseful and finally severed head' of Macbeth was brought on stage by Macduff. A copper thunder-sheet hung down on the left side under the overlooking balcony. A props table supplied necessary accessories to the actors. The cast deliberately numbered thirteen. Trevor said in 2019 that he could still remember the heavy breathing near-silence of the cast around the perimeter of the stage before the play started. Ian began the action by striking the copper sheet three or four times, before launching into his darker longings, informing them with genial irony, even laughing bravado, and foaming rage during which, as he later said, 'unwanted snot poured from my nose.' Cottrell remembers with a shudder his delivery of 'I 'gin to be a-weary of the sun before' when he commandingly gestured down to a naked light bulb.

It was the development of a hitherto undreamt-of sexual chemistry between Dench and McKellen upon which this production rested, and a delineation of a marriage in disintegration which Ian was able to achieve with an actress of equal emotional weight to his own. One could truly say that in Judi, Ian had met his mimetic acting double. McKellen showed Macbeth guided by his passion for his wife more than lust for power, while Judi's Lady Macbeth lusted for the crown for her husband and not for herself. In the end, here were primarily two human beings in an intensely personal relationship. In this intimate locale you could see into their hearts as they concocted together the results of their shared egos, not of two monsters or friends but flesh-and-blood vulnerable victims of a downward spiral of temptation neither could resist. For Shakespeare, Macbeth was not an evil man but one who is drawn into evil, and deeply troubled by his actions and his awareness. The poignancy conveyed was well-nigh unbearable. A priest used to attend the production regularly and hold up a crucifix. Not to protect the audience or himself, but to protect the cast. He really thought they were liable to be assailed; evil was really present, Ian told Joy Leslie Gibson. Macbeth's evil was of a weak, ambitious man, dominated by his wife. 'I'll go out on a limb and say,' Ian is quoted, 'without really being able to remember, that Macbeth lives entirely in the moment and what happens is happening to him as it happens.' To say the whole exercise, played with a nightly audience of 160, was sombre, dark and full of fear, conveyed little of the impact. 'She actually asks to be made cruel,' commented Judi, acting against her instinctive good nature, while the production ratcheted up the terror by having no interval.

How did she do it? As Kenneth Branagh says of Dench in his memoir, *Beginning*, 'She seemed to be able to embrace every emotion wholeheartedly. There is an amazing, childlike quality in her acting which allows her to cry or laugh with the abandon of a child. She assumes nothing, doubts herself constantly, but without indulgence.' With Judi, McKellen could do something that was difficult for him: connect with the female side of his personality. It may be too, if I may speculate, their similar non-conformist upbringings (Judi boarded at the Quaker Mount School) contributed something to their rapport.

The demands on willpower and physical stamina were immense. McKellen did not spare himself, for on the Saturday before the press night of *Macbeth*, he did a matinee and evening of *Romeo and Juliet*, drove three-hundred-odd miles to Edinburgh, performed his new one-man show *Words, Words, Words* in St Cecilia's Hall on Sunday evening, and returned to Stratford for *Romeo* on Monday night. He simply could not get enough of performing.

'We see the gradual tearing away of Macbeth's public mask until we reach the driven psychopath beneath,' wrote Michael Billington in his *Guardian* review. 'He marvellously achieves that blend of the practical and the introspective; and establishes with his wife a rich relationship, full of affection, desire, awe, inspiration and protectiveness,' averred J. W. Lambert in the *Sunday Times*. Yet, and quite uniquely for him, it was a woman's inspiration that drove him to it. 'When I work with Judi, I really have to pull myself up to her level.' Physically he was nearly a foot taller than she. The erotic charge was evident throughout each performance, especially when Judi kissed her husband on stage: 'I have to go right up on tip-toes to reach him, right up to the toes of my boots.' Sober Ian brought things down to earth, calling the experience 'a corrective to my work'. 'It's so rare in the theatre,' he said in *Playing Shakespeare*, 'to get that intimacy in which the audience can catch the breath being inhaled before it is exhaled on a line and feel the excitement and certainty that what is happening is for real.' Up on the stage at the Royal Shakespeare Theatre it may be live and it may be real, but it's nothing like as real as in a 160-seat tin hut. According to Nunn, there was a technical advance in the intimate speaking of the verse in that season, which has not been spoken of before. Nunn held up Bob Peck, playing Aufidius in *Coriolanus*, as an example of this, and he had been listened to carefully and followed by Ian Hogg, who was Coriolanus, standing in the wings. This brought a new approach, which was to engage with the naturalistic thought pattern behind the lines. As Trevor expressed it, 'everything was to do with the thought – and this of course was to break down the rigid adherence to mood music, to the form of the verse.' Peck, who also played Macduff, commented on the animated and heated discussions between Trevor and Ian. These were 'not unusual in rehearsal', but Trevor persuaded Ian 'to simple ideas . . . he tends to thrash around in rehearsal but Trevor anchored him down. Trevor's very clever.'

Trevor's contribution should not be underestimated. Peter Hall wrote in his diary, verifying what Nunn said about the change in the speaking of the verse:

Monday 26 September 1967

Off to the Warehouse for Trevor's *Macbeth* production. It is magnificent: refreshing, invigorating, utterly clear and original; also the only *Macbeth* I've seen which works. And my admiration for the subtlety of the acting is unbounded. But by doing Shakespeare in a tiny room you do actually sidestep the main problem we moderns have with Shakespeare – rhetoric. We don't like rhetoric, we mistrust it: our actors can't create it, and our audiences don't respond to it. So how on earth do you do a great deal of Shakespeare? It's the problem that will often confront us at the Olivier and at the Barbican. The subtlety I saw in this *Macbeth* would have delighted the eyes of Leavis, but it was only possible because of the scale. In a large theatre something different would have happened – not intellect, but passion; not irony, but emotion. I am sure that historically the tendency in the seventies for the classical companies to work in tiny spaces will be seen as a cop-out. For all that, it was an evening which made me proud of my profession again, and full of admiration for Trevor. He is now a master. He has done the play three times before, and it has obsessed him for five years. This time he's really made it. He is now one of the four or five directors whose work I would cross mountains to see.

The performance won Ian the *Plays and Players'* London Theatre Critics Award for Best Actor of 1976. They transferred the production to the main house. In the Other Place the cast had shared a dressing room with a communal room with a curtain down the middle to separate the men from the women. When they moved to the main auditorium all, from Ian down, had their own single room. But when Trevor went round after the show to give notes individually to the cast he found they had all moved into the chorus room at the top of the theatre 'and put up a curtain down the middle again!' But here in the main auditorium it flopped: the atmosphere and contact with the small audiences were lost.

Nunn took it off after three weeks then moved it to London to the Donmar Warehouse, and later the Young Vic. With a variety of tricks, speed-runs and silly backstage pranks, such as tossing bras and pants over the partition in the scant dressing room, or even sticking pink luminous spots on themselves on stage to show the others without the audience noticing, the cast members revitalised the essential sexual thrust of the tragedy. One or two critics cavilled at the triumphant progress, notably Bernard Levin who found it 'hideous and empty', while B. A. Young called Ian's speaking of the verse 'eccentric beyond the bounds of acceptance'. Benedict Nightingale felt, he told me recently, that Judi's performance did not entirely engage him, 'in comparison with McKellen's Macbeth, unable to cope with horrors she was incapable of seeing, she seemed, inevitably, somewhat superficial. The thing about Macbeth is that he has inner qualities she doesn't have or doesn't think she has and certainly disdains – and gets a horrible shock.' He turns his back on her in the end, leaving her to weep alone.

In 1991 Trevor Nunn tried to sum up the production as a landmark, invoking the great god Larry, which pleased Ian, saying that Ian's version 'is referred to as the great Macbeth of the century. It's a Waterloo of a play, which Olivier never pulled off. A text that most people think of as rhetorical, even overblown, was suddenly conversational, immediate, domestic. Because it was completely recognisable, it was harrowing and therefore unforgettable.'

When Antony Sher talked over Ian's performance with Greg Doran, who was to direct him in the role, Doran remarked, 'What Trevor did wasn't just simplicity. It was inspired simplicity.' To this Sher responded, 'Hmm. [Greg was] absolutely right, but "inspired simplicity" is just code for "great art". Aiming to do an inspirationally simple Macbeth is as difficult and dangerous – that word again – as setting out to paint a masterpiece.'

Billington's final words on Ian's Macbeth: 'If this is not great acting, I don't know what is.'

Ian now had fame, acclamation and rapturous reception in more than plenty, for he was utterly adulated and pursued by fans, one of whom was the newcomer Rupert Everett. In the hot summer of 1976 at Stratford he hung around the stage door with all the other 'freaks' and became an obsessive fan. He described how, when Ian appeared, the ladies, as he put it in his memoir *Red Carpets and Other Banana Skins*, whined and snivelled, arms outstretched for the miracle of physical contact. 'In one brief moment of climax, cards, cakes and keepsakes fell on him like a plague of locusts and then it was over.'

His own way was more menacing; positioning himself to full advantage, he stood back and stared, and never asked Ian to sign anything. He became something of a stalker, learning Ian's every move by stealing his rehearsal schedule, waiting in the mornings to see him leave his house, but never speaking or intruding.

Six months later, once at drama school, Everett got a job at the Donmar when *Macbeth* transferred there. As a ticket-tearer, he would scold latecomers until the house manager told him the 'leading actor' complained. He played the voyeur 'through the crack in those felt curtains, like an imprisoned wife in purdah, making eyes at Ian on the stage as his clothes were torn from him by the little witches in their dirty lace mittens'. He wormed his way into McKellen's dressing room, returning Judi Dench's little voodoo dolls after her mad scene, but managing 'to look sultry as I passed through the men's dressing room where Ian sat half-naked and smoking in front of the mirror'. The stalker was in the house!

McKellen was flattered, even complicit. Everett's pick-up tactic worked, because soon he was on the back of Ian's scooter for a tête-à-tête in Camberwell, exulting in his triumph over another persistent fan, a tall, slightly hunched girl with pebble glasses, a high forehead and long scarves. He would never forget 'her utter disbelief' as he 'strapped on Ian's spare helmet', a tartan Sherlock Holmes deerstalker, and 'put my hands around his waist before speeding off. You could have knocked her over with a feather.'

They continued to see one another, and it led to more than just that. The climax of Everett's fan-dangling came over a year later when he was round at Ian's home drinking wine and sorting out make-up. Drunkenly they made themselves up. Everett painted on a Ziggy Stardust look, and McKellen a chalk-white geisha, before both sprayed on fixative. Ian suggested they play rock-stars and fans, so Rupert, standing on the sofa, plucked a string-less guitar over Ian on the floor writhing and screaming.

This cameo of an off-duty Macbeth, which Everett described in July 2012, had more in it than was shown in his memoir, and ended with Rupert uttering 'Good evening, Camberwell,' and bursting into tears. Later, on a more serious note, he was to confess that his 'liaisons ranged from Paula Yates to Ian McKellen,' so there must have been much more to the off-stage romping with Macbeth. In 2013 Everett said specifically, 'I did sleep with Ian McKellen. I loved stalking. Now it's illegal, such a shame. Such fun!' Everett liked danger: 'Everyone at the time lived on a knife edge . . . in the shadow of AIDS. You went to lunch with family friends and would see someone taking your plate and washing it separately.'

To like danger, with the ghost of the dead father in the background: is this yet another strand of the McKellen mystery?

TWO

Atrocities and Absurdities

'Those who can make you believe absurdities, can make you commit atrocities'

Voltaire

14

Enter Ganymede

'I think, as Ian's boyfriend, I was very much in his shadow'

Sean Mathias

Sean Mathias and McKellen met at a party after the show in 1978 in Edinburgh where Sean was performing in the National Youth Theatre. Ian was playing at the Festival on the RSC small company tour. He was thirty-nine, on the cusp of forty. Tipped to be the greatest actor of his age ten years earlier, still single and very much on his own, he might be forgiven for a rush of blood to the head when he spotted this Adonis figure, with flowing golden hair, with altogether the manner and personality of a 1970s rock star, and an easy, outgoing charm. But there was an apparent contrariness or rebellious streak too, which must have struck home to Ian's off-beat personality, an eclecticism of appearance which showed in the glasses with thick black rims like Michael Caine's in *The Ipcress File*.

Sean was twenty-two, and an actor at the time, although he dreamt of fame as a playwright and director. He was born in Sketty, the smart area of Swansea. The buzz for him was of danger, as he said to Andy Lavender of *The Times*: 'I like the high wire.' It was as if he was proclaiming to the world, 'I'm up for anything.' Little surprise then, that Ian and he fell straight into bed. Ian must have enjoyed the feeling he was dangerous, both in creative work and in his private life. As Richard Eyre commented later when they rehearsed *Richard III*, 'He likes the smell of napalm in the morning!' Trevor Nunn, too, when I met him in 2018, emphasised Ian's taste for danger. There had been some lonely years on his own since he had left Brodie and moved on from the affair with Gary Bond.

Keeping apart from the rest of the RSC company, Ian stayed in a large Edinburgh mansion rented by John Drummond, that year's festival director, with other female and male guests of Drummond. Mathias was appearing on the fringe, Ian was in *Three Sisters*. 'Could I bring a friend?' Ian asked Drummond. Straight away he and Mathias were sharing a bedroom. For all Sean's charm and attraction, he did not make a hugely favourable impression on Ian's friends. He was tolerated and welcomed everywhere with Ian, for Ian's sake. Ian meanwhile wanted his privacy respected. His attitude, as stated on his website, is, 'I think it's one thing to declare your sexuality, if you care about what that is. It's another to start talking in public about what you do in private and who you do it with. It's not that they [my significant others] don't want to be identified as gay, but that they don't want to be identified as . . . with me.'

But wait a minute. Sean did not mind at all being identified with Ian. Would he be a good match for the restless, even pernickety, Ian? Sean, who has always been open and outspoken, even rude, described them as different people. 'Ian's more of an academic, and I'm more of a maverick. We approach things in different ways . . . He would have to know all the reasons for doing something. I can go along with something more abstract.' More appositely, Ian had the borough engineer mind of his father: he always weighed things out and measured everything carefully into pros and cons.

The long-standing older friends of Ian such as Drummond and Roger Hammond, who went back to his Cambridge days, felt protective of Ian. But the mutually shared egotism was in-itially productive to both parties, at least in that first full flush of sexual exploration and contentment, while Sean now had a much older guide, mentor, sponsor and protector. It was not a match made in heaven, but more on a terrestrial plane, for even on a day-to-day basis there would seem to be disputes.

Sean and Ian now engaged in what he called a 'quasi-marriage', though Ian remained 'very suspicious of the institution'. In spite of their differences, or perhaps because of their differences, there is no doubt Sean made Ian happy in a way partners in a gay relationship were still not supposed to be happy – judging by what Sean says later in recounting the effect on Billie, his mother. It took Sean some time into his relationship with Ian, eight years in fact, to tell his mother that they had been living together. Even though they were seen on trips abroad, still Billie did not know they were lovers, or that Sean was gay. The immediate catalyst was that a book of his was about to be published, and the publicity about the book would make it clear that he was a gay man. Sean went over to see her and tell her. He thought that she must have already guessed, because he had been living with Ian for all that time. 'People may know certain things but don't always want to address them explicitly.'

Her response was so cold that he was convinced she had not known. It was an uncomfortable weekend, for they had been so close, and now were upset and awkward with each other. He remembered his mother saying something about grandchildren, which struck him as absurd because she already had grandchildren. She tried to understand, but 'it is a generational thing, in that my mother grew up at a time when gay men were supposed to live very unhappy lives, and Billie wanted me to be happy – so it was hard for her.'

Gradually over months and years, it got much, much better and she became reconciled to it. 'At first I would say, yes, there is someone in my life and I am happy – I am happiest in a relationship – but Billie maybe didn't want to talk about it.' In later years relations were to improve: 'Billie and Ian get on very well these days, much better than when Ian and I were together,'

Sean told the *Mail on Sunday* much later, after the end of their relationship.

A year or so after he had met Sean, after the speed and the euphoria of their affair had worn off a little, Ian was still the good looking, decent, nice boy from Bolton, as Margaret Drabble described him at Cambridge: self-effacing and ruminative, very thoughtful. But, like the iceberg, this was the public tip of the personality. Something had remained unresolved. Sharp-eyed Caryl Brahms wrote that he is 'in the shadows'. He was not quite (or at all) himself. This was a frequent observation of those who spend an hour, a lunch, or a whole day with Ian: he switched moods and was often self-contradictory. He was still travelling determinedly. A spiky quality could be seen when Ian met Ingrid Bergman, arriving late after a performance of *A Lily in Little India* at a dinner party where Bergman was the guest of honour. They were discussing what was wrong with the theatre. Straight away Ian said, 'It's the star system.' 'But we have to live,' pleaded Bergman, with perhaps a degree of false modesty, 'won't you give us a chance?' Ian turned on her his peeled and steady look, and into the silence said a very firm, 'No!' He subsequently denied any memory of ever saying this, but in essence this was undoubtedly how he was.

Meantime the money kept pouring in as he appeared in an Anglo-American TV version of *The Scarlet Pimpernel* in 1982 as the wily evil Chauvelin, who pursues Blakeney, with Jane Seymour as Marguerite (with a part, too, for Sean).

In 1981 Ian had been up to see Sean appear at the Glasgow Citizens Theatre in *The Maid's Tragedy*, but Sean clearly felt his liaison with Ian, widely known in theatrical circles, hardly promoted his fortunes as an actor. According to Sean, he was sitting feeling very bored at another play in the Edinburgh Festival, while the audience loved it. 'I can do better than this,' he thought. He turned to play-writing, latching on to the well-known theatrical figures of Noël Coward and Gertrude

Lawrence as a schematic device. This turned quickly from 'a scream from inside me' into a fully fledged play called *Cowardice*, which subsequently Anthony Page seized from his hands at a dinner party, and which Duncan Weldon, with the star backing of Ian and Jill Bennett in the two main roles, decided to produce in the small West End Ambassadors Theatre.

The brilliant *Times* critic Anthony Masters (whose life was later tragically cut short) was not complimentary at all: 'In the theatre where the Master [Coward] gave a celebrated prompt from his stage-box on the opening night of *Hay Fever* and fumed when [Hermione] Gingold and [Hermione] Baddeley went a bit too far in *Fallen Angels*, Ian McKellen and Janet Suzman now play a brother and sister in a Peckham basement rehearsing a Cowardish play, supposedly dictated by Sir Noël from the grave, with champagne bottles full of supermarket ginger ale.'

Jack Tinker, the *Mail* critic, in his review explained, '[I] bent over backwards' to be kind to Mathias, who was 'among those who were on the small personal side of my Christmas card list ... By contrasting slightly shabby pastiches of Coward's high-life wit with the desperate low-life remoteness of their existence, the play tackles with varying degrees of success such absorbing themes as the nature of theatrical illusion itself; that hazy divide between adult reality and childish make-believe that is also the borderline between sanity and madness.'

Daunted by the grand West End opening of McKellen and Suzman impersonating Noël and Gertie, and Page's formidable directorial talents, Tinker concluded, after gently pointing to the overall lack of focus, 'I cannot help feeling, almost ashamedly, that the public would have been better prepared had they been allowed to discover Mr Mathias's undoubted talents at their own pace and in their own good time, under less hot-house conditions.' The outcome had been total disaster.

But Mathias was not to be daunted. Sean's philosophy, in his own words, was, 'This whole business works on people wanting to do favours for their mates, but it also works on self-interest.'

Years later he proudly recalled how actor Edward Hardwick at the post-opening party handed him a pen with the words, 'Please write another play immediately.' Mathias took up Hardwick's exhortation and wrote an even worse play, called *Infidelities*, a labyrinth of sexual encounters of every conceivable kind, and *Poor Nanny*, a family play about the aged nanny of a rich, grotesque, dysfunctional family. McKellen declined or was too busy to be in either. Of *Poor Nanny*, Milton Shulman said, 'Why did Mathias write this?' while Tinker called it, 'A gross folie de riguer mortis'.

Yet Mathias's skill with dialogue attracted others. *Infidelities*, directed by no less than Richard Olivier, son of Laurence, enjoyed a week's run at the Donmar, also starring Jill Bennett, then went even further down the slippery slope of critical disfavour, although according to Sean, Jill Bennett 'wouldn't let it [the production] go'. Sean took it to Paul Raymond and his seamy Boulevard Theatre, calling the venue, 'tatty but charming, like an off-Broadway lounge'. Again with Ian's backing, Sean and Bennett formed the Avenue Theatre Company. Here it would seem to have stopped. But then, remarkably, showing he had talent after all, another Mathias play, *A Prayer for Wings*, was taken up by Anne Mannion and directed by Joan Plowright no less at the Edinburgh Festival, where it won critical plaudits, played to full houses and then enjoyed a spell at the Bush Theatre in London. Sean seemed to have a somewhat contradictory play-writing career, although he did write another play, for, as one feature put it, 'had he not been so well connected in his world, his story would not read quite so much like a chapter from *Who's Who in Theatre.*'

Ian was the faithful lover. They set up home together in Ian's dockland, a quiet riverside nest near to The Grapes, the finest pub in Limehouse. So how do we view and characterise this attachment, which lasted ten years in intense form, and then as a curious and unusual ongoing friendship – a 'post- or ex-quasi-marriage' – for the rest of Ian's life? It was quite stormy over the years they were together: for, as Tony Kushner writes in *Angels in America*, 'It's not always kind to be gentle and soft, there's a genuine violence softness and kindness visit on people.' And then, elsewhere, in *The Illusion*: 'Love is the world's infinite mutability . . . it is the inevitable blossoming of its opposites, a magnificent rose smelling faintly of blood.' This was love more *à la* Tennessee Williams, encompassing paradox. It was not quite the same as that permanent, non-conformist Christian devotion Ian had seen in Denis and Margery, and then in Denis and stepmother Gladys, but perhaps sometimes not all that far from the spiritual union that was so prevalent in Shakespeare:

> Let me not to the marriage of true minds
> Admit impediments. Love is not love
> That alters when it alteration finds.

The truth about McKellen and Mathias's attachment to each other is that it has lasted.

15

Validation

According to McKellen, he was in bed with Sean in 1978 when he threw over to him a script which Robert Chetwyn had sent, asking 'Should I do this?' To this, Mathias replied on reading it with a highly enthusiastic 'Yes'. The play was *Bent* by Martin Sherman. Mathias remembers this quite differently, telling Marianne Macdonald this never happened: 'He was chivalrously courting me, it was two months before we went to bed. He's wrong. The whole point was that he wouldn't go to bed with me.'

Sherman was an American playwright who had had several plays performed in the States, including a try-out of this one in Waterford, Connecticut, in 1978. Jewish, openly gay, charming and much liked by everyone, he settled in England where he later enjoyed a long and illustrious career. The main character in the play is Max, who McKellen decided to play himself. Max's father is a rich industrialist who is so appalled by his son's sexuality that he disinherits him. Yet his father turns a blind eye to Max's uncle, who practises homosexuality secretively. Ian's enthusiasm grew strong. As he put it in publicising the play: 'Such hypocrisy is current today in the argument that gays and lesbians should be seen and heard only when they pretend to be straight. Homosexuals are thus encouraged to disguise their true feelings. Is that why so many become professional actors?' He made the plea that Sherman's character embodied a universality of gay problems, but there were personal echoes, too, of his own situation.

Bent begins with a very contemporary feel. Max is shown as a misfit who drinks too much, is unable to pay the rent, and is a cocaine user. He is unfaithful to his lover, who earns a pittance dancing in a drag club run by a man called Greta. 'Max may not be the sort you care for,' admitted McKellen. If the beginning of the play suggests life today, it is soon clear we are in the brutal 1930s when Hitler has just disposed of the services of the murderous SA homosexual Ernst Röhm. The homosexual gangsterism of the SA or Sturmabteilung leaders was unambiguously cruel, just as its members were murderous thugs. Yet they carried out Hitler's orders to treat homosexuals the same as Jews or the mentally ill. (Though *Bent* made no mention the SA leaders were homosexual.)

That Max refuses to acknowledge his love for Rudi, established in the modernistic first scene, does beg a few questions, especially as Rudi is to become a martyr for the modern audience. Horst, who is Max's next lover, tests Max's survival strategy because he has rigged himself up with a yellow Star of David claiming he is a Jew, instead of the pink triangle of a homosexual. The two central love scenes between them caused much consternation before the first night, for it was feared they would outrage the public and critics. The first love scene is quite graphic, but only verbally so, as Horst, wearing his pink triangle as a homosexual, and Max, cunningly hiding himself with the other side of his victim status in Nazi eyes, as a Jew, do not physically touch. They stand side by side facing and speaking out to the audience and bring each other to tumescence.

HORST: Down . . .
MAX: Yes.
HORST: Down . . .
MAX: Yes.
HORST: Chest. My tongue. . .
MAX: Burning.
HORST: Your chest.

MAX:	Your mouth.
HORST:	I'm kissing your chest.
MAX:	Yes.
HORST:	Hard.
MAX:	Yes.
HORST:	Down . . .
MAX:	Yes.
HORST:	Down . . .
MAX:	Yes.
HORST:	Your cock.
MAX:	Yes.
HORST:	Do you feel my mouth?
MAX:	Yes. Do you feel my cock?
HORST:	Yes. Do you feel . . .?
MAX:	Do you feel . . .?
HORST:	Mouth.
MAX:	Cock.
HORST:	Cock.
MAX:	Mouth.
HORST:	Do you feel my cock?

The restraint here was shockingly innovatory when one considers the more or less routine heterosexual bonking that had by now taken (and still continues to take) over stage and screen. Acted without them touching, it had an icy, intense purity. The second scene, equally remote, was tender and chaste, as it was played, but similarly linear or even naive.

HORST:	Just hold me.
MAX:	I'm afraid to hold you.
HORST:	Don't be.
MAX:	I'm afraid.
HORST:	Don't be.
MAX:	I'm going to drown.
HORST:	Hold me. Please. Hold you.

MAX:	OK, I'm holding you.
HORST:	Are you?
MAX:	Yes. You're in my arms.
HORST:	Am I?
MAX:	You're here in my arms. I promise. I'm holding you. You're here . . .
HORST:	Touch me.
MAX:	No.
HORST:	Gently.
MAX:	Here.
HORST:	Are you?
MAX:	Yes. Touching.
HORST:	Gently.
MAX:	Touching. Softly.
HORST:	Warm me.
MAX:	Softly.
HORST:	Warm me . . . gently . . .
MAX:	Softly . . . I'm touching you softly . . . gently . . .

Both scenes moved audiences at the first Royal Court performance in May 1979, and later, in the transfer to the Criterion, to a standing applause for Tom Bell (who was full of qualms about them) and McKellen.

Bent opened just as Margaret Thatcher assumed power in Downing Street, and McKellen's CBE, awarded a month later, was followed by what were now fairly regular awards, to which Ian submitted himself with customary good manners, perhaps checking the impulse he had to rebel with the comment, 'I suppose there is a side to myself which the Establishment wishes to recognise.'

Bent brought visible validation to homosexual passion on stage, and gave McKellen an extra thrill in that it enabled him, as he declared in an *Evening Standard* interview years later when the play was revived, 'to act out on stage the secret I refused to share publicly'. McKellen and Sherman went round from door to door handing out publicity about the play. Keeping his secret, he stopped short of public avowal. It might be claimed that quite publicly he was already acting out his gay commitment. He attacked the *Telegraph* critic's contention that *Bent* was titillating, vulgar and shoddy much of the time, claiming its value was educational. It showed that gay people were vilely murdered by the Nazis in 1934 when Hitler saw that his homosexual enforcers of terror led by Röhm were no longer fit for purpose. Ian's courage as well as *Bent*'s riveting effect on audiences advanced McKellen's standing in the theatre, the gay community and in society at large. Brian Cox described the admiration for *Bent* as 'part of an expansion which had not been expressed before'.

Whatever the argument over dates between Ian and Sean, and who first suggested doing *Bent*, Mathias's enthusiastic support was crucial. There was a Svengali element in Sean, who had great social ease and confidence, as well as a carelessness about what people thought of him, which sidestepped the explaining, self-justifying rationale of McKellen's personality. He brought Ian out of his shell, but the view expressed by McKellen's older friends, most notably by Ian's lifelong friend Roger Hammond, who never had an unkind word to stay about anyone, was that Mathias, as Roger expressed gently, 'was not very good for Ian'. Along the path of McKellen gaining confidence as an extrovert celebrity, Mathias had a strong influence. He helped Ian to enjoy and maximise his celebrity. Sean notes that McKellen was always 'too mean on himself . . . When I met him, he was wearing old jumble-sale coats and driving a stupid old scooter, which I refused to get on. He didn't have a licence to drive a motorcar.' Sean encouraged him to take a driving test and earn some money to buy nice clothes. 'People say that I styled him.' Sean was far from the romantic pillion-riding Everett. He made Ian dress like a celebrity, give up his Vespa, groomed him into star behaviour. The common-or-garden bloke or everyman from Bolton lineage was subsumed in that of the star – but so far only of theatre, not of film, which always rankled a bit. Mathias encouraged Ian to socialise more and be seen with him by audiences at award ceremonies. It therefore became quite usual for Ian to be photographed with 'a close male friend'. The love that 'dare not speak its name' was out in the open both in New York and London, some years before positively and very publicly it declared itself. Simon Callow had supper with Ian in Los Angeles in 1984 at about the time his book *Being an Actor*, in which he declared he was gay, was published. Ian asked him, 'Should I come out?' adding, 'If *I* do, I hope to do it as gracefully as you did.'

At the Tony Awards in 1981, to which he now took along Mathias, McKellen said thank-you to the New York audience in true showbiz style – they 'lift you so high that sometimes you feel you want to fly for them'. He said thank-you to colleagues. He said nothing about Sean, sitting next to him all evening. But now he was putting his private life first. Sean had a few more acting and film jobs but, his restlessness unfulfilled, he turned not only to writing but also to directing.

Ian could never see himself sustaining into permanence a homosexual affair, even though by nature he was monogamous and loyal. 'He has to know what the motivating force of life is on an everyday basis,' Sean commented. He self-confessedly was half Irish and half Welsh. 'What a dreadful combination, full of the poetry and the alcoholism, the Dylan Thomas dark-ness and the mournfulness. Perhaps I am more drawn to the dark stories,' he later told the *Financial Times*. Sean was never one to mince his words. He craved the urban, angst-ridden experience of London theatrical life. By contrast, Ian's private life was rather austere.

Mathias picked on the puritan that came out in Ian, in contrast to the expansive figure: 'He's uncomfortable if people

135

talk about sex in public . . . I love to do the opposite . . . But I don't know. He's the most extraordinarily private person. Very secretive. I'm sure I prised him open a lot as well . . . I used to have to pin him down to talk about anything that was to do with an emotion or life, really, before. Now I think he is more open.'

Everybody remembers the past differently, particularly about intimate relationships, according to their present mood and situation. Ian at one point blamed the fact he never came out as gay earlier, regretting leaving it for such a long time, on Sean: 'Oh yes, it would have been much better to have done it earlier.' He gave the reason he was inhibited was Mathias, just starting out as an actor . . . he felt himself to be the junior partner. 'A lot of gay people don't come out because their partner doesn't want to be defined as being "the friend". So only when we split up did I feel a free agent to come out, and shortly afterwards he found someone else.'

But this was to come later. After *Bent*, it was another ten years before he took the step to be open about his sexuality.

16

The Robot Factory

'I don't believe in labels like success and failure'

Paul Scofield

The 1980s

The last time I saw Peter Hall, the Cambridge Mafia Godfather, before his death in 2017, was when I sat next to him in the front row of the Donmar production of Derek Jacobi's *Lear* and we had a drink in the interval. I had liked and admired Hall ever since I joined the first Royal Shakespeare Company as an assistant director in 1962 and met him time after time, after I stopped directing, with each theatre biography I have written, drawing on his eloquence and rich fund of knowledge.

The National Theatre under John Dexter had been anti-Oxbridge, with Dexter humiliating Derek Jacobi for his poor make-up. When Derek messed up during one performance of *Saint Joan*, became entangled with a huge cross, and slithered across the stage, Dexter accosted him afterwards, shouting 'Fucking university actors! Go back to Cambridge!' Cambridge had ultimately captured the National when Peter Hall usurped and unseated Olivier, and from then on the anti-Thatcher liberals were in charge and the theatre for a while lost any infusion of right-wing playwrights. Olivier might have used Tynan as his left-wing gadfly to prick and provoke, to encourage in-fighting and rivalry, but when Hall took over, it was the arrival of the apparatchik rule and dismissal of dissenters.

Hall never considered directing in itself to be a satisfying creative activity, but instead saw it as a dedicated profession. He constantly needed to have his identity confirmed by being passionately in love, at least until his older years, and if unhappy in this as he frequently was, could counterbalance it with his achievements as a director and company leader. He thrived on his judicious choice of talents, while juggling with insecure and unpredictable circumstances: 'a truly creative talent that makes something out of nothing is never uncertain,' he wrote in his diary, constantly proclaiming his own insecurity. Reading through Hall's diaries of the years 1971–80 one is struck by his undoubted determination and attachment to artistic quality, whatever his faults and his overreaching ambition. Hall knew what was good and what was bad in the theatre for his generation and was drawn to what was good like a magnet.

Dexter was not the only one resistant to the Cambridge mafia and Peter Hall. Brian Cox says Hall 'hijacked the theatre'. Anthony Hopkins was uneasy at the dominance, while the 'boardroom' method of direction had made a particular casualty of Albert Finney's *Hamlet*. The criticism of these and others was that the 1950s post-war generation 'Up for grabs' attitude relied on the traditional feudal hierarchy of Cambridge to spread its influence through the theatre and allied artistic professions.

Ian's first encounter with Hall as a director was in 1980 when he took over the role of Salieri in the New York production of *Amadeus*, which had been premiered in London with Paul Scofield as Salieri.

McKellen, together with Jacobi, had been on John Dexter's original list of potential Salieris, as the play had been initially intended as his directorial vehicle at the National. Gielgud had been another possibility but was considered to suffer from problems of memory and energy, while Scofield's problem, wrote Dexter to Hall, was saintliness. None had or could show expertise in the expression of passion for 'tit and slit', as Dexter charmingly put it, but the younger pair were considered to be unflustered by Shaffer's habit of constantly changing his text. While Shaffer offered the play first to Dexter, it seemed Scofield was not Dexter's first choice, and anyway he had said at first he was not keen to do it at the National. Disagreements were resolved when Hall, the second choice, took it over. Dexter spent hours on the text, and after Hall had firmly taken over direction, Dexter demanded a percentage.

Hall had from the start only one choice for Salieri – Scofield. In fact the imbalance the ever-perfectionist (or change for change's sake) Shaffer found in the London production, was that Mozart was shown up too much as the villain. Salieri's own evil aspiration was not sufficiently strong, as Shaffer explained in revising the play for Broadway.

In his own 'mini-biography' Ian writes, 'I originated the role of Antonio Salieri in the Broadway production of *Amadeus*.' This is perhaps a slight exaggeration, for the production had been a resounding success in London in Hall's production. While there was a distinct difference in their performances, nothing could disguise the fact that it had been Scofield who originated the role, but had turned his back on the success and fame that would follow from doing the role again on Broadway. Michael Winner expressed utter incomprehension and surprise, as in his opinion no one ever did anything like that just to tackle Macbeth, which was Scofield's reason. According to Winner, Scofield could have been the toast of New York and earned a million dollars.

McKellen did just that. A big PR exercise was made by him and his court to establish how much 'better' his performance was in New York compared to Paul's at the National. Simon Callow, who played Mozart in London, though not in New York, and saw the new production there, stressed how very different it was from Scofield's extraordinary baroque performance, emphasised by substantial changes Shaffer made to the text. 'One of the faults I believe existed in the London version was simply that Salieri had too little to do with Mozart's ruin. Now, in this new American version, he stands where he properly belongs – at the wicked centre of the action.'

McKellen took every opportunity the text offered to make Salieri more explicitly evil. No one could ever deny he made the text entirely his own. When he had seen Scofield in London he could 'only glimpse him through half-closed fingers lest a particular moment be etched on the eyeballs and later inhibit me'. His triumph was complete, his control total both of the anger and envy, and the ecstasy of his resentful envious denunciation, with its erotic and sexual undercurrent of misogyny (in the seduction of Constanze) utterly convincing. Walter Kerr, in a rapturous description of the performance in the *New York Times*, referred to his 'uninvited ecstasy' of listening to the voice of God, namely Mozart, 'which had not come from Salieri himself, but from a man whose voice is that of an obscene child'. Kerr commented on McKellen's 'extraordinarily small gestures'. The production was a sell-out. The triumph was unalloyed, with Ian making the million dollars instead of Scofield, and Peter Hall, strapped for cash and in the throes of wooing the temperamental opera star Maria Ewing, making three-quarters of a million.

Ian, the cast and the production were showered with awards, chief of which was the Tony Award for Best Actor. He and Sean Mathias wallowed in the New York adulation, with limousines, universal fêting and recognition, and Ian gratified his hosts, saying he had always wanted to be on Broadway from the beginning. The old puritan reserve would kick in slightly, and he would become circumspect, claiming, a bit coyly, that what was delightful about New York 'seems to me to be what was delightful about childhood. There's always something to look forward to. A parade. A birthday. And they give you such wonderful presents. Gift-wrapped. None of this is very important, but it's so nice.' The Tony Award, he conceded, was helpful to his case, and getting things done. 'I went to the laundry and the man said he couldn't get my suit back till Monday. I said, "But you've got to! I'm on the Tonys on Sunday." "You're on the Tonys! Great! Sure!"'

Scofield had said his year-long New York run in *A Man for All Seasons* was enough to last him a lifetime and he vowed he would never go back. Taking a leaf from the previous Salieri's book, Ian refused the US tour, and withdrew exhausted from the fray, saying he had lost all interest in the theatre, and could not even think about work. He lamented he had not been more interested in financial investment now he was well off. 'Americans are still forty-niners at heart,' he said. 'They like to dig for gold. They're always mining. They are not good gardeners. To create fine theatre you plant little seeds. You should nurture and cross fertilise your plants, and try to produce a black tulip.' But he spent his earnings well, buying his riverside house in Limehouse.

Ian always claimed that Scofield deep down was pre-eminently the actor's actor. Here Ian was following in the footsteps of the master of self-conservation and integrity. But there was a sting in the tale of Ian's involvement with *Amadeus*: he was seriously miffed when the film role eluded him in favour of F. Murray Abraham, who won the Oscar.

After *Amadeus*, Ian was no less sceptical than others of coming under Hall's wing, which was now offered at the National Theatre. He was, as Anthony Holden reported in 1984, 'wary' of joining it, 'hating the place' and 'all it stood for'. Donning his journalist's cap in a radio assessment, McKellen observed that Hall was the new breed of artistic director which runs the British theatre, and elaborated more kindly, but still with a touch of hubris: 'It's still too early for me to speculate as to how Sir Peter balances his burdensome responsibilities as the leader of such a large army. Sometimes you see him in the staff canteen, concentrating a little too hard on his plate of French fries, as if avoiding a stagehand with a grievance! At the other end of the canteen, there is likely to be a huddle of actors complaining, as actors tend to do, sometimes justifiably . . . the director [i.e. Hall] slumps neglected and lonely at home or, just as probably, gets down to planning his next show.'

This criticism is very typical McKellen, borderline accepting, but passing judgement from a quite magisterial position (and just having made Hall three-quarters of a million dollars in New York). 'All artistic directors of my acquaintance are workaholics, divorced and very charming,' he goes on.

Hall set Peter Gill to direct Ian first in Thomas Otway's *Venice Preserv'd* in which he somewhat unexpectedly took the role of Pierre, a greater challenge than he might have wished. Perhaps Jaffeir, which Michael Pennington played, might have given him more scope for self-torture, irony and treachery. But he had done plenty of that recently as Salieri, and as Pierre Ian produced resonant echoes of Scofield's darkly sonorous performance, in an earlier famous production with Gielgud at the Lyric, Hammersmith, and gathered considerable plaudits for an unselfish restraint. He did cavil slightly at the unhistrionic nature of the role, saying, 'I wish I had a more spectacular death.'

Wild Honey, Michael Frayn's adaptation of Chekhov's sprawling untitled first play usually referred to as *Platonov*, brought Ian enormous scope playing the lead, again a meticulously detailed and yet carefree performance in which he completely dominated the stage with his volatile character, in contrast to the surrounding company. Once again, as he had with Face in *The Alchemist* in 1977 for the RSC, he was playing a heartless creature. In his review of the earlier production of Ben Jonson's play, J. C. Trewin wrote how Ian always surprised: 'You never know how you may find him. He is a man of peak-end value.' Here was a hint of Ian the man.

Face and Platonov, with their auspicious appearances, have much in common. *Wild Honey*, unperformed in Chekhov's lifetime, is farce and tragedy in one. Platonov, the wannabe Byron schoolmaster who berates his villagers with the truth about themselves, descends through drink and reckless seduction, mixed with high-minded principles, to suicide. 'His reactions are always two steps ahead,' wrote Wardle of Ian's performance.

Milton Shulman, never easy to please, wrote of Platonov in *Wild Honey*: 'McKellen is superb, and then superbly funny, lancing his self-frustration by taunting the company with eloquent supercilious humour and placating the women who love him with increasingly desperate stratagems until finally vodka and self-pity take control. His Platonov manages to be both Chekhovian and Fraynian and still utterly true to life; it is a brilliant dual creation.' McKellen confirms Shulman's point in the old adage 'you can't begin to be funny without being truthful,' adding, 'a good reason why today so many comedians are so remarkably unfunny.' Platonov was both effortless, easy and completely unforced, with Ian's timing and responses, further to Wardle's comment, always two thoughts ahead. This kind of electricity aligns him as an image with Prometheus, who stole fire from the gods. Prometheus's punishment was to be forever chained to a rock, Ian's to be forever chained to his career and self-image.

These first two plays were done in the Lyttelton Theatre, and just as Nunn had bided his time at Stratford before he did *Macbeth* with Ian, Hall waited before he cast Ian as Coriolanus, directing the play himself. This was Ian's third National Theatre production. Once again Ian had the chance to rival Olivier and assume his mantle, and once again McKellen chose a modern parallel to base his character on. This time it was Muhammad Ali at his height, with a different slant. Coriolanus is fighting not on behalf of himself, as an athlete tends to do, but on behalf of his society, his city, and the country he had lived in. 'I see that side of him as being admirable . . .' Continuing the sporting hero idea, he also based Coriolanus's arrogance on John McEnroe, the tennis star, who had won Wimbledon a third time and quarrelled with the umpire.

As usual both before, during and after the production which ran on the open stage of the Olivier Theatre, McKellen eloquently gave his exposition of what he was doing, a habit operating sometimes in inverse ratio to the finished result. As his magnetism charms wherever he is, he virtually took over the PR department of the National. With an arm (metaphorically if not actually) around everyone's shoulder, he was the master of 'Trev-ing'. 'He arrives late to the party and then takes the party over,' said Brian Cox.

Apart from the five scenes he played with Volumnia, who was Irene Worth, the physicality of this performance was remarkable. His complete and near naked athleticism in his fight with Aufidius was achieved by many hours spent in the gym, under the tutelage of a fitness trainer (so that he could match the fourteen-years-younger Greg Hicks as Aufidius). But the mixture of classical and modern in Hall's resident designer John Bury's costumes and set, unnerved and puzzled Ian, as well as the rest of the cast. 'Oh, dear,' said Bill Moody, one of the citizens, 'they were sort of "eclectic".' One member, Sean Bean, just out of drama school, and cast as the First Citizen and Ian's understudy, left after a day, while Hall's notion to have members of the audience on stage paying £2 each to join in the action as the Roman rabble, increased the stress level.

Hall fell ill and missed parts of rehearsal. Hicks and McKellen rehearsed on their own, incorporating the homoerotic engagement which had worked so well in Tyrone Guthrie's production at Nottingham when Ian played Aufidius opposite John Neville. Jacqueline Fletcher, who took the role of Virgilia, recalls, for Barratt, Ian slumped unhappily on a stool in the Green Room, all on his own, with a bottle of champagne in a bucket unceremoniously in front of him, not coming over to talk to anybody, while no one went over to talk to him. Usually he was 'such an upright person'. He managed to wriggle out of the mustardy-coloured, timeless costume Bury and Hall had picked for him, and chose his own 'white cashmere belted overcoat slung around the shoulders and a blue shirt and tie with his sword nonchalantly slung over his shoulder'. Underneath was a brilliant white suit, and he sported shades (but without McEnroe's tennis racket!).

Later, in one preview, when Coriolanus is about to be killed for betraying the Volsces, delivering the lines, 'Cut me to pieces, Volsces, men and lads . . .' he began to rip off his jacket, but could not divest himself of his trousers over his ankle boots. In the end he did get down to the loin cloth. It was often extreme as he tuned in to the vitriol, the anger, the hatred in the role as he singled out members of the audience to aim the lines directly at them, so some became scared and wanted to break the eye contact. His was a love affair with the audience, but also a love-hate affair as he projected his anger, in a very visceral way. So where did Coriolanus end and Ian take over?

The first-night critics had grave reservations, baulking at the on-stage exhibitionism of the privileged rabble Hall had placed there. Benedict Nightingale noted,

> I've seen more suddenness and ponderosity in the throng at a bring-and-buy sale than at the National Theatre last Saturday. Early in Coriolanus one of the Roman generals exotically claims that he's as good at telling the sound of the title character's 'tongue from every meaner man' as shepherds are at distinguishing thunder from tabors. One knows what he means, because the tongue in question belongs to Ian McKellen and has just been heard transforming the simple sentence 'Come I too late?' into 'Caahm Ai too laiyate? . . . At the point of death the word 'boy' becomes a weird gurgling wail of "booyaahayaaee". In fact, there are times when one feels that Mr McKellen's tongue has invented a new tongue.

Nightingale, a great and affectionate McKellen advocate, still stuck out for his 'present eminence' becoming 'pre-eminence'. According to Joy Lesley Gibson, Ian's first biographer, he totally mis-said, 'My gracious silence', that lovely line indicative in Shakespeare of a man's love for a woman, although much later he was to kiss Wendy Morgan as Virgilia with sexy rapture.

Maybe it was because Peter Hall had never been much in evidence, but after it opened, as by now almost a habit, McKellen's persistence and determination as it worked itself into the production turned what was an eclectic muddle into a resounding triumph. Audiences cheered, while the cast attested to how great Ian was in leading a company, behaving without any air of superiority, and even making tea for them.

The rest of the second spell at the National, while he eschewed any chance or pressure to assume a more managerial role, was spent running a group enterprise with Edward Petherbridge, his old colleague and friend from the Actors' Company. Hall had divided his company into five different groups of actors, and decided to give McKellen his head by putting him in charge of one group with Ted Petherbridge so they could go their own way. The actor-manager in Ian, out of Hall's direct control, was given free rein. By this means Hall, often guilty of having his cake and eating it, kept Ian's prestigious name in his regime as director.

'You've got to have someone you can blame,' said Roy Kinnear in an interview in the *Observer* in 1985, and the McKellen–Petherbridge choice, Philip Prowse from Glasgow Citizens Theatre, came in for a lot of stick with Webster's *The Duchess of Malfi*, the first production of this new group. Ian played Bosola, ideal villain-casting which he relished and could really let himself go in, unshackled from the romantic lead image that dogged him. The image lingered, and when a young woman came up to him with obvious intent after a performance, and he told her, 'I'm gay,' she responded,' Surely, you're still gorgeous.'

Prowse undoubtedly put his actors off, with Ian commenting at a public seminar that Prowse was a director 'capable of admitting publicly that he is not in the least interested in actors' opinions and would as soon work with marionettes'. Later that year in his *South Bank Show* appearance, Ian said to interviewer Melvyn Bragg that at one rehearsal Prowse told him he 'couldn't act' and had no truck with actors' attempts to understand their characters' psychology.

No one thought this continuation of the McKellen–Petherbridge partnership was a great success. When Kenneth Branagh in the year before had proposed to Terry Hands that he'd like to act in and have a company of his own, Hands told him, 'Don't. Ian McKellen tried running actors' companies three times and still hasn't got it right.' But it drew the crowds, had its moments, and when it played New York on tour, as was often the case, it received a higher level of gush and a lower level of critical discernment than back home. The company went on to perform a double bill of Tom Stoppard's *The Real Inspector Hound* and Richard Brinsley Sheridan's *The Critic*, with Ian as Hound and Puff, another echo here again of Olivier, although Olivier had done Oedipus in *Oedipus Rex* in an adventurous leap from the sublime to the ridiculous in his Old Vic double bill in 1945. Ian only went from the present-day ridiculous to the period ridiculous. Brilliant crowd-pleasers, yes, although John Peter fired a familiar warning shot across the forging bows of his relentless, arch bumptiousness and bizarre North Country accent, like a cross between Gracie Fields and Frankie Howerd: 'It isn't always easy to tell him apart from the characters in his play.'

The Cherry Orchard, their last play, translated by Richard Cottrell, was pure redemption. Performed in the smaller Cottesloe (now known as the Dorfman) Theatre at the National, with Ian as Lopakhin, it created the perfect atmosphere for Chekhov's last play, to which the director Mike Alfreds applied the Stanislavski method of spontaneity. So performances varied from night to night but were commended for their naturalism. But later on tour it would seem to have lost some of its freshness and subtlety, and it was a bit affected by Ian's tendency to add a nightly touch of improvisation, which slowed down the performance. This sealed the fate of this experiment, and in May 1986 Hall disbanded the group.

Ian's variable fortune tossed him here and there in the 1980s and had in its wallet of oblivion a further production of *Wild Honey*, in the US, and two hundred performances of *Acting Shakespeare* – his one-man show, which had risen out of *Words, Words, Words* – for an eight-month trek across the States, which left him deciding in late 1987 that he was clear he had absolutely no desire to do a play on Broadway again.

Acting Shakespeare, one of those simple formulas where a great actor could cash in on his own fame and wow crowds by the tens of thousands, was an entertainment, or solo extended cabaret act, which went back to McKellen's RSC days as Romeo and Macbeth. Its genesis was the informal, almost casual *Words, Words, Words* which he devised prior to Macbeth, and which made a virtue of its unpreparedness. It exemplified the passion of someone who simply could not get enough of performing. In this prototype for the more polished later product, *Acting Shakespeare*, McKellen would intercut snippets from roles he had played with extracts from Samuel Pepys's diary, bureaucratic communiqués, entries from Roget's *Thesaurus* and even that old chestnut, the great star standby, the alphabetically listed London telephone directory (as Ralph Richardson had done).

This was a dressing-up occasion for the middle-class, gala-frequenting audience who loved Ian and Shakespeare in a joint cultural event. Ian was instinctively 'to the manner born' a master of this sort of entertainment and would indulge his passion for being the travelling provincial player whenever he had a gap in his schedule. He would not bring it to London, not at least for the time being, and he was extraordinarily generous in putting this crowd-pleaser at the service of a charity he

Not Gandalf's Middle-earth, but down-to-earth: Burnley birthplace; Bolton middle-class abode; on the terrace before 'the brown god'; co-proprietor with Sean Mathias of riverside pub.

The 'Cambridge mafia', photographed by John Bulmer: Peter Cook, satire king; Ian McKellen as the sullen Son in *Six Characters in Search of an Author*, with Alison Prior, Margaret Drabble and John Wood, later Fortune (as Mother, Stepdaughter and Director); McKellen in Richard Cottrell's *Deutsches Haus* with Drabble.

Divine-right Richard II to 'Should the play be called *The Footman?*' – as the pageboy with a boil on his bum, McKellen had audiences in hysterics in *Ruling the Roost*, with Caroline Blakiston as Arnadine.

As drunken rogue Toby Belch in *Twelfth Night*, duping Andrew Aguecheek (Roger Rees).

Shavian burglar advocating social change in *Too True to Be Good*, with Judi Dench as a Cockney nurse.

Francesca Annis as Juliet cuddles a dead Romeo.

Incestuous supplicant Giovanni in *'Tis Pity She's a Whore* with Paola Dionisotti.

Puppet master Dr Faustus.

Murder, guilt and sexual chemistry in *Macbeth*,
acting alongside Judi Dench.

Naked combat: as Coriolanus with Gregory Hicks as Aufidius.

Balaclava'd Face in *The Alchemist*; with Paul Brooke as
Sir Epicure Mammon.

'Salieri socialising' after the show with Anna Calder-Marshall (Constanze) and President Carter in Washington.

Facing the press at No. 10 after his meeting with John Major.

Joining forces with activist Peter Tatchell to protest outside the Russian Embassy in London.

'Put money in thy purse': as 'honest, honest' Iago in *Othello*.

approved of, and schoolmasterly too, in insisting on its educational outreach and value.

Everyone in the performance arts loves one-man shows for obvious managerial and financial reasons. By the late 1980s Ian had morphed *Words, Words, Words* into a prodigiously accomplished, top-of-the-range entertainment product, with no longer scribble crib sheets to hand, and not quite so much of the knockabout informality of the earlier show. This was not quite so possible in thousand-plus-seater theatres in Washington or in Cleveland, Ohio. It was the old Bolton Silcocks Brothers kid, happy to stomp the fairgrounds in barnstorming style, but now on a hitherto unforeseeably gargantuan scale. This was the tough, coarser side of his touring, but there was equally the ex-Cambridge prestige of British Council tours of continental capital cities, and even, if the gap materialised, Broadway. The great chameleon, shifting nimbly from role to role, male to female, analytical to gawky, emotional to cold and heroic, was a marvel to everyone: all embraced and encompassed in his huge Protean stage presence, so beautifully controlled 'that the tears pricked the back of your eyes; it was so skilful a manipulation of an audience'. When Benedict Nightingale followed it on the tour for his *Fifth Row Centre*, he noted that McKellen, as well as saying that the most reliable director of his plays is Shakespeare himself, asked 'the odd question – "Can anyone name a single happy marriage in Shakespeare?" When someone suggested *The Taming of the Shrew* he grinned and said, "I try to do the jokes in this show!" Yet there are happy marriages in Shakespeare, and many happy marriage endings.' Not for the first time McKellen the politician and activist was marshalling Shakespeare to endorse his own opinions.

So here McKellen was, in his own clothes, jeans and T-shirt, or tweed, seated in a chair in front of the curtains conjuring up the greatest conjuror of all time.

*

149

One day in January 2012 in The Grapes, the picturesque Thames-side pub near McKellen's Limehouse home, I explored with Ian who Shakespeare was for him. Built in the early eighteenth century, The Grapes is redolent with history and literature. Charles Dickens visited here in 1820, describing it in *Our Mutual Friend*: 'A tavern of dropsical appearance . . . suspended over the water [like] a faint-hearted diver who has paused so long on the brink that he will never go in at all.' Advertised at the Tower Hill tube station is 'The Jack the Ripper Walk'.

Ian and I were snugly seated at a small table in a corner furthest away from the river. He told me about a trip he and Derek Jacobi made to Derek's house in France:

'What I remember most about that trip . . . was that I had had a conversation late at night with Derek and Richard Clifford about Shakespeare and who he was.

'"Let's not talk about that," said Derek, "because you'll get angry."

'"Oh no," I said, "I won't."

'"Yes, you will," said Derek.

'So I said, "No, please tell me, I want to know."'

'So they started together [on their belief the Earl of Oxford was Shakespeare]. I said, "Whoah, hang on there a moment! All I know about whoever wrote the plays was that they were *steeped* in theatre; the idea that whoever wrote the plays was an actor makes absolute sense to me. It's the overriding thrust of all the plays that all the world is a stage. He didn't write novels, he was perfectly capable of doing that, he didn't write epic poems, he wasn't Homer. He didn't preach other great ideas or anything, he wrote plays. So what has the Earl of Oxford got to do with plays?"

'"Oh well," they said, "the Earl of Oxford had a theatre company." – I didn't know that.

'"And how could Shakespeare learn about plays?"

'"Well, theatre companies used to go through Stratford."

'"Yes, yes, yes, we know about all that . . ."'

No longer faint-hearted, The Grapes bustled with customers as we talked, its walls proudly displaying oils and watercolours of Limehouse subjects. Over the noise, unguarded, Ian lost his usual reserve, sounding off to the top of his compass.

'And then we got on to school! And I said, "Well, he went to the grammar school in Stratford." And they said, "There is no evidence he went to the grammar school in Stratford!" So I said, "There is no evidence that anyone went to the grammar school in Stratford because they didn't keep records, so where does that get us?" At which point I cried out, "Oh Derek!" And completely lost my temper, which is what Derek said I would do, so the discussion was very short, was volcanic at the end from my point of view, and I thought they were talking absolute rubbish, and they'd clearly had it so many times with other people, so many of their friends, that they didn't want to have it any more . . . I think some professional historian told him there was no evidence . . .'

'I believe it was Mark Rylance who convinced him of this,' I suggested as Ian's indignation wound down.

'Mark is a romantic and a conspiracy theorist,' Ian says quite sharply. 'Not an intellectual at all.'

'But, like Derek, Shakespeare came from nothing and yet was a genius.'

'You got it!'

Yet Ian had his own different agenda on Shakespeare's sexuality, which notably emerged in a disagreement with Anne Barton, John's wife, a Trinity College, Cambridge, fellow and Shakespeare authority. Ian's view could be summed up as 'Did he sleep with another man? I would say yes.' Anne said Ian was 'barking up the wrong tree. I don't think for an instant Shakespeare slept with a young man. You won't find an academic consensus that Shakespeare was gay.'

Ian's argument that he had, rested on the understanding Shakespeare had of gay relationships. This argument would have had Tennessee Williams and Terence Rattigan sleeping with women.

But the arguments about Shakespeare apart, Ian had demonstrated a breathtaking range of endeavour and shown himself fearless in taking on a challenge, becoming almost in one breath the toast of Broadway and a dangerously unconventional Coriolanus back home. He embraced danger and he liked walking on a tightrope. He was about to find a new trial, having learnt that what looks like disaster, with time and a few different twists, could become victory.

17

Body and Soul

'The body is the garden of the soul'

Tony Kushner, *Angels in America*

Many have pointed to Ian's enigmatic nature. Throughout the years of the 1980s, perhaps from the very beginning of his match with Sean Mathias, overwhelmed as he was with his passion for the romantic image of this inspiring, flamboyant beauty, he had felt an inner emptiness encroaching on his soul. He had played the great roles, he had demonstrated to himself a mastery of control, conditional, if not absolute, to whom he was. He had also given hints that at heart he was a staid Lancashire man. And he had, in a raw, even ugly, statement, pronounced that he prepared to risk, to the absolute limit, making a fool of himself – 'cutting myself open and then going out on stage and showing everybody,' was how he phrased it.

This had fulfilled him. Intense competitiveness and an openness and ability to express and expose himself at every opportunity both in word and image, had brought him to a position where he was the most talked about and written up actor of his time, wholly inhabiting that role. On stage, he could convert himself instantly. Yet off-stage, away from the security of being in a role, he sometimes looked uncomfortable, Sheila Hancock noting one day that 'he flops about like a sort of over-grown puppy.'

A talking head, voluble, sensible, well supplied with facts

and reasons, Ian had for years been a champion for worthy causes (restoration of the salvaged Tudor warship *Mary Rose*, more state funding for theatre, rights to perform for English actors in the USA). He was a tireless benefactor in his one-man performances of *Acting Shakespeare*, with over two hundred performances in the US, raising money for the increasing number of AIDS victims, many of whom were artists or performers. Ian Charleson, Ian's close friend, was a particular case in point. This empowerment became the fuse, but the big barrel of gunpowder was below and hidden, long hidden, ready to explode under the English Establishment.

AIDS, by the end of 1987, was now becoming worse every day, especially in New York where attitudes to the epidemic were being changed from fear and self-distancing by such plays as Larry Kramer's *The Normal Heart* and William M. Hoffman's *As Is*. The deaths of famous people from AIDS occurred more and more often. Fired by his visits to America, Ian now believed that *The Times* should state in its obituaries when respected and respectable people died from AIDS. 'AIDS is a disease of transformation like no other,' said Christopher Spence, director of London Lighthouse, the AIDS hospice. The epidemic was raging at its height. The whole purpose of Spence's Lighthouse project was health. 'You realise,' said Spence, 'if you put your attention on dying well, that what you're talking about is living well. The whole focus of this project is health. Dying is a perfectly healthy thing to do.' No positive spiritual or belief system could fault this.

Sheila Hancock, even in January 1988, did not see his support of AIDS charities as a coming-out gesture. 'One of his closest friends had died from AIDS,' she says. 'It was a gift from God to be able to do something to combat a disease which has struck many fellow artists.' (When the much-loved Ian Charleson, who had been performing Hamlet while affected, died, Ian and Richard Eyre flew up to Edinburgh to attend the funeral).

London Lighthouse enjoyed McKellen's support to the tune of hundreds of thousands of pounds.

Mathias's departure set the fuse alight. McKellen told John Lahr, who interviewed him many years later in New York in 2007, that he and Sean had been 'a great couple. We would swagger out together and it was good. I loved his friends. He didn't much care for mine. He thought they were too stuffy.' Sean had made McKellen take down all the posters of himself, saying, 'I'm living with you, not your reputation.' On the support McKellen gave to Mathias's career he told Lahr, 'It was exciting to see him growing in front of my eyes.' But Mathias wanted to move forward in the relationship and have a life in which McKellen didn't always put himself first. He said, 'He was constantly bickering and an irritant to me, not easy to handle. We had dreadful arguments. I don't like getting angry.' The tipping point came before he went to New York with *Wild Honey* in 1986, when Matthias said, 'If you go to America, I can't come with you.'

Ian was almost fifty, and his lover had left him, but he never showed any rage or resentment.

Ian's explosion, if so it may be called, was measured and very English, so much in keeping with the good manners and traditions of his country, and his faultless educated background, that he gained from it a higher proportion of approval than dissent. Importantly, too, his revolution was made on Radio 3, the hallowed cultural outlet of the British Broadcasting Corporation. Forever a self-analyser, searching after fact and reason, Ian further explained how he had been affected by talking with the novelist Armistead Maupin and his then-partner, Terry Anderson, during his visit to San Francisco in September 1987 with *Acting Shakespeare*. Maupin has it that McKellen was, in the tradition of such expatriate Englishmen as Christopher Isherwood and David Hockney, 'Californicated' into a greater sense of individual freedom. The discussion had centred on the 'closetedness' of certain Hollywood stars, and whether an openly homosexual actor would be limited in 'selling his sexuality'. He began to realise 'the fact that I know that a man is straight doesn't stop me fancying him. If that was true, why should it stop a woman fancying me even though she knew I wasn't straight?'

Mulling this over, McKellen had met a casting director in Los Angeles, where he was up for a part in a movie, and asked her if she thought he could work in Hollywood if it was known he was gay. She answered, 'Well, why not? The director's gay, and so is his wife.' The names of the famous pair were taboo to reveal. 'The point, if it is true, is that a lesbian and a gay man got married. And not, of course, to fool their friends or themselves, but to fool the world . . . I went right off Hollywood.' Such open secrets had been the practice going back many years, as far back as Lord Montagu's trial in the 1950s and Kenneth Williams' indiscreet confessions. Elton John, never hiding he was gay (even while for a short time married to a woman), while never completely admitting it either, wore glittering coats, feather boas and purple tights on stage, while in an issue of *Playboy* David Bowie called him 'the token queen of rock 'n'roll'.

On 4 January 1988, when Ian was collecting in a bucket for the London Lighthouse, Carole Woddis, a journalist, stopped him, thrusting a sheaf of papers into his hand about that 'nasty and brutish', as he called it, Section 28 of the Local Government Bill of 1988. He phoned her back about 1.30 the next morning. She said that they chatted about how difficult it was for him to come out, because he might lose work. Then he said he had this idea: What about holding a big press conference, and getting heterosexual couples to come with their babies and protest? She took him to a meeting, in the smoky bar of the London Drill Hall, of the Arts Lobby, a mainly gay group, intent on stopping Clause 28 on the basis that it threatened censorship of the arts. The purpose of the Clause was to make it illegal for local authorities to 'promote homosexuality' or to give money or assistance to anybody who did. The implications were alarming.

A number of actors, such as Simon Callow, had for some time made no secret that they were gay, but there was a reluctance on the part of journalists and the media to proclaim this publicly, and so these admissions were still kept under wraps or ignored. But this was to be overthrown very dramatically when, because of his high-profile collecting for AIDS charities, BBC Radio 3 invited Ian to take part in a debate on Clause 28 on the programme *Third Ear*. He would be in conversation with Sir Peregrine Worsthorne, editor of the *Sunday Telegraph*, with Robert Hewison presiding.

Worsthorne had stated unequivocally in his leader column the Sunday before, 'viciously parading his ignorance', according to Ian, that homosexuals provoked intolerance towards themselves because of their 'proselytising cult'. It was by no means a new theme or perception in the Establishment or among the elites. Noel Annan, Provost of King's while both McKellen and I were undergraduates, had said as much in his book, *Our Age*, in a chapter on 'The Cult of Homosexuality'.

Radio 3 had invited Ian on before his evening show on 27 January. During the twenty-minute discussion Hewison taxed McKellen that he was overreacting to the Clause, while Worsthorne argued cautiously that its target was education, not the arts. But then Ian, having guarded his cold anger with perfect manners, made the public admission, when asked if he would like to see Clause 28 disappear altogether. Yes, he said, because it was 'offensive to anyone like myself, who is homosexual, apart from the whole business of what can or what cannot be taught to children'.

The argument grew, then, into one of whether homosexuality was 'a perfectly normal and desirable condition,' which Worsthorne believed it wasn't, and whether it should be promoted as such, to children at an extremely impressionable age. The argument and controversy hinged on the question of what was meant by the word 'promote', leading to Worsthorne's clearest expression of prejudice: 'I regard homosexuality as being a great misfortune. I see it as something the less frequent it is in any society, the better for that society.' (This in spite of the fact that he elsewhere admitted to experiencing a degree of gay dalliance – a 'deflowering' as reported in the press – with the jazz musician George Melly while at Stowe School.)

Ian didn't exactly rise to this. 'The heart of the matter,' he said, 'is whether homosexuality can be promoted and taught, and people could be converted to it.' Here the essential division between the pair lay.

It became a more polarised and personal argument but still conducted in unheated tones, when Worsthorne declared in a patronising but eminently smooth way that he was not saying that gay people living openly, as in San Francisco, was 'necessarily a bad thing'. He goaded Ian by saying, 'I know a number of pubs in London, I can give you their addresses, except that they are so well-known, where . . . they are known as gay pubs and they—'

Ian interrupted here, and couldn't resist retaliating: 'You mean the Garrick Club? You must accept that there are very, very few famous homosexuals in this country.'

He went on in an even voice but with passion to hammer home the inequality:

There are no sportsmen who declare that they are gay because they don't like to because they are frightened of what will happen to them. And this is the area in which schoolchildren, to get back to the Bill, the schoolchildren who, having no role models in society discover – fear – that they are gay, they go to their parents where they get a dusty answer. They go automatically, of course, to the other adults in their lives, they go to their teachers. And their teachers need to be in a position to be able to discuss that sexuality and reassure them that it is not against the law, it is not wrong and they must feel at ease with it, if they have decided at the end of their experimentation with their sexuality that they are one thing or the other. And this Bill will restrict dangerously that perfectly proper activity of the schools.

Worsthorne's response to this was palliative, declaring that more discretion was needed by homosexuals, and more understanding that the majority of the country did worry about homosexuality. He had lost the debate.

Ian wound it up by stating that 'the country would be healthier if people in public life who are gay announce that they are gay, and left it at that, that the majority in society would understand that homosexuals are their friends.'

This discussion, conducted in an *echt* English manner with hardly anyone ever raising their voices or using extreme language, was finally what brought Ian to this new resolution. He would keep quiet no longer. He no longer feared public reaction. Very quietly, very firmly, he had declared his gayness. When he explained it later, to *Vanity Fair* in June 1992, he said Worsthorne 'was being very rude about homosexuals, saying why couldn't they stay in their clubs? And I said, "You mean like the Garrick Club?" – a gentleman's club of which he is a member which I wouldn't be seen dead in.'

It was the 'they' or 'them' that did it for him, Ian claimed in hindsight. 'It was a good debating point. And having done it, I've not stopped doing it.'

Immediately after this admission he was drawn into Terry Wogan's primetime TV show, on which he declared, 'I've been a homosexual all my life.' Next morning the press loudly proclaimed, 'Ian McKellen's coming out as gay'. It was now public knowledge, and such it was to remain.

The manner of his coming out, the simple unadorned Shakespearean style, was of infinite importance in the way subsequently it was accepted. The avowal of homosexuality had been statesmanlike, a declaration of faith as well as identity. It could have been mawkish or embarrassing, but it was not. But a degree of disguise and ambiguity could also have played their part in his direct action, because the theatrical sense of timing was perfect. This was very hard to determine because he'd enjoyed the flirtatiousness of being in the closet while everyone knew, like Elton John. The whole, dignified way Ian's avowal of being gay was conducted at the highest level of studious modesty and integrity and, dare we say it, would have won approval from the Nonconformist stepmother, and his deceased father and mother, even if they had disapproved of the principle behind it.

Lifting the shadow or oppression of living with a guilty secret had a profoundly liberating effect. Ian found it unnervingly easy saying more, telling everyone after this public avowal, including his sister and her family, friends and colleagues, encouraging them to do the same as him. When he told Gladys, his stepmother, she said she had known he was gay for years and couldn't care less. The most dangerous moment, Napoleon declared, comes with victory, yet Ian's self-outing, relaxed and under control as it was, became a moment of light that expanded and spread everywhere. It then, like a rocket, impelled him into eminence as the cause's leading figure.

For the rest of 1988 the espousal of the gay rights cause took off. In Manchester in particular it exploded, with participation from the sympathetic town council and its leader Graham Stringer, into a backlash against Clause 28. It drew 20,000 people, both gay and straight, onto the streets to sing with Tom Robinson 'Glad to Be Gay', and applaud the speakers including McKellen, who had been drawn into it after his initial contact with Carole Woddis and the gay rights lobby in January. The event was celebrated as a wonderful turning-point. 'The best show of the year,' McKellen called it in *Capital Gay*. 'I marched with Michael Cashman, Stifyn Parri, Peter Tatchell . . . wearing my "Out and Proud" T-shirt. At Westminster I met our lawmakers . . . The Whip in the Commons – [who said] "I'm sorry about Section 28 – it's just a bit of red meat thrown to our right-wing wolves." The Whip in the Lords – "I'm sorry about Section 28 – but you appreciate my job is just to get our chaps to vote the right way.'

Here was a new script and a new role of enormous dimension and proportion, of gargantuan breadth to meet his superabundant energy. You might have said he had just been waiting for such a moment. It would fill that inner sense of isolation and loneliness he had felt for fifty years. The down-played manner was in the *No Sex Please, We're British* tradition. Many now would be the declarations of people, in all walks of life, which could be directly linked, as Anthony Sher says of his own coming out, to McKellen's. Callow, who came out in 1984, mischievously claims, 'I was John the Baptist to his Jesus.'

Would this become the defining moment of his life and career as an actor? Had it all led up to what he now declared? 'Coming out, coming out, coming out. That's the only thing I've ever done, really. That's what it can say on the gravestone. That will be the obituary,' he told Ben Brantley in 1992. Until then he had spent his life as a publicly closeted gay man – though always very comfortably 'out' in the theatre community and never given to telling interviewers he was simply 'waiting for the right girl'. It was something for which he no longer needed to flagellate himself. And clearly, too, there was an element of grief or at least coming to terms with the end of his partnership with Mathias, the younger, volatile and unpredictable yet tantalising figure.

Yet again, well prepared over several months, he had transformed well-digested and painstaking analysis into fresh, almost throwaway, performance. It was steady not impulsive. The preacher, the puritan, the precision artist, were all evident in the following months.

For forty-nine years, as he famously says, Ian had been living a lie. How late he left it to come out was a repeated question put to him, with different reasons each time. 'Why did you wait so long?' asked Stephen Sackur on the BBC's *Hardtalk* in

November 2017. 'I was the second to be knighted who came out, after Angus Wilson,' McKellen answered, jovially fielding it, evading the question.

Matthew Parris had earlier also picked this up, commenting in a *Times* interview: 'When you do [come out as a gay man] your sense of reproach toward yourself for all that wasted time, all that stupid and unnecessary timidity, is transferred – unconsciously I believe – on to others.' 'Transference', that magic word of explanation in the chemistry of relationships, carries so much relevance to those who 'but slenderly know themselves'.

With the truth now out in the open, this very complex man had found a new and exciting role to cut in public life (almost like a new marriage), and a new and stronger focus for his life and career.

Two theatre directors who had extraordinary insight into Ian's inner being might provide clues here. The first was Toby Robertson. He went back to the days of the Marlowe Society and the Prospect touring company. Even four years on from 1988 he said, 'There's the funny feeling that Ian – at fifty-three – is still in many ways very much a young man. You don't feel here's someone of great maturity: the man is yet to come.'

Hall made a similar prophecy after Ian's coming out: 'It now went without saying by now that Ian belongs (like Derek) to the Olivier tradition – a performer of genius who will do anything. He has great daring.' One could also see, said Hall, as you could with Olivier, the wheels going round.

It is only in the last few years that Ian has started to reveal bits of himself that were private and personal. I can best describe it by saying that to me Ralph Richardson was an actor of genius – someone who seemed to be switched into the most complex of human emotions – whereas Olivier was a performer of genius. Ian has been like Olivier, but I think he is moving into the great-actor class as he shows more and more of himself . . . I believe

now that his public and private honesty is one, we may be going
to see his greatest years.

But still physically, as he reached fifty, Ian's feeling of awkwardness was overridingly apparent. 'Do I think of myself as
a misfit? I mean you know, I think it would be up to someone
else to write this . . .' Simon Russell Beale once remarked of
the gay community, 'Once you're over fifty you're finished.'
Of course this was nonsense but off-stage there was sometimes
a very ungainly physical presence. McKellen reminds me of
Jonathan Miller, the *Body in Question* TV doctor and brilliant
director (again a two-sided man), or of John Barton. He stam-
mers, and is given, again in that Cambridge manner, to long
pauses of reflection. Sometimes focused and sharp, his face can
drop any sense of coherence and cohesiveness, and he can, as
in the picture of him as the Son in *Six Characters*, look hopelessly
fatigued and befuddled. He still covers his face like a shy boy –
even for Ben Brantley, who interviewed him for *Vanity Fair*, 'the
immense hands seem suddenly like cumbersome props, and he
often covers his face with them between sentences.'

But beware. He can convert himself to anything. He is a
chameleon actor. Would Hall's prophesy come true?

18

The Other Strong Yearning

By the 1970s, film companies had not come knocking on Ian's door as they had with other actors of his generation. This is an integral part of the McKellen mystery. Why had this not happened? What was in the way? When he had a good part in a film no one knew who he was: 'Not that I wanted to be a film star, but it should be useful in the theatre.' He found that 'a vicious circle exists in the theatre'; to get 'an excellent part in an excellent play', he had first to be established in a wider medium than the theatre as a box-office draw to satisfy the backers.

Moreover, he felt it was a little annoying when people in theatre and film who should know him, did not. 'I am always going after films and not getting them, which is upsetting at the time . . . Films are absolutely the worst of all. The actor is never told anything. It is so insulting, so rude and so despicable. I would be glad to not only cut them off but cut their heads off.'

Another cause for fear and alarm had been highlighted when, back in 1980, years before coming out, he had met Sam Spiegel at Spiegel's house when Harold Pinter had suggested him as the possible heterosexual lead in a film of Pinter's *Betrayal*. 'We chatted,' he told John Lahr in 2007. 'I was shortly going off to do *Amadeus*. Spiegel said, "You're going to America?"

'"Yes."

'"Will you be taking your wife?"

'I don't know why I said, "Well, I'm not married. I'm gay."

'"Oh!" he said. "Look at the time. Lovely to meet you." I was

164

out of the house like that.' McKellen snapped his fingers. 'I had never come out to somebody before.'

In 1980 Christopher Miles, the brother of the actress Sarah Miles, cast McKellen in his first film after a long gap in the role of D. H. Lawrence. Miles had been the director of the early aborted Gregory Peck film, so here at last was a substantial leading role in a film.

McKellen seems, at least from my perspective, an extraordinary choice for Lawrence. Surely it was not going to convince anyone that McKellen could be made to look like Lawrence, but McKellen's blue eyes, similar to those of Lawrence, as well as the oval-shaped face, clinched it for Miles. 'Authenticity', that dreadfully misleading word, was the name of the game, so filming in exact locations like a Lawrence travelogue, would make the biography *A Priest of Love* by Harry T. Moore come alive. Ian concedes that the original book was 'stodgy', but the auburn-dyed hair and extra false moustache and hair around the chin, plus Lawrence's 'surplus energy and a lot of things gnawing away at his innards', created its own brand of wishy-washiness.

Ian claimed he was searching to find the inner man. At a pre-filming cast do given by the American millionaire who put up the whole £1 million budget, he asked Alan Plater, who wrote the screenplay, how Lawrence would be behaving at such a party. Plater told him to sit in a corner and watch. Still, Ian could not find the inner Lawrence: 'Have you noticed how Freud, Shaw, van Gogh and Lawrence are the same person! When I put on a beard I could be any of them,' he told the *Sunday Times*. When Kenneth Branagh came to play Lawrence in a later television film, again written by Plater, he struck out for an image different from the vituperative woman hater and tortured intellectual, who was 'wonderfully sunny, a great mimic and marvellous company'.

You can tell from the way Ian recounts making the film on his website that this was a performance that was not going to strike fire into the hearts of screen audiences: 'By Lake Garda, an old lady who had served breakfast to the honeymooning Lawrences 65 years previously took one look at me in costume and rewarded me with a huge smile of recognition: Lorenzo!' He also describes his first encounter with one of the co-stars: 'I flew out alone to Oaxaca in Mexico . . . and was shown up to a hotel suite overlooking the valley surrounded by a distant mountain range. The dusk was pierced by lights twinkling in the town where D. H. Lawrence had stayed and written. Through the fronds of the palms on a level with my veranda, the swimming-pool reflected the fading blue of the sky. A lone bather in a bright green one-piece was breast-stroking in my direction. She waved: "Hello, Ian!" It was Ava Gardner and I felt I was in Hollywood.' Gardner, who played Mabel Dodge Luhan, a rich American patron of the arts, had light brown hair which 'fell wispily against her pale, celebrated cheekbones'.

What could McKellen have been thinking of during the filming beyond 'I have to become a famous movie star'? Janet Suzman, cast as the writer's wife, Frieda, was hardly an inspired choice: a gifted classical actress in the Peggy Ashcroft tradition, the fluidity and sensuality of a Laurentian heroine was not her forte.

The consequences of *Priest of Love* were dismal in advancing his film career. The jobbing actor, always having to be at work, was taking on any old film role. He was asked by Melvyn Bragg to feature in a diary of his year for a *South Bank Show* film in 1985, in which he declared glumly, 'The joy's gone out of the job, even the acting.' In the stream of interviews he gave, he engaged as the charismatic, great actor in complete modesty, underlining that he could not help it if people wanted to talk to him, photograph him and know all about him. He was also, as the other side of this, a workaholic, quite happy sometimes to play the heroic martyr to the demands made on him, underlining his lonely position.

I can't see beyond this treadmill of work. I am usually in the office [where he planned his work] by 9.30, and if I've got a performance I don't finish until eleven. Then, while I was rehearsing the double bill [of Tom Stoppard's *The Real Inspector Hound* and Sheridan's *The Critic* in 1985], there was also some learning to be done. It's daft. No way to carry on. If you're not used to it, making decisions that affect other people's lives (meaning theatre personnel as well as staff) is much, much more worrying than making decisions about your own life. It's exhausting – and then you have to forget all that and go on stage.

Screen fame stubbornly eluded McKellen, and in the wider world if you were not a film star you did not rate. 'Ian McKellen is Ian Mc-who? to all but the country's slim group of theatregoers,' wrote a journalist in *Woman*. Duncan Weldon, the leading producer and theatre manager, told me his name was not even a big draw for audiences when he presented him as the star in 1980s West End theatres.

While Ian protested to Tim Pulleyne in the *Guardian* that he was more excited when an unsolicited film script hit the floor in Camberwell than a play proposition, film or TV roles in the UK and US such as *The Scarlet Pimpernel*, *Zina*, *The Keep* and *Plenty* made between 1982 and 1986 brought him none of the kudos enjoyed by, say, Christopher Plummer, Sean Connery or Peter O'Toole. And by then Jacobi had become an international star and household name with *I, Claudius*, in which Ian turned down the role of Caligula, possibly, one might speculate, so as not to play a smaller role than Jacobi's. It was played instead by John Hurt. Others in his peer group happily combined screen and stage success. But now Stephen Frears, another Cambridge figure, who had since leaving built a successful career as a director, stepped into the breach.

Frears had worked primarily with writers such as Alan Bennett, and in 1982 teamed up with novelist David Cook to make *Walter*, about a boy with physical and learning disabilities, for Channel Four's new and ambitious *Film on Four* slot. McKellen was performing *Amadeus* in New York when Cook sent McKellen the script of *Walter*, which was based on his Hawthornden Prize-winning novel, inspired by his time spent working as a hospital nurse. Perhaps this extremely subjective and emotional role would prove the Janus other side of the Plantagenet royal princes' coin. The part caught Ian's imagination, with the added attraction that here, too, was a striking serious social theme about a victim of the present-day underclass, the mentally ill.

Frears could not have been a better operative to cut Ian's acting down to size, to reduce his powerful work ethos and his impatient need to analyse to a simpler essence of just 'being'. The important factor was that Ian was just at the right moment ready for it. While Frears is a very self-deprecating and self-critical personality, he was challenged by ex-Cambridge McKellen (they thought and spoke about the same kind of serious mission in art), to put to one side his use of anonymous, unknown people and take on board 'this immensely flamboyant actor . . . I found that tremendous and very exciting.'

This was a work on a great social theme, influenced by Ken Loach. The film, more explicit as might be expected from Loach's influence, was not going to be for people who had read the book. Ian could use his native accent for what little dialogue there was (Walter lived mainly through his imagination which he found difficulty in sharing). His thoughts 'swam like goldfish inside his innocent head'.

Ian visited a psychiatric hospital, saw similar patients at first hand, and did a complete makeover for the physicality of a disabled Walter. He was prepared to immerse himself in the humblest possible way. He spent a week with an ex-psychiatric nurse at a large hospital, where he met after-hours with other nurses to act out episodes from their working day. Stephen Frears dropped in each day. He told McKellen, 'De-focus your eyes and it will seem that your thoughts are more confused and complete [as the character Walter] than your own.'

With bucked-teeth dentures and flat cap, Ian then went out to test the role with the ex-nurse in Marks & Spencer, and behave in public as he thought Walter would behave, making a beeline for the rack of ladies' underwear and giggling to himself, then charming fellow shoppers at the check-out with an innocent, toothy grin. This was a far cry from putting freshly picked raspberries on your breakfast cereal in proximity to Gregory Peck in Gstaad.

When screened as the inaugural Film on Four, *Walter* kicked up quite a furore because there was a degree of no-holds-barred violence as well as a very gentle, humane, even sweet side. Denounced by some as a new low in television obscenity, Walter, Ian claimed, was the most amazing job he had done up to then, wholly changing his perception of human beings in the two weeks of its filming.

Frears says later he learnt a trick from Ian during this, which he passed on to Helen Mirren when making *The Queen*. (David Frost asked McKellen in 2006 what he thought of Frears' film. 'You can see she was jealous of Diana,' he said, but surely what he meant was 'envious'.) When Tony Blair says to her in one scene, 'You were very young when you became Queen,' and she replies, 'Yes, just a girl', Frears directed her to do what Ian had done in *Walter*: 'As you say that line, let your eyes drift across the camera.' Frears added, 'She did it, and I thought, you'll win an Oscar – and she did!' Ironically, though, the Oscar would go on eluding Ian.

A sequel, *Walter and June*, was made and shown two years later, in which Walter has sex with mentally ill June, played by Sarah Miles. Serious critics appreciated the performance and applauded, but once again no major film role materialised as a result. Ian's film ambitions of playing leading roles remained unachieved, until in 1988 another chance came along, this time to play John Profumo, the UK War Secretary, in *Scandal*, with John Hurt as the society pimp Stephen Ward, the film which exposed the liaison showgirl Christine Keeler had with Profumo and which significantly damaged the Harold Macmillan government.

David Suchet was mooted as a possible for Profumo, while Donald Pleasance turned the role down. McKellen's self-justification for doing it was that it was a very important social and political theme for his country, and given that this was in the immediate wake of his coming out, he wanted to show he could still convince the public as a straight lover. In the usual style of his approach, McKellen wrote to Profumo to try and engage him in conversation, but twenty-five years on from the shameful event, Profumo only wanted to be left in peace. Ian did have a chance to talk to Christine Keeler when she visited the set, but did not seize it.

The film, not altogether a great success with critics, had its moments, particularly Hurt's haunted osteopath Ward and Joanne Whalley's enticing Christine Keeler. But it was a disaster for McKellen. His risible hairstyle made him, even he confessed to *Time Out*, 'the laughing-stock of five continents'. Yet he seemed puzzled why it was a failure, for he stated in his declarations about his career moves, this time in August 1989 (when perhaps hubris was at its very height): 'It's a slight mystery as to why bigger film roles haven't come my way, but now I've been left behind.'

19

Pay-off Performance

'I despise the Ian McKellen of the first 49 years of my life'
Ian McKellen, *1991*

To me there is no doubt that until the new century, together with Macbeth, McKellen's other greatest Shakespearean role was that of Iago, which he played in Trevor Nunn's production of *Othello* at the Other Place at Stratford-upon-Avon in 1989. As it was a year-and-a-half on from all the public, and no doubt private, turbulence and furore of his coming out, he could make a welcome return to his main career: 'I am all actor; there is nothing more than the actor McKellen. It is my passion, my life.'

Iago is not one of the great four tragic heroes generally identified by critics as the peaks of Shakespeare's art and is often brushed aside in the reputation game of great performances. Yet the part is a towering, dominating one. Says his friend Ted Petherbridge, 'The acting instrument is the most difficult of all to play because it is the most complicated. It is the human personality itself.' Ian's acting instrument was about to be put to the test.

Trevor Nunn was a supreme casting entrepreneur. He had noted that the black operatic star Willard White had never been able to sing Verdi's Otello because the role was written for a tenor and he was a bass-baritone. He had cast him in his *Porgy and Bess* triumph of 1986. Nunn said to him, 'You can't sing

Otello, why don't you play it in the theatre?' Nunn was proud, he tells me, to make White the first black actor to play Othello since Paul Robeson (who had played it in the 1920s with Peggy Ashcroft as Desdemona). Nunn cast Imogen Stubbs as Desdemona. He was to marry her five years later, after his divorce from his second wife, Sharon Lee-Hill.

Trevor commended White's 'tremendous insight and heightened naturalism in the heightened language.' The thrilling deep, rich voice, the size and beauty of the man, meant there would be a combat, a contest of equals, not least physically. For Iago, Ian would set out to inhabit the part's very character, up to the right body size to measure up to White. His body, his face, his hair, he has said many times, 'they're only interesting in terms of my work. Every haircut I've ever had has been for a role.'

Ian's method of searching for contemporary parallels – for Richard II the god-Emperor Dalai Lama; for Macbeth the Kennedys and Ali (or the steely Coriolanus with the steroid-stiffened backbone of John F. Kennedy and Ali) – would not be possible with Iago. For there would be no escape possible from drawing upon all his resources, both inner and outer. He recreated a childhood memory, reported an old schoolfriend from Bolton, of an ex-army gymnastics master who smoked from a little box and saved half-cigarettes for later. 'His Iago is very much of the barrack room, a soldier in his fussy fingertips, forever straightening his blanket, wiping used glasses, putting brandy in the basin of wine which he prepares for the drink scene,' wrote Joy Leslie Gibson. 'There was one magic moment when he realised he had caught everyone in his own trap . . . slowly, very slowly, his face went sodden, a look he used right at the end when he refused to say why he had done what he had.'

He didn't know why. I saw Ian's performance very much as a self-portrait: a man searching for himself. This was the actor of whom John Tydeman said to me in 2017, 'When Ian looks at himself in a mirror, he does not know who he is.' His Iago was perplexed, even overwhelmed by what inside him was unknown, but outwardly pursuing his plot for their downfall.

Iago's evil was of a different dimension altogether from Macbeth's. For Ian to deal with a classic without bringing to it the usual trappings of thought and analysis was a different experience both for him and for the audience. He saw at once that he needed to look no further than himself to be able to manipulate Othello's emotions. 'I haven't even to delve into my past experience,' he says. 'Willard is so very athletic, very beautiful and attractive that when I see Imogen Stubbs, who is also very beautiful, in his arms, it doesn't take much to be jealous of them.'

When I spoke to Nunn in 2018 he told me, 'I saw the key to Ian as Iago was his apparent transparent honesty – "honest, honest Iago" – and that he induces jealousy in Othello because of his own jealousy of Michael Cassio.'

Why Iago was such a great part, and a great autobiographical role for Ian, was that he was by now able to understand in every way the skill of being able to turn a scene, create an impression, fabricate a feeling, lie plausibly and be a master of fake news. As Nunn put it before the play opened, 'That chameleon quality in Ian makes him a wonderful person for Iago,' adding (in reference to the fact that Ian was godfather to Trevor's son Jacob), 'and his ability to slip into another personality means he is wonderful with children; he becomes the best uncle that anyone could dream of.'

This may seem a sinister understatement for Iago, but what Nunn puts his finger on is that Ian is (as Olivier was) a great pantomime or music-hall entertainer. This is what he would bring to Iago. His Iago would be a W. C. Fields, an Arthur Askey, a Morecambe and Wise, as well as a serious evil demon.

As with *Macbeth* in 1976, Nunn's production was conceived and then, in Benedict Nightingale's word, 'carpentered' for the Other Place. (Nunn got Adrian Noble, the RSC artistic director, to postpone his proposed closure of the theatre. As he said to me in 2018, 'I opened the bloody place, I want to close its stay of execution.') As with Nunn's Macbeth, the detail was perfect, this time with an Edwardian flavour in set and costumes, with a graphically accurate army camp in a hot steamy Cyprus which Othello is defending against the Turks. Ian showed the hunger, the stealth, Iago watching himself helplessly as the darkest longings fired by his ambition for power overwhelmed him. I was in the first-night audience, and wrote in *Plays and Players* that 'there was an almost doleful striving after identity . . . in McKellen's masterfully structured performance.' The key to this was the way he was driven by envy, that most childish of emotions. Yet at heart 'his distortions came from a lot of good qualities finely bent: he was a puritan, a protestant, a profession- al at anything he set out to accomplish . . . a clown, architect of disaster, dapper courtier and ageing, disillusioned NCO with racist leanings.'

The nonchalant way McKellen carried this off, offering all aspects of the character with a disdainful shrug of the shoul- ders, showed Iago's heart was not in any of it. Why? Because, as he showed as Iago, he did not really identify with any of these roles. Crucially, he would just as soon be Othello, and as such would make a much better job of it than the Moor himself does. Yet in his vengeful pursuit of Othello's downfall he brought out many facets of his character.

'McKellen's careful interpretation was dangerously experi- mental, that of an uncommitted character, observing himself at every stage, evaluating his own performance,' I wrote in *Plays and Players*. It was chilling, yet for all the impeccable surfaces, McKellen also succeeded in demonstrating the extent to which Iago remains a child at heart. What he and Trevor Nunn's pro- duction managed so beautifully to convey was that the play is as much Iago's tragedy as Othello's: if Othello's jealousy is blind and extreme, so is Iago's envy . . . I concluded my review: 'almost anything he [McKellen] does is memorable – something to be assembled afterwards in the memory – if not instantaneously affecting.'

Other critics were similarly enthusiastic: '[McKellen] with his ramrod back, swinging arms and clipped Northern consonants is the absolute embodiment of the professional soldier . . . he is an old sweat warped and corrupted by fantasies of power . . . he also induces compassion for this pitiable creature,' said Michael Billington, while Benedict Nightingale summed up the long-term significance of the performance: 'It is his Iago that theatre historians will surely be discussing, with its cast of twelve, drilled to precision, in a hundred years.'

There was an extraordinary episode in early 1988. It concerned a thin, sickly-looking girl. Her name was Rosemary Varne and from the balcony during a performance she screamed at Ian, 'I love you! I'll always love you' over and over again. A security guard tried to take hold of her, and she fastened her teeth on to his arm and took a chunk out of it. And then she produced a knife and slashed her wrists. They managed to take her out and both she and the guard needed emergency treatment.

This highly explosive episode has to be compared with the obsessive behaviour of a deranged fan to Derek Jacobi, which shows both a remarkable similarity – and yet a distinctive difference. Jacobi's crazed fan was a slow-burn stalker who out of a sense of rejected love took a poison-pen letter to Derek's devoted parents, saying their son had tried to seduce him.

Many years later, at an Arts Society lunch given in his honour by the Critics' Circle, Ian was on sterling form. He regaled the company with expressions of debt and gratitude to the critics. In particular, he said, he pays attention to the bad reviews. He expressed great affection for Harold Hobson and revealed that as Gandalf he didn't get a whole lot of cranks writing to him, that fans were mainly quite well behaved and reverential. He reminisced about Justice Shallow at Cambridge with Michael Burrell as Slender.

He was still at his most boyish, his posture reminding me of Paul Scofield's, head forward when seated, shoulders rounded, knees together, in a disposition of listening and surrender, occasionally turning and giving me a wink. And over a cigarette in the garden, he told me about a revealing moment in the *Othello* production. Willard White, somewhat upstaged by Ian, he suspects, not only was driven into homicidal jealousy by Iago's manipulations, but inflamed equally by Ian's performance.

'One night he grabbed me by the lapels as he came off – "You're talking to the audience. YOU'RE TALKING ABOUT ME." "Well," I told him, I said, "well . . . yes."'

Willard, who found the part made him anxious about portraying Othello's murderous jealousy – something he found much more difficult than singing the operatic role – went on, 'I saw you, you're talking about me! You're getting them on your side!!!'

'Well,' said Ian, 'Othello's in a world of his own . . .'

The green-eyed monster had taken over Willard in a wider than just sexual, conjugal sense . . .

20

Not So Much in the Cupboard
but in the Safe

'A wholly relaxed attitude towards cooperating with others,
coupled with a crusading zeal for reform – a really burning sense of mission – are formidable in combination and
rather rare in the world of gay politics'

Matthew Parris

From early 1988, once the cat was out of the bag and everyone
knew what his sexuality was, Ian's 'engagement' in a musket-
eering sense was increasingly savage, tooth and claw. But on the
threshold of fifty, he would now, as he had as a schoolboy when
a woman in front of him had giggled at Gielgud's Lear, take a
swipe at Mrs Grundy. He had a rare quality, rare in actors at
any rate, to project simple and credible sincerity. He could keep
a lid on his anger and outrage and win over hearts.

As Peter Tatchell, leading human rights campaigner, says, 'Ian
took considerable personal risk to his acting career by coming
out as gay. At that time there were hardly any "A" list actors
open about their sexuality. He was quite apprehensive about
possible negative consequences of being out. He trailblazed
where others have since followed.' He had left the dark closet
of secrecy for self-exposure and liberation. This galvanised
him, energised him in a direction he had never thought himself capable of. Identified now as a chaste, never promiscuous,
completely dedicated general and leader of men, as an activist

he displayed an inner mobilisation of force and direction of power in the social, political field. He began writing letters to the papers, signing articles, making responses on television and radio, constantly expressing his views on the cause to which he now dedicated himself.

The Stonewall movement had been founded after a police raid on the gay clientele of the Stonewall Inn in Greenwich Village in 1969. It had developed and spread from there to lead the campaign for gay liberation and the recognition of LGBT rights in the USA. Keeping this agenda, it was now established as a growing charity in the UK and Europe. Ian would call and hold meetings to discuss and direct the campaign in this country from his riverside house. He came to be seen as the responsible public figure for gay equality, with his CBE for the arts, lobbying politicians and peers (Viscount Falkland, Baroness Cox, Local Government Minister Michael Howard and so on) who all lent an ear to his powerful supplication to abolish Clause 28. The example, too, of what was now to all appearances a lonely and celibate existence, also reinforced the example of integrity. At his fundraising efforts for the cause, no one saw him arrive with an attractive young consort, no one saw him or reported him partying at gay clubs, there was no triumphal flaunting of gay sex and no proselytising. It was entirely direct, normal, as Ian wanted gay people to be seen, dispassionately as 'us', with 'them' abolished.

Ian became religious in his supplication and desire to learn. He wanted this new direction in himself to be established as real as possible.

There is no doubt he relished the somewhat pathetic reactionary or homophobic backlash that was inevitable in this new tide of social awareness. He took gleefully to promoting the annual Gay and Lesbian Pride March, having a swipe at Graham Turner, a well-known columnist, who suggested tolerance of homosexuality should be suppressed, and at a *Sun* leader that warned that such approval brought society 'to the brink of disintegration'. Ian argued in the *Sunday Telegraph* along the lines of Shylock, another member of a persecuted minority, that gay people had ears, eyes, organs, dimensions like everyone else, and of course that they were by no means a cohesive community. There were shades of John Milton (the Roundhead Puritan poet whom he was to play in a 2018 radio dramatisation of *Paradise Lost*) when he showed how persuasive a polemicist he could be: 'morality,' he said, 'is properly a subject for rational debate . . . we have to allow each other to differ; not all homosexuals are promiscuous, just as not all heterosexuals are continent.' Convincing, too, was his very personal note: 'Heterosexuals should consider the painful moral process most homosexuals have to go through in admitting the fact of their sexuality to themselves, to others close to them and to the world at large . . . We can't say marriage is immoral because most child abuse occurs within the family.'

Until the early 1990s Ian, by his own admission, had not been connected with a deeper sense of self, an inner freedom that would allow him to realise himself fully both as an actor and as a human being. To say his coming out was spontaneous or a shock to himself was far from the truth; it had been carefully under preparation in many ways, most of them below the level of consciousness until the break-up with Sean Mathias. There was the rapid and sudden increase in awareness of HIV because of the 'gay plague', which scared him until he could check he was not infected, the death of his close friend Ian Charleson, and the year-long tour of America, when he met up with prophets of the gay movement who put the final seal of approval on his 'conversion' and public declaration. These experiences were important triggers of change. But most important of all was his need to move forward.

McKellen's commitment to the cause of gay equality has some aspects perhaps surprisingly similar to Alec Guinness's conversion to a right-wing obedience to Roman Catholicism. For Guinness, this did not quite do the trick and still kept him in thrall to inner guilt over his unresolved sexuality. In Ian's case the commitment to the gay cause was the Full Monty, the real thing.

He was awake now with a rich, vivid self-awareness, an almost romantic religiousness not apparent before, and a burning social purpose that went beyond a need for personal love, a stable giving relationship, the need for a family. He was driven by secular idealism – a romantic, moralistic, social consciousness – which was all-consuming and highly inventive. It gave his life a passionate course: the principle of honesty had turned on an inner switch.

Robert M. Pirsig writes in *Zen and the Art of Motorcycle Maintenance*: 'To the untrained eye ego-climbing and selfless climbing may appear identical . . . But what a difference! The ego-climber is like an instrument that's out of adjustment. He puts his foot down an instant too soon or too late. He's here but he's not here.' Ian's coming out was selfless climbing in tandem with the ego climbing of his acting. The description by Stonewall member and director of the London Lighthouse, Christopher Spence, of the depth and compassion voluntary AIDS workers applied to their task of care, managing the crises of life and death, points to how much of Ian's conversion was selfless climbing. Spence said, 'If I think of the number of significant people in my life who've died because of HIV, I don't think I can draw a single conclusion. I just know I can't deny my emotional responsibility at loss. Unless the relationships we make with people in a setting like this are real with all the usual components: like, love, hate, anger, aggression, you may as well pack up.' And for this reason Ian's acceptance of his sexuality was rock solid, backed up by his past, the deep religious faith of his parents and his stepmother Gladys, and their Nonconformist genealogy. His existence was now suddenly meaningful to him, as it had never been before: this was a kind of self-surrender to a lifelong cause, a goal.

Was there also an element of ego-climbing in McKellen's devotion to this cause? If so, it had a pattern, a burning relevance,
which made it popular, important for its own time. It became
a red-hot faith as he found in the assent he awoke in others'
validation of his own act of assent.

First of all, in spite of his worst fears, coming out had no
effect on his personal life or the offers that came in. Questioned
about Margery at this time, he said that her death was certainly
the major fact in his upbringing. But he had a very good stepmother. She lived in a Lake District village. 'When I came out,
an old friend said, "Oh, poor Gladys, this means she'll have
to leave the village." Of course she didn't. She is a Quaker,
very sensible and far-sighted. I'm a huge fan of the Quakers.'
But then, he said, when in 1999 he tried to tell her again his
'shocking secret', perhaps forgetting he had already done this,
she said, 'I've known for thirty years. I thought you were going
to tell me something dreadful!'

It had taken him so long to come out and only the phrase
'born-again' could describe 'the relief from the millstone of
lying, the release of energy which would flow . . . I am born as
a gay man who is now happy to acknowledge on any occasion,
and to anyone in the world, his sexuality.' Everyone interviewed
him remorselessly about being gay, but over the next ten years
he played more romantic or serious heterosexual roles than ever
before. Some interviews could become tiresomely repetitive. He
would sound off that bisexuality was the norm; he had confessed
once he loved to be touched by women and to touch them, and
that 'any number of women' had asked him to go to bed with
them, 'to convert me to heterosexuality'. When he was elected
Visiting Professor of Contemporary Theatre at Oxford University in succession to Stephen Sondheim, a breathless hush fell
when he said one of the reasons he became an actor was that
he hoped he would meet some queers. Why had he used that
word? 'I was quoting myself: in those days, we were called queer,
and referred to ourselves as queer. It is coming back, now, as a

statement of defiance: "I am queer. I am out of the ordinary. I am unusual. I'm queer, and I'm proud of it." There's a club called Queer Nation over there' – he indicated Covent Garden – 'but I prefer to be gay than queer, quite honestly.'

It took some six years from January 1988 before there was a proper debate in the House of Commons on lowering the age of consent for homosexuals to sixteen. On 21 February 1994 after a heated debate in the Commons, which McKellen watched from the gallery, a free vote failed to endorse the lowering of the homosexual age of consent from twenty-one, which had been fixed in the legalisation of homosexuality so long before in 1967, to sixteen. The twenty-seven-vote majority against the age of sixteen had been achieved by the abstention of Scottish MPs frightened to upset their constituents (as MPs were in those days), a hardcore of traditional Labour MPs as well as Conservatives who did not include John Major and his liberal-leaning following. In angry scenes of demonstration outside the House, Peter Tatchell said he did not rule out criminal action against the Bill, but Ian's response was more muted, saying he was 'very disappointed', and that 'we will be back to the Lords'.

When the shit hits the fan, as the cliché goes, you find out how much tolerance is worth. It was hard not to be carried away by Ian's passion, but intolerance sometimes over the next few years gained the upper hand. Ingrained attitudes died hard, and in a poll in 1994 still two in three people condemned homosexual acts and lifestyles. Not until 11 February 2000 did the Sexual Offences (Amendment) Act reduce the age of consent to sixteen. Clause 28 was not fully revoked until 2003, while in 2009 the Conservative Party leader David Cameron apologised for backing earlier legislation that was 'offensive to gay people'.

Ian was adept at putting his finger on the confusions in society. In 2006, for instance, he attended the union of Michael Cashman, with him a co-founder of Stonewall, and Paul Cottingham when, as a witness with Michelle Collins, he became a bit weepy:

> There was a groom's side and a groom's side, and you had to decide where to sit. They didn't call it marriage, although you can call it anything you want. The one thing you cannot mention is God, that is absolutely verboten. I suppose I'm a bit mean-spirited, but I really can't see why the government couldn't just say gay people can get married . . . But that hasn't been done because they couldn't face the furore. So they've passed a law that is not available to straight people – straight people cannot have a civil partnership, they have to get married – extraordinary!

In the conversation Ian and I had on this matter in 2012, we discussed why Derek Jacobi had no particular interest in coming out or the gay cause. I pointed out that his parents had known about it all the time, all the way through. Yet he was still reluctant to come out as a young man.

'Richard Clifford's' – Derek's partner (and now in 2018, spouse) – 'parents – he had a father . . . who had a thing about it, and it's always complicated, people get distracted by what other people will think. But we [Derek and I] never had a big, a great bust-up about it and I was very glad when he didn't sidle out of it and they have a civil partnership, don't they?' said Ian.

'Again privately,' I said, 'I think it's a private thing that's important to Derek, whether he's gay, heterosexual, and—'

Here Ian interrupted. 'How many people do you know who have a private heterosexual marriage? It's something to do with being gay, it's very rare . . .'

'But some people don't like to talk about their private heterosexual marriage . . .'

'Oh yes they do,' countered Ian, 'they're always parading their heterosexual marriages, showing you photographs of their children, their wedding rings, their marriages . . . A friend of mine said the other day, "I don't ask anyone I meet if they're gay, because if they're straight they'll tell me in the first paragraph, with the things they say, they refer to their families, their wives, their children, they can't help it. It's the first thing they do." It's not straight people, but the gay people who [keep quiet] ... Derek and I are out of our generation, we're both victims really of society's view and its effects are ... what makes us nervous of such things ...'

'Surely,' I said, 'there's no need to feel nervous about such things?'

'When you grow up feeling you're breaking the law, that affects you ...'

'People in various gradations all get hung up about sex ...'

'Well, that's true,' Ian replied. 'I agree and I know a lot of gay actors felt, oh my God ...' Ian went on more about this, and at other times and in other places. '"Well, if I come out," Nigel Hawthorne felt, "I'm going to have to talk about it all the time." You don't. You don't at all. All I have, all I believe is that people shouldn't lie about it – it's bad for society, bad for themselves. Young actors now, they leave drama school where they are openly gay, and they're out. But it's taken time.'

In spite of contrary expectations times did really change, and gay marriage was legalised in 2013. In the final episode of the sitcom *Vicious* in 2016, in which Ian and Derek Jacobi, as the bickering gay couple, finally married, Ian addressed to cheers the studio audience, celebrating the legalisation of gay marriage, something for which by now he had been striving for years.

21

Self-Awakening to Spirit

Bent had had its first and fullest season nine years earlier, first at the Royal Court and then at the Criterion. In 1990 there was a revival of the production, with Ian as Max and Michael Cashman as Horst. (Cashman soon left the cast to become a politician, and was elected as an MEP in 1999. Christopher Eccleston took over the role.) It was directed by Sean Mathias. Robert Chetwyn, *Bent*'s first director, had felt that he had done what he could, and found it hurtful that no one had even bothered to invite him to do it again. Much later, when McKellen had asked who were his favourite directors, he answered Guthrie, Chetwyn and Nunn.

Time was turning back the clock here because on a personal level, and apart from the impact it made, the controversy shown, and rapturous tumult it stirred up, the revival somehow must have had an elegiac resonance for McKellen and Mathias. It was their joint shared enthusiasm that had led to the original production.

The original statement of *Bent* was made nine years before McKellen came out. When he first performed Max, Ian had been unhappy that the part had not led him out of his 'musty cupboard, with nothing more stimulating than a skeleton for company'. But he had found it 'a thrill to act out in public the inner drama and secrets, and publishing the secrets I had in my heart . . .'

Even though Denis was dead, the fear that had he known he might still have disowned his son must have stayed centrally with Ian. Yet ultimately in *Bent*, in the barbarity of the extermination camp life, no feeling is carried through: the feelings of love are transient. In his ruthless survivor's streak, Max coldly turns a blind eye to the death of Rudi, his previous love (in an echo here of Romeo's previous passion for Rosalind in *Romeo and Juliet*).

Why was the Royal National Theatre now giving Ian stage-room? he asked. 'He's certainly not the first misfit I've played there. Bosola, Coriolanus and Platonov all leave Max standing. And after Max, I'm doing Richard III! His most reprehensible fault is one I have shared. When it suits him, Max denies he is gay. I shan't spoil the plot by telling you the extreme form of his deviousness.'

Although instantly affecting as it was played by McKellen as Max, and Christopher Eccleston as Horst (who unlike Tom Bell was not fearful the scene of mutual orgasm would provoke laughter and not reverence), it was the star vehicle aspect of the play, as well as its boost to a new wave of the nakedly gay-rights agenda, which propelled *Bent* to public recognition. Productions all over the world followed, and then a film directed by Mathias.

When the earlier production had opened, McKellen had guardedly sidestepped the issue of total personal identification, refusing to be pinned down: 'I had no hesitation in being in a gay play and to be publicly associated with a cause as well expressed and relevant to people in the modern world as this.' Was he being carefully political? Or was it just that he knew that the moment was not right for him? There had been, too, the suspicion voiced by his new agent, James Sharkey, to whom McKellen had moved on the retirement of Elspeth Cochrane. (Elspeth lived to the age of ninety-four, having been at one stage duped or betrayed in some real estate scam. Ian attended her funeral.) According to Robert Chetwyn, Sharkey had distinct worries about the effect *Bent* might have on his client's career. Instead the reverse happened.

On the occasion of the transfer in May 1990 of the *Bent* revival from the National to the Garrick, Bryan Appleyard interviewed Ian for the *Sunday Times*, under the headline of 'The Portrait of an Actor as a Gay Man'. Appleyard resisted the initial outpouring of McKellen charm, and his opening salvo of how in Wigan market square as a child, Ian told how he was sexually attracted to the romantic, wild-looking gypsy-like men, and wanted to run off with them.

'Aha,' [Ian] says and points triumphantly, 'I trailed that piece of meat across your path!'

Appleyard pointed out, 'he has, more aggressively, more insistently, more relentlessly than any previous gay in public life, "come out",' and astutely added, 'Yet there remains the uneasiness – that little trick to bring the subject up while leaving it open to himself to pretend that it was me all along.'

Appleyard probed to the extent of making Ian confess to the torture behind the issue, the self-drama, the subtext of the coming out. What had made him so angry, Ian responds, was that he had been conforming and destroying something right at the heart of himself, so much so that he asked, 'What it is in our society that has made me do that is cruel, and as near evil as I can imagine?'

The reviews for this revival were in general favourable. Not as good as the previous production, was the general verdict, but Michael Coveney noted in his *Observer* review how the play now came across with a shattering intensity because the tragedy of AIDS had taken a turn for the worse, and was now 'necessary', while before, in the 1979 production, it was 'merely mawkish and sensational'.

Among the heterosexual majority, said Coveney, there was still strong reluctance to accept homosexual love, with commentators such as George Gale, in the *Mail*, in August 1989, 'suggesting all homosexuals were likely to spread AIDS, and therefore incipient murderers'. The audience was electrified by those love scenes in which, in breaks from lumbering stones from one side of the stage to the other, Max and Horst 'make physical love by auto-erotic suggestion . . . getting your rocks off while keeping your socks on' (quipped Coveney). '*Bent*'s rallying cry – better to be out and dead than furtive and alive – is both cruel and harsh.' Powerfully effective in creating tolerance and compassion, Ian demonstrated again, as he had effectively in Iago, the power of being both evilly obnoxious and pitiable. 'One of the most stunning things I've ever seen,' Martin Sherman told John Lahr for his profile of McKellen in the *New Yorker* in August 2007, came when the SS guard forced Max to beat his boyfriend to death to prove he wasn't homosexual. 'He was sitting there and he defecated. It was very subtle – but you saw in his body the spasm, which is what a person does in a period of such shock.'

The character Max stands for all the mass of people who died nameless, uncelebrated and forgotten. I identify here, undoubtedly, that again McKellen was stealing fire from heaven and playing, for the world to witness, a very Promethean role – this time willingly and exultantly chained to the rock of his sexuality.

But on occasions it could well seem that McKellen's life from the beginning of his new celebrity was more than anything else about stardom and survival, and keeping those who worshipped him happy, rather than enduring love and forming relationships at a personal level. Perhaps he was already, now he was fifty, a fully paid-up member of that Establishment. 'I hate authority,' he told *Vanity Fair* two years after the *Bent* revival. 'I'm part of the Establishment and all that so I can dismantle it . . .'

22

Who Was Olivier's True Heir?

'I want to know the mind of God. The rest are details.'

Albert Einstein

Richard III – 1990–2

In 1983 Laurence Olivier had informed his guests in the studio when recording *King Lear* for television that you cannot just go and be a king: there has to be an element of sanctity. 'In the Coronation service it would seem it's God who makes a king.' Upon his death and funeral held locally near his home in Ashurst, Sussex, where he had attended church, lobbying began for his ashes to be buried either in St Paul's or Westminster Abbey. The Abbey finally upstaged St Paul's in the competition, claiming it would be more suitable they should be interred beside David Garrick and Henry Irving than Nelson.

On Friday 20 October 1989, at the memorial service for Olivier in Westminster Abbey, all the theatrical and film acolytes carried relics of the regal personage to the organ sounds of three great English religious composers, Edward Elgar, Ralph Vaughan Williams and William Walton. There was a touch of the Archie Rice ridiculous as, to be laid on the high altar in reverence, Maggie Smith carried up a tea set, and Michael Caine, Olivier's lifetime achievement Oscar. Significantly, in this pirouetting of rivals for the crown, Ian McKellen carried the *Coriolanus* laurel wreath, while it was Derek Jacobi who bore from the sacrarium the crown Olivier wore as Richard III in the film. Sadly, Olivier had upstaged Anthony Quayle, who died the same day with hardly a mention.

Uniquely for an actor, Olivier had been elevated to the peerage, and substantial books about him continued to be published after his death in 1989, right up to 2013 and beyond. The biggest auditorium in our prestigious National Theatre still carries his name. The Olivier awards each year signify the peak of theatrical achievement.

The Olivier way was to be absolute ruler, to dominate in whatever he did, in fact to be God, or even worse, a tyrant. Stories abound of Olivier's will to power and power games. When Jacobi joined Olivier's original National Theatre Company in 1963, at Chichester playing Ladvenu, the young but aesthetically fine-drawn Dominican in *Saint Joan*, at his first rehearsal in Chelsea Olivier came in with Joan Plowright, cast in the title role. The cast were all lined up. Olivier came down the line like a king, shaking hands with all, saying a word or two, with Joan at his side, and as he came nearer, 'the shirt,' recalls Jacobi, 'was sticking to your back, and then he shook hands, and he absolutely locked eyes with me. He was talking to me, and it was just "Who is going to drop the eyes first?"' He had superabundant ego-fuelled energy. As the director Casper Wrede wrote to Angela Fox, 'If Olivier had not been a great actor he would have been a great murderer.' When Jacobi took over the role of Don Pedro in *Much Ado About Nothing* from Albert Finney, he could not emulate Finney at blowing out a smoke ring to end the show, and instead 'blew out' the spotlight on him. Olivier at the end of the dress rehearsal rushed forward to hug him, exclaiming, 'Baby, darling, baby boy, great – and I so wondered what you were going to do! That was marvellous! I've got a better idea, darling, baby boy. I think you should jump up on to the banquette, pull off your wig, and shout "Je suis un homme!"' . . . Jacobi saw it as a very involved joke about Olivier's own sexuality, at which he laughed dutifully, but thought what he really meant was that he had not got Albert's balls. 'Maybe it was a bit cruel . . . it was this sexual thing he had, this hang-up. He adored his boys, us I mean, but he was always wary if we were effeminate – if we were gay . . . he couldn't have been happy with that side of himself . . . He was very finely tuned in that area, and a bit hung up too.'

Notice the 'power control'. Jacobi had been 'adopted', so to speak, as Olivier's acting 'son' and felt flattered when Olivier called him into his office and said so. He was invited to Olivier's Sussex home at weekends when Olivier brought him break-fast in bed, took me in his arms and said, 'You are my third son,' meaning after Tarquin and Richard. So there was warm humour attached to the notion he considered fanciful, that he was Olivier's or anyone's 'heir'. In 1988 a prominent profile in the *Sunday Times* said Jacobi was the 'era's Gielgud to Ian McKellen's Olivier', a shorthand comparison on which the bril-liant director Clifford Williams poured scorn. 'How absurd can you get . . . Derek doesn't want to take up any mantle, he runs a mile from reputation. He's just interested in acting.'

For McKellen, the ambition to be deemed Olivier's successor was fierce and real. On his online CV (which he approved and vetted if not entirely wrote) is this: 'He always keeps on "solidi-fying" his "role" as Laurence Olivier's worthy successor.' The point is further emphasised that he made three Shakespeare films in common with Olivier: *Hamlet* (Olivier 1948; McKellen 1970); *Richard III* (1955; 1995); *King Lear* (1983; 2007) adapted for TV.

McKellen hungered after Olivier's status and had long hungered to emulate him. Without the physical closeness and shared productions Derek had had, Ian followed the urgings of his acting soul, adopted Olivier as his idol. He had the same urge to power, but without quite the same means to dominate or advance himself directly as Derek had. He had fallen back on his non-mainstream Cambridge roots, and eventually, as an outsider in the perhaps old-fashioned actor tradition, built up his reputation from his Cambridge background (something Olivier never had).

Yet in Ian's own reckoning and frequent assertion, Laurence Olivier remained through all his life his main and constant inspiration. Jonathan Miller may have said that 'Many of us felt enormous sentiments of love, of longing to be approved by him, and patricidal feelings at the same time,' but for Ian there were no patricidal feelings, only unconditional love.

In one important way he was decidedly Olivier's successor, as Antony Sher elegantly pointed out when he and Ian were working together in the National Theatre production of *Uncle Vanya* in 1992: '[H]e's an actor to his fingertips, he lives, breathes and loves it; he says yes it's about showing off, yes I can do that, and then some. From day one, he's there performing, needing to entertain the director, the other actors, stage management, anyone who's watching. He'll interrupt a scene to invent some comic business, people will laugh and applaud. I found some of this irritating at first, yet was quickly won over; his charisma is irresistible.'

Few would dispute Olivier's greatest role was Richard III – Shakespeare's pure egotist creation, realised when the playwright was an immature, fantastically gifted wordsmith. Richard III is an unrepentant megalomaniac, a tyrant, an avalanche of power that sweeps down and destroys all before it, especially women. During a discussion of Shakespeare with Simon Callow years earlier, when Callow was an unknown young actor, Ian, who 'could be casuistical', firmly announced that 'Shakespeare is always on the side of change.' Callow tentatively put it to the famous Shakespearean actor that this was perhaps not entirely true, that order and 'degree' were what Shakespeare was attached to, that instability was the thing he feared most and that all the plays represent a movement towards the re-establishment of order. Somewhat to Callow's surprise, Ian said, 'Well, you're obviously right. What I just said was complete rubbish.'

*

Richard Eyre was McKellen's director for *Richard III*. 'It's impossible for a director to stage a play without revealing something of his politics,' said Eyre later in 1995. 'Every director wants to be God – or godlike.' And so it was to be in this production. McKellen was busy in the evenings with the West End transfer of *Bent*. He had wanted Deborah Warner to direct *Richard*, but she was directing *King Lear* with Brian Cox, in which Ian was playing Kent. Eyre was asked instead. Both directors had very different methods of work. Eyre saw himself as the builder, as well as negotiator, diplomat, translator and mediator of the play. He liked to have all details worked out beforehand in a careful plan. Warner wanted to sit back in the eleven weeks of alternating rehearsals to let the cast invent and improvise, so she could choose and shape the best results.

Ian was on the side of the meticulous and well-planned production effects, with Eyre observing he was ever so slightly wary of Ian's attention to this kind of detail. Unbounded as he was in admiration for Ian's breadth and power, 'He monitors his effects and orchestrates them . . . Searching for external effects – It's a criticism you'll still hear of McKellen's stage acting, however much he himself feels coming out or working in small theatres has changed him.' After two weeks of rehearsals things were no better. 'Ian is particularly exhausting,' writes Eyre in his diary. 'It's difficult to divine his true feelings and he fusses around and over-decorates.'

Rehearsals had begun on 19 March 1990, with Ian throwing a champagne welcome to his cast. Eyre found the rehearsals a strain also because his father was dying; he was tired and felt low much of the time. 'Ian was remorseless,' he told the *Sunday Telegraph Magazine* in August 1992. 'He would go on and on about parts of the show that weren't right.' But, then, *Richard III* was an immature, broad-stroked work. Here perhaps we see Ian's need for rich, many-sided complexity overreaching itself. As Nunn said of him, 'Ian has the intelligence to push the directorial process. Simple answers just won't do. There are complexities . . . that he is aware of and wants to be explored.' Eyre hardly ever imposed his ideas, wanting to provide the happy environment for his cast to work in, and being the solid and sometimes slightly dull director he was, always achieved a sound result.

But Ian worried Crookback was a politically incorrect character, aligning disability and evil, and because of this had shied away from ever playing Shylock, whom he also saw as politically incorrect. Eyre, McKellen and Bob Crowley, the designer, came up with an imaginary version of Britain in the 1930s with Richard taking over as an Oswald Mosley-like fascist dictator. The key moment was when Richard and his followers change into fascist uniform, and he greets the crowd with a stiff-arm salute. In the second half the back wall was adorned with a huge, nude portrait of an idealised Richard, painted in the mythic/heroic vein beloved of the Nazis, with withered arm miraculously healed. At first Eyre insisted on the penis being redone, claiming it was out of proportion, i.e. oversize, although McKellen maintained it was drawn accurately from life!

McKellen's doggedness prevailed and at last Eyre surrendered to what he calls the perfectionism. Brian Cox (Buckingham) voiced his unease at the Eyre-McKellen, or cut-glass, English and 1930s posh accents. In his general's uniform he spoke with a Sandhurst accent, and 'talks of "wintah" and "myajestea" in a blend of drawl and blimpish staccato,' as Benedict Nightingale reported in his *Times* review. In the coronation scene Richard was given a red cloak to wear, the size of the whole stage. This was cut before the opening, but Cox still found the staging uninteresting, the stiff-arm fascist salutes grating. 'It all goes back to the business of everything being pre-digested,' he said, 'all the discoveries are already made before we get to rehearsal and it's just a question of filling in. I find that way of working frustrating and dead . . . You stand around working on technical things which have already been created on the model or whatever . . . I'm sorry, I can't find any enthusiasm for *Richard*

III whatsoever, I'm feeling really low about it, quite frankly it bores the ass off me.' Yet his Buckingham was considered by the *Sunday Times* 'the perfect foil to McKellen's dictator as the corrupt civil politician' – as was McKellen's loyal Kent to Cox's maddened Lear.

They ironed out their differences before the first night, with Eyre surrendering to the more powerful, stubborn will of Ian. 'He's a perfectionist,' he conceded, 'and I love that.' Eyre was the master of tact, the outstanding National Theatre administrator who ticked all the right boxes, with his liberal, left-wing leaning, a sensitively aware leader of a secularist multicultural establishment. But there was something more serious, too, in Ian's shortcomings, which made his Richard III weak by comparison with Olivier. No gloating sexuality towards Anne came over in McKellen's misogynist virulence. It seemed McKellen was seeing Richard as the victim, responding – as he had with his Iago and Macbeth – to their lack of love in their own lives, so surely there was a hint of a personal issue here. Richard III was far from Olivier's triumphant, humour-relishing villain of pure evil. A homosexual undertone could be detected in Richard's approach to Tyrell, admitted by McKellen: was there a parallel between the hunchback, the withered arm, causing detachment, anger? The explanation Nunn expressed to me was that, as he saw it, Ian's Richard was not lovable. There was for example no allure in his delivery of the line 'Since I cannot prove a lover . . . I am determined to prove a villain.'

As Ian put it, 'Richard's an old show-off. An actor. A liar. He fools the audience. "Richard loves Richard. That is, I am I." If you can only love yourself, you exist; life is worth carrying on with. And he needs to do something. I can sympathise with that. If he'd just stop, he'd be pathetic. He needs motion. Give a chap a bit of weaponry, or a uniform . . .' Ian's Richard was a lively outsider villain.

This is the very opposite of evil passion, of Olivier finding lightness and exhilaration in violence, the relish and humour in no longer being able to hold down his violence. Roger Lewis, in his biography of Olivier, explains that 'what is chilling about Richard, Macbeth, or the demon dentist, is that with Olivier thinking, suffering and feeling, living through each moment, and drawing us in, they can still commit their deeds.'

Updating *Richard III* to the 1930s worked well in some areas and not in others. The scenes of dark-suited, paranoid men in dimly lit meeting rooms made the politics of the play clear and vivid. But the sudden intrusion of armour and swords on the battlefield, not to mention 'a horse, my kingdom for a horse', was hopelessly anachronistic. 'What the fuck are we going to do about the ending?' Eyre exploded after they had just tried it out. And when Richard was winched into the air on a plat-form to address a Nuremberg-style rally, it looked as if Eyre would rather have been directing *The Resistible Rise of Arturo Ui*, Brecht's parable of the rise of Hitler, transposed to the Chicago gangland. In *Playing Shakespeare*, John Barton says the great danger with putting Shakespeare into modern dress is that 'it can reduce rather than resonate'. In other words, a play that has something universal to say about, say, tyranny is reduced to a patronising spelling-out of narrow historical parallels. Barton preferred 'timeless' productions, set in no one particular period in an attempt to say something about all periods.

Inside Ian it had not gone quite right. There is a loss in making Richard a 1930s case study, which as the *Sunday Times* critic Robert Hewison wrote, 'traps . . . and prevents him exploring Richard as thoroughly as he did stealthy, ravenous Macbeth . . . or the dry cold Iago'. Ian's portrait of an entirely possible fascist is convincing, Hewison felt, 'but when the interpretation bears a matter of historical comparison the imaginative possibilities are lost.' From the self-effacing start of his engagement with this supreme role of Olivier (in which Ian had consciously to 'prove himself' – 'I have to do something every day to feel good about myself'), Ian's approach smacks of a rather patronising dismissal of the play as not fit for modern consumption. 'Before

1990 I had had no interest in playing Richard III.' Once he had embarked on it it became evident he had adopted an academic tone: 'Richard's wickedness is an outcome of other people's disaffection with his physique . . .'

At once the thesis of victimhood has been applied to Crookback, and for much of the time all we see is a military and aristocratic mask. Benedict Nightingale, in his *Times* review, asked, 'Is this Richard punishing the world for childhood rejection? Or compensating for the lack of an arm, as Hitler supposedly did for the want of a testicle?' (Others suggested it might be that Ian showed this feeling because it was about his own sense of victimhood as a gay man.)

Olivier had decided, following in the heroic footsteps of Henry V, that in all Richard's qualms and uncertainty, even strong defiance of his own murdered ghosts dismissed as indigestion, mastery and concentration were the keynotes of the performance. McKellen's Richard III may have been a soul-searcher, a technical perfectionist, but the actor had remained full of doubt over obtaining the right effect. Michael Burrell told me that he pointed out to Ian his shortcomings. Burrell had been closer to Ian's performances than most friends. In particular, having played Richard III himself, he was very aware that when Ian opened at the National he was shocked and disappointed at the poor response from the critics. Burrell reassured him, saying his performance was really so genuine and natural, for, by having a small hump and only a lifeless right arm, Ian was underplaying the histrionic aspects of the role.

Only once did Ian become vitriolic in the Olivier tradition, when he dressed down Hastings, and pulled a cork from a bottle clenched in his right arm. In the long scene in which he is wooing Anne, he argued skilfully that he killed the others, including Anne's husband, 'only because I loved you'. Nightingale's review probed the lack of an interior life when he asked, 'Why for instance is his Richard less than credible when he emerges from his pre-battle dreams bent, bunched shuffling forward querulously groaning out his fears? Is it Shakespeare's fault, or his, that this most inner of moments seems so unmotivated, so unprepared?' Even so he was compellingly attractive as Richard. Of the hordes of female fans who followed him, Ian said, 'They are barking up the wrong tree.' They would have to wait till the tour, and in particular New York, for the praise to bear comparison with those earlier triumphs of Macbeth and Iago.

Brian Cox had had his doubts about the initial lengthy rehearsals and London run, and been sceptical of Eyre's approach, but he came round to liking the production in the end. While Ian was in his element touring, Cox missed his family and home life: 'You're in the theatre all day, every day – fourteen hours a day, or twelve hours, it's just too much.' But this was not at all McKellen's feeling. There was no family at home to test his patience or worry about. His single-mindedness was such that he would never have to feel like Olivier, who, when sleeping next door to his son Tarquin when he was a baby, commented, 'I'd rather play Othello eight times a week than do this again!'

Once they were free of this country, and the carping critics here, they began a world and European tour, beginning with Tokyo, to last for the whole of 1990. At one stage, when they had been playing in Madrid, a certain demoralisation set in. Two attendants standing at the back in the Queen Elizabeth scene fainted. The theatres were on strike and they had to shift with changed plans. McKellen grew morose, saying, 'I don't think the company likes me, I don't know what I've done.' Peter Brook came and didn't like the production. Yet all this soon passed as they went on touring: Ian discovered that the audiences everywhere revealed a paradox, namely that the more specific a production, the more general was its relevance. While Richard was so obviously English, in Hamburg and Leipzig, Richard's black-shirt troops 'seemed like a commentary on the

Third Reich'. In Bucharest, when Richard was slain, the Romanians 'stopped the show with cheers, in memory of their recent freedom from Ceauşescu's regime'. In Cairo at the time of the Gulf War, it 'seemed like a new play about Saddam Hussein'.

In the early summer of 1992 the National Theatre company and Ian, now in his fifty-fourth year, after having performed in other plays, including *Uncle Vanya*, revived *Richard III* for a tour of America that lasted for sixteen weeks, seven shows a week. The penis had armour over it in order not to offend American prudishness, although Ian had in the flesh revealed all at the Brooklyn Academy of Music in 1974 when he played Edgar in this earlier tour production of the Actors' Company's *King Lear*. Visibly at ease, he exuded affection and warmth to everyone he met. He often felt theatre was superior to other jobs, for here he had family and work without loneliness, could always eat in company, always share the experiences of travel. He was married to Melpomene (or Melpomen in his case) his muse. 'It's even rumoured that we sleep together,' he observed ruefully. He had no stress, no relationship or the problem of how much power to assert, or not, over another person.

Ian beat the drum for the modern setting more and more, claiming it was impossibly 'confusing to distinguish between a multitude of characters who are all done up in floppy hats and wrinkled tights'. This was humorous but possibly wide of the mark, for by now no one, except in Blackadder send-ups, ever performed Shakespeare in floppy hats and wrinkled tights. But even so, the zeal was unabashed and infectious.

New York labelled him grandiloquently 'The World's greatest classical actor' and who was he to deny it? But all was not smooth sailing as on tour there were concert-size auditoria to fill with audiences, and even some dissenting reviews, which were quite outspoken. The *Village Voice* called for a parliamentary investigation into 'a near total disgrace' and for a thorough fumigation of the National Theatre's London headquarters, while the *Washington Post* lambasted a 'lame production' and 'a ranting cast'. Frank Rich in the *New York Times* more than redressed the balance by warming to Ian's 'original charac-terisation' of 'a most contemporary tyrant', whose gargoyle make-up reminds him of 'Michael Crawford's *Phantom of the Opera* or perhaps Jack Nicholson's *Joker*'. Later his 'grinning demonic death mask' evokes the Weimar caricatures of George Grosz, as well as latter-day photographs of Kurt Waldheim. When he asks about the murder of King Edward's two young sons a cigarette dangles from his mouth at 'a sly Noël Cow-ardesque tilt' while his 'sheer wily persistence and battering-ram personality, not charm of eroticism' define his wooing of Lady Anne.

This eclectic feast of chameleon string-pulling is continuous-ly relished by Rich with McKellen wielding a pocket bible to adopt the public pretence of piety, then discarding it with a contemptuous flick of a wrist so that he might lead the masses in a blackshirt salute. After his spirited description Rich ends with a bit of an anticlimax that McKellen cannot show, except for one beautifully done mea culpa near the end; how much 'his acting has grown in emotional depth since his last bravura performance here as Salieri'.

During the tour Ian attended a White House theatre fund-raiser where former president Ronald Reagan was present and was quite moved when the elderly president said, 'If only we could understand everything in Shakespeare, the world would be a better place.' Only a few days later he caught Reagan on television addressing a Baptist audience. The president was recalling the words of a wise old man: 'If only we could under-stand everything in the Bible, the world would be a better place.' Ian marvelled at Reagan's artistry. The holders of offices of state had entered first accompanied by 'devastatingly attractive cadets'. Then in ran Ronald and Nancy – two septuagenarians telling us they were not old. Ian watched from a sofa as the

Reagans kissed, slapped backs, reached out and touched cheeks, finding the appropriate response for each person. 'It was utterly exhausting and an utter waste of time. He could have signed a cheque and got on with being President.'

23

Underneath All the Tolerance

In November 1990 Ian and his *Richard III* company played Paris, at the Théâtre de l'Odéon, which was for Richard Eyre, its director, the realisation of an adolescent dream: 'My favourite auditorium in the world'. When it was reported Thatcher had resigned, they were jubilant and cheered. A day later Eyre was woken by a phone call from Ian.

'Can you come to my room?'

Ian lay on his bed, looking anxious but elated. 'I've been offered a knighthood,' he said. 'Do you think I should take it?' Eyre told him he should and saw he was relieved, but 'being Ian wouldn't show his elation'. At this juncture Ian also phoned Sean Mathias and Michael Cashman.

It was a characteristic irony for Ian that Thatcher, before she resigned, should have awarded him his knighthood (indicating how politicised actors had become), and that on the same list the 'homophobic' Manchester police chief was also awarded a knighthood.

Surprisingly, and in spite of various polls that strongly disapproved of a gay man receiving a knighthood, in the New Years' Honours list of 1991, with John Major now as replacement Prime Minister, Ian was knighted. There was an immediate debate, loud in the media outlets, between street-level activists and those in the corridors of power. Film-maker Derek Jarman was up in arms, outraged at his acceptance, finding it impossible to react with anything but dismay to an acceptance from a government 'which . . . is poised by means of Clause

28 of the Local Government Bill to take important steps towards recriminalising homosexuality . . .' He vented his anger
in the *Guardian*: 'Why did you accept this award, Ian? It has
diminished you.'

Straight away, eighteen well-known theatrical people, led
by Antony Sher, called Ian's recognition, from a government
he had accused of homophobia, a significant landmark in the
history of the British gay rights movement. Wishing to 're-
spectfully distance ourselves' from Derek Jarman's letter, were
Simon Callow, Michael Cashman, Nancy Diuguid, Simon Fan-
shawe, Stephen Fry, Philip Hedley, David Lan, Bryony Lavery,
Michael Leonard, Tim Luscombe, Alec McCowen, Cameron
Mackintosh, Pam St Clement, John Schlesinger, Antony Sher,
Martin Sherman, Ned Sherrin and Nicholas Wright. Others
argued acceptance was a step towards the demarginalisation of
homosexuality.

Jarman replied that 'the McKellen 18 seem, sad to say, to
see no further than the end of the artistic arena'. What, he
wondered, 'of gay footballers or cricketers, lesbian tennis players and athletes, gay miners or lesbian diplomats, gay building
labourers or lesbian doctors?' Did the supporters of the Mc-
Kellen knighthood 'seriously say to these people, "Come out!
Sir Ian has shown that you're safe. It won't damage your
career." Of course not.' If there was any suspicion that an element of pique or small-mindedness lay at the root of Jarman's
reaction, bringing in Derek Jacobi – a bitter cry of 'What about
Sir Derek?' – his clear-sighted and passionate concentration on
what he believed to be the very real and harmful issues at stake
allayed it.

Sir Derek was a question in point. He wanted to have nothing to do with each side of the divide. I mentioned to Ian that
he had once had a slight falling-out over Derek's not coming
out as a gay. Ian quickly interrupted: 'It's all in his imagination. Entirely. I never fall out with anybody over that, I just feel
sorry for them. Did I fall out? No, I don't think I ever had a

conversation about it. Does he remember a conversation?'

'Only vaguely,' I answered. Antony Sher, arguably as great a stage actor as McKellen, was spurred on further by Ian, simply tired of flannelling in interviews, or having to disguise 'my true pride in shows like *Torch Song* . . . I was impressed and humbled by what other gay actors, like Ian McKellen and Simon Callow, were doing for the cause.' But perhaps, most important, he was about to publish the book of his paintings and drawings called *Characters*, and 'I refused to lie about the relationships and interests portrayed on those pages. It was one thing to be dishonest as an actor – that job fools around with the truth all the time – but somehow quite unacceptable as an artist.'

When Sher did come out in 1989, via an interview about the book in *The Times*, there was no fuss. 'Ian had stolen all the thunder . . . In fact, rather disappointingly after all the time I'd spent agonising, it made no impact whatsoever. If I'd been a movie or TV star it might've been different. That Sunday the phone rang in our Stratford house and a voice said, "Hello, Ian McKellen here, we don't really know one another – hope you don't mind, I got your number from the stage door – but I just wanted to say one thing. "Thank you".'

There were a dozen or so nasty slanging matches following Ian's knighthood, ranging from complaints that his publicly admitted homosexuality had been honoured rather than his acting talent, to accusations that some gay people were 'making careers out of their sexual preference, as opposed to intelligent homosexuals who chose to keep quiet'.

An especially bitter exchange took place between Ian and Nicholas de Jongh, who mockingly awarded him the Golden Vanity prize in an article titled 'Men Are the Real Bitches'. Ian retaliated he never claimed to be, as de Jongh called him, the 'leader of the gay and lesbian movement in Britain'. He was also assailed on Radio 4 by callers making highly technical claims about the tensile deficiencies of the rectal lining. 'How dare you presume to know about my sexual practices?' he replied with soft and measured equanimity.

In July 1991 Ian accompanied John Major to see Eduardo De Filippo's *Napoli Milionaria* at the National. Afterwards Richard Eyre, as the NT's director, hosted a supper party at which Ian sat next to Mary Soames, daughter of Nicholas and chairman of the National Theatre, while on her other side sat Prime Minister John Major. Somewhat cheekily, one might say, Ian bantered over the top of Soames's presence, offering voice projection tuition to Major as long as he did not make use of it to win the election. He then sprang the challenge to Major: could they talk together about a 'social matter'?

It seems Major, unworldly as some might say he was (according to Anthony Seldon, his biographer, he loudly remarked over dinner that Archbishop George Carey of Canterbury was 'a very good chap', meaning tolerant and broad-minded, which caused a lowering of eyes round the table who had a perception that Carey was anything but), quickly fell in with McKellen's request.

Ian came to Number 10 at 10.45 on a wet 24 September dressed in a suit and tie and armed with a paperback title *The Pink Plaque Guide to London*, which had a photo of Number 10 on the jacket. This was a politically provocative gesture. When Major questioned Ian specifically over this, he had prepared his script, claiming that 'from the available statistics it is likely that 10 per cent of the people currently working here are homosexual. But the celebrity in question is one of your predecessors – William Pitt the Younger. He never declared himself as gay and I wonder if the burden of his secret led him to the alcoholism which rapidly killed him. Maybe his benign ghost will hover over this meeting.'

They took coffee. While the result from this meeting was virtually nil for McKellen, it became part of an inexorable change in rolling back intolerance and prejudice towards the gay community. A young female admirer pointed to one important ingredient when she first met him with this comment, on how the charm always worked: 'I first saw him at a *Guardian* party in Soho – I was a student and he was the guest of honour. He asked me for a light and handed back the matches with such courtesy and such a gorgeous smile I remember thinking: "How amazing. He is even nice to the small people."'

A wag commented that as one had the more mellifluous speaking voice you might see McKellen as a sort of gay Major: 'both were supposed to be calm, reasonable, unassuming alternatives to the harsher, shriller voices previously associated with their respective causes.' Like meets like when one chameleon meets another. In this case the chameleon took on the colouring of his surroundings.

Derek Jarman, who was by now diagnosed with AIDS, from which he was to die, poured scorn on the Major–McKellen meeting, saying Ian should have arrived dressed in a frock.

During these spats Sir Ian (or Serena, as Stephen Fry had jokingly dubbed him) remained at least outwardly serene. As Steven Berkoff, his neighbour, recorded the day after the knighthood was bestowed, 'These titles become the theatrical profession and endow a certain majesty.' Berkoff caught the real McKellen as he underlined the shadow side: 'He is a ceaseless prowler around the body of the English theatre and sometimes reminds me of a stalking wolf, ready to seize his prey and tear it to pieces.' Later, Berkoff noted in his autobiography, his roles have all been of villains and he was developing a nice rogues' gallery. 'There is a quest in his face, a hunger which, like the wolf, will never be satisfied; his eyes reveal nothing to tell you what he will be.'

John Major was arguably one of those small people to whom Ian was nice. But the tolerance, easy to Major, had its limits. There had been a problem gaining cross-party reform 'under Roy Jenkins' stewardship of the Home Office', comments David Owen, former Foreign Secretary, and joint leader of the Social Democratic Party when it split from Labour. Others in the House considered the battle to be won when the Sexual Offences Act had been passed in 1967 and didn't see the value of handling the repeal of Clause 28. 'There was,' says Owen, 'something of a dilemma in government as to how to handle the welcome change'; Owen as a doctor at St Bartholomew's Hospital had witnessed 'at first hand the physical tragedy of elderly closet gays committing suicide because of the law'. He applauded William Whitelaw and the Conservative government's acceptance that they 'needed to be seen to be tolerant'.

When in June 1998 the age of consent for homosexuals was lowered to sixteen by a majority of 207 in the Commons Ian and campaigners clapped and cheered from the public gallery when the result was announced. Yet intolerance not far from the surface grew on both sides.

Some years before, there had been a young diarist who followed McKellen around with the idea of outing him. The diarist approached him on public occasions when he was with Brodie and would be flattering and friendly. He worked, McKellen found out, for the William Hickey column in the *Daily Express*. He was making Ian's life hell with 'his attitude . . . which appeared to be very friendly but wasn't'. Relating this to Marianne Macdonald, Ian's tone was neutral as he set his coffee cup on the floor. She was shocked by his next words: 'He was blown up by the IRA.' He showed a similar short temper when MP Michael Portillo declared he might contest the Conservative leadership election in 1999. 'Mr Portillo', whose earlier record on gay rights was 'appalling and hypocritical', according to McKellen, had to recant. Were the Tories ready for their first openly bisexual leader?

Ian incurred the wrath of his erstwhile admirer Lynda Lee-Potter when, at an Olivier Awards ceremony in 1991, he announced before the assembly, 'I'm doing my best not to bump into Jason Donovan in case anyone thinks I'm straight.' She pointed out this was as unjust as anybody who says Donovan was gay. But his defenders would say it was just a joke. And when Edith Cresson, a rather scatty French Prime Minister who met McKellen at Number 10 the same day, just after he saw Major, commented that 25 per cent of Englishmen were gay, that they did not like to look at women and the female body, and were in some way a little maimed. McKellen countered a day later that if one in four Englishmen was gay, Britain would be a better place.

In November 1994, at Edinburgh's Lyceum Theatre, Ian was on stage alone, performing his touring Shakespeare show in aid of the gay rights group Stonewall, and had just done a highly mocking impersonation of the firebrand Unionist politician Ian Paisley (drawing no doubt on his Northern Irish blood). He picked up a bible set on the table in front of him, and turned to Leviticus, from which he proceeded to read: 'Thou shalt not lie with mankind as with womankind: it is abomination' (Chapter 18: xxii). 'If a man also lieth with mankind, as he lieth with a woman, both of them have committed an abomination; they shall be put to death; their blood shall be upon them' (Chapter 20: xxiii). Ian then ripped out the pages and tore them up, denouncing these passages as 'dangerous pornography!'. The audience laughed and cheered. He urged the audience to do the same, and to do as he did, whenever staying in a hotel – to rip out these pages from the bedside bible.

He knew what he was doing, of course, and that it would whip up a tempest, which was duly led by the Scottish Tory MP Sir Nicholas Fairbairn, who accused him of being profane and blasphemous, and said he should be locked up. A Church of England bishop, asked for his reaction, feared to give his name because of reprisals but didn't mince his words, calling the gesture a 'product of a twisted mind; defacing any book is sad'. More conciliatory voices were heard, too, one from an Edinburgh minister who in a very soft-voiced reaction pointed out that gay Christians who sympathised with Sir Ian would regard this as dangerous, while a non-committal Church of

England spokesman commented, 'Generally speaking we don't encourage people to tear pages from the Bible!' As Tolkien said in one of his letters, 'You can't fight the Enemy with his own ring without turning into an Enemy.'

Someone from Stonewall, which was making a fair bit of money from the evening, defended the gesture. It was a piece of theatre and had to be seen as that. The audience clapped and cheered. George Bernard Shaw, in his 'Epistle Dedicatory' to *Man and Superman*, called such gestures 'the heroism of daring to be an enemy of God . . . From Prometheus to my own *Devil's Disciple* such enemies have always been popular.'

Ian subsequently and wisely never responded to the complaints about this display. From then on his demonstrations were more muted, as befitting his gentler side. Time maybe might have mellowed his outspoken atheism.

McKellen's roller-coaster ride on the gay rights cause had undoubtedly been selfless climbing, with unstinting financial support to AIDS and, later, LGBT charities. He demonstrated that he was successful as an instrument of public change. He was never sloppy and ill-tempered, and he took victory in his stride without stridency and triumphalism. He had felt happily rewarded that *Bent* was accorded its full National Theatre revival at the Lyttelton Theatre. Peter Tatchell emphasised for me how, this Edinburgh episode apart, Ian and Michael Cashman, as gay rights activists, were wedded to the Stonewall model of working for change from within the system: 'suffragists' rather than 'suffragettes', demonstrating that 'it takes many very different styles and teaching to win a campaign.'

24

Shining a Light through Celluloid

'Nobody is ever first choice. Peter O'Toole wasn't first choice for Lawrence of Arabia. But there's not much point in saying it was Albert Finney.'

Ian McKellen

Ian had performed Richard III a hundred and fifty times and now felt he should make the film. He felt empowered to do anything he chose. No alimony to pay, which hamstrung so many of his contemporaries with ex-spouses and children, no mortgages – he was, in the words of Racine, 'master of myself as of the universe'. The image may seem rather frightening, but fortunately, as a keynote of his character, Ian had not the hubris or dictatorial ambition to be carried away too much by his power.

He set out to craft his own film version, yet still with the notion of being Olivier's successor and heir. Ian had been dismissive of the idea that Richard's physical deformity was related to his villainy. Before he was fifty and played the role, Ian had believed the play's sell-by date had expired 'once modern psychology had questioned the cruel assumption of Shakespeare's contemporaries that physical deformity was an outward expression of some inner moral turpitude'. In accordance with the zeitgeist of the early 1990s, he believed that 'Richard's appalling behaviour [was] the outcome of other people's disaffection with his physique.' By 2019 this all looks old hat: what do we still

see in Richard III but Trump, Putin, even Assad, all quite unashamedly 'playing the villain'? Here is Shakespeare's timeless
resonance. Yet Ian's interpretation, which puts his supreme
villain into the category of a misfit let down by society, shows
also Shakespeare's adaptability to contemporary mores.

Ian interpreted Richard's self-identification with his victimhood as making him a tragic character – his choice and lack of
self-knowledge identifies him with his disability. This obsession
with filming Richard had begun when he was at school. 'In 1958
I saw Laurence Olivier's *Richard III* at the Odeon Cinema in
Bolton. The spell was cast as I watched the shadows of great
actors and I had confirmed my juvenile sense that Shakespeare
was for everybody. I hope that today's young audience might
feel something similar when they see our film.' What differen-
tiates him remarkably from his hero, is this: 'I would like to
come in every day for the rest of my life and film Richard III.
I never want it to stop.' He loved its triumphant moments, as
when Buckingham proclaimed 'Long live King Richard!'

McKellen's systematic fastidiousness and self-demanding
nature came to the fore during the implementation of the
script, which he wrote with the director Richard Loncraine.
The contemporary Richard was now a Hitlerian tyrant (and
still a victim). There was even a certain presumptiousness when
he made the claim that Shakespeare would approve, although
he hastily added, 'Not having him present to consult, I think
of his having just left the rehearsal room, soon to return with
the gentle query I've sometimes heard from living playwrights
– "What the hell do you think you're doing to my play?" . . . I
believe Shakespeare would never do that – nor would he have
been at a rehearsal.'

He was keen, he wrote in his introduction to the screenplay,
and having just played Iago, 'to explore Richard's humanity
rather than reducing him to an emblem of wickedness'. Poor
Crookback is to be understood, empathised with as suffering
inner turmoil in his riot of destruction. This was to be no relish

or celebration of evil, and thus rather surprisingly, given his hero-worship of Olivier, he dismisses him, drawing attention to his own Richard III, which had 'already been fixed for posterity on 26 May 1991, when three cameras were let into the Lyttelton Theatre . . .'

He schooled himself beforehand by acting for the screen with numerous film and TV roles – nine altogether, including an unmemorable turn as a repressed gay English cowboy in *The Ballad of Little Jo*. He also drew on the subservience of Hollywood (MGM) to classic English thespian knights in order to obtain finance and set up his film.

As for casting, he high-handedly dismissed Al Pacino, who had been a celebrated Richard III, in his personal approach to Ian to be in it, responding, claimed the *Evening Standard*, 'God . . . that ham!'. He aimed first at having Danny De Vito to play Buckingham, and Meryl Streep, Queen Elizabeth, but got neither. But he persisted: 'We can't make our film until we get the famous names to be in it.' Interestingly enough he had *Star Trek*'s Captain Picard, Patrick Stewart, as his first choice for Clarence, given Stewart's distinguished Stratford-upon-Avon status and that Gielgud played the role in Olivier's film (Gielgud of course was the actor closest to Olivier). The first choices did not agree, for as the pragmatic Ian pointed out, they never do, either in this case for director (Richard Eyre had said no), producers or cast.

McKellen, undaunted, went on exploiting his networking skills to land Annette Bening and Robert Downey Jr and then to add the illustrious Maggie Smith, Nigel Hawthorne, Kristin Scott Thomas and other illuminati. Every setback over the three years it took, whether financial or artistic, only served to make him more determined, and in the end he said the only person who couldn't turn him down was himself. 'Nobody was first choice. Except for me!'

The film when it was released was generally considered in the respectful notices it drew to be an extraordinary and

British film limelights: misfit and disabled Walter; passionate Priest of Love as D. H. Lawrence (with Janet Suzman); Mosleyite Richard III.

Hollywood calls: in *Apt Pupil* as the ex-Nazi villain Dussander, with Brad Renfro as Todd; film director James Whale with gardener friend (Brendan Fraser), which secured Ian his first Oscar nomination, for best actor; mutant Magneto with the magnetic Mystique (Rebecca Romijn).

Gandalfs galore: 'more dangerous than anything you will ever meet'. Gandalf the Grey, sword in scabbard, morphed into Gandalf the White, wielding it.

Screen royalty: with Cate Blanchett, the elf queen Galadriel, for the royal film performance of *The Hobbit: An Unexpected Journey.*

Late old stagers: as Vanya with Astrov (Antony Sher); as an outrageous Widow Twankey in *Aladdin* with Roger Allam as the villainous Abanazar.

'The Bromance': *Waiting for Godot* as Estragon with Patrick Stewart as Vladimir.

At the Empire Awards: 'What I love about Patrick is that he's so predictably myself. I think we are the same person … I think Derek Jacobi is trying to be the third at the party.' (*ES Magazine,* 1 Sept 2016)

'Married at last': Derek as Stuart and Ian as Freddie in ITV's *Vicious.*

The disputed
Shakespeare
patron the Earl
of Southampton
in *All Is True*.

Very aged Sherlock
inspecting evidence, in
Bill Condon's *Mr. Holmes*.

'Tsarist Lear' in 2007 at the Court-yard Theatre, Stratford. 'Thy truth then be thy dower' – with Romola Garai as Cordelia and Ben Addis as the King of France.

Lear reprise in 2018 on the cliff-top of redemption at the Duke of York's, with Danny Webb as the blind Gloucester.

eccentric work, 'a magnificent scrap between Shakespeare and the 1930s', something even completely bizarre, 'a marriage which fails all the time'. For Simon Callow the adaptation was deeply clever. McKellen hadn't directed it himself, like Olivier, but 'came at it from behind, creating the environment in which it could happen.' For Callow, it finally erased the stranglehold of Olivier's sublimely melodramatic conception. This was an entirely credible human being, and all the more alarming for that. For Richard Cottrell, it was cut too much. Typically, it became a triumph of a very personal kind. Richard III on both stage and in film demonstrates a McKellen at the peak of his powers, both as born politician and commander. He saw it as a step towards greater command in his own career: a new control over the use and direction of his talents. That hankering for independence always dogged him. 'On my own terms. It had always bewildered me why an actor of my experience and ability was not allowed to play large parts in films.' When he makes such seemingly egocentric statements they are without ostensible vanity. He is quite objective about his talent, relaxed about acknowledging his own, as he is free in his acknowledgement of others. It does not offend. He might not like the comparison, but Lady Thatcher, too, spoke of her achievements not as a boast, but as a fact – as a successful carpenter, or mountaineer, or soldier might do: 'This is what I have done; this is what I am capable of.' Matthew Parris adroitly summed up McKellen: 'Beneath the breast of this literal, pacifist, creative artist, barks a commanding officer who is trying to get out.'

Not altogether happy with the mixed reviews, it seemed, McKellen afterwards was in heroic martyr mode: he explained how difficult it was to make the film, and insisted that, of course, in extreme contrast to Olivier, in his film he had extracted from Shakespeare the message for his generation. The image of the fifty-year-old McKellen on his screenplay jacket is of a haunted victim, with ill-fitting moustache, staring furtively over his shoulder. He is not a king, but he looks well enough like the young

Enoch Powell and Oswald Mosley. And once again the contrast with Olivier is strong because the latter as Richard is always enforcing subjection, yet with McKellen you feel he has not quite found himself. Olivier's characters may have unruly desires but they always keep a hold on their identity; Roger Lewis writes; 'notice how Olivier does not laugh . . . but simply opens his mouth wide, like a mask . . . he affects intimacy, people think he's understood by them, but he has no intimates, no family life in the usual and natural sense . . . [when] one of the princes goes too far, making a joke about Richard's misshapen shoulder . . . what we get, for a split second, is a glimpse of Olivier's primitive power, a glimpse of the abyss inside him.'

In McKellen's Richard the actor, self-serving or self-regarding, would so often seem to be playing to an image of himself. Here of course is the big test: did McKellen, as did Olivier, love the part, or love himself in the part? All the time there was the opposite to self-love, an enviable, dogged determination to improve – and so it was to continue. He had not yet quite fully risen to lasting stardom either as a Shakespearean actor or a movie celebrity. His Richard had a puritan Roundhead determination that was to some degree still inhibiting great performance: only keep cameras rolling and theatres open if they have a poignant and well-executed social message!

As for the London opening of the film, it did nothing for him: 'It's the oddest thing in the world, a film premiere. I mean it's a total non-event. A man just shines a light through some celluloid and casts shadows on a wall. And you're sitting among an audience you can't talk to and who can't respond. It isn't happening. It's happened.'

Yet even so, indisputably, the film was an affirmation of Ian's personal triumph. The Society of Friends of Richard III, meeting momentarily at York, objected strongly to the portrayal, but the blackshirted tyrant won Ian his fifth Olivier Award. And yet the Oscar still eluded him. 'I'm not worried about myself, but I know how the big bucks are affected by these things,' he said tartly. The ending, though not of the stage plays, was resounding and memorable. Ian's armoured cars and machine guns rendered Bosworth Field a Bond film finale of awesome pyrotechnics. When it was revived to mark the 400th anniversary of Shakespeare's death in 2016 the *Guardian* called it 'terrifically exciting and lucid', commenting how McKellen 'does some outrageous takes into camera – like Olivier, in fact – although the effect is terrifically personal and distinctive'. The final 'Cagneyish catastrophe, accompanied by Al Jolson's "I'm Sitting on Top of the World" is nightmarishly good.'

McKellen's extraordinary face gives clues to experts in facial analysis to divine or reveal character from its curious pattern of lines. Admittedly this is speculation, but even so Lailan Young, one such expert, suggests that these lines denote the divisions in Sir Ian's personality: 'Particularly one [line] which runs across the bridge of his nose, and the fine line rising from the inner end of his right eyebrow.'

Young observes, for those intrigued by this approach, the network of scalloped creases below the eyes, and a gentle scallop close to the lower eyelid, underlined by patterns each more deeply etched than the last, while these intersect each other. This pattern of creases is further complicated by a curved, nearly vertical line that drops from the outer corner of his left eye, and lines extending into his cheeks below the deepest of the bags already altered by sensitive experiences. It indicates a fluctuation between elation and defeat. 'Many actors have dimpled chins or a "split" chin,' she says. 'These are signs of conceit and a craving for attention. Ian McKellen has only a hint of this actorly characteristic. We can conclude that he is not a natural extrovert – more a thinker with an analytical mind.' So far we can concur.

In the parallel bands of creases in his forehead, taken together with the good-natured twinkle in his eye, and his rueful, even doleful expression, Lailan suggests in her perhaps far-fetched analysis that he is nervous and insecure, and conscious of envy if rivals sometimes outshine him. The smile conceals envy, which he knows is an emotion as destructive as jealousy. His face signals to her that loneliness is what he tries to hide, fear of failure, or being let down by someone he trusts. His eyebrows tell the world their owner is quite selfish – 'but capable of great courage when the going gets tough'. Whatever one may make of such analysis, and some might find it speculative if not specious, there is no doubt the face is a very complex one, and while Lailan sees it as a fixed map or chart of character, the reality is that it is ever-changing, ever in movement. The contradictions were by now a very public phenomenon of this unique and extraordinary actor.

For the 1992 production of *Uncle Vanya* at the National, in which Antony Sher was to play Astrov, McKellen wanted Sean Mathias to direct, and while he believed Mathias was good at directing him, and capable of pulling him up short if he didn't like what he was doing, others demurred. According to Sher in *Beside Myself*, Richard Eyre took him and Ian aside, telling them, 'I'll line up any director in the land for you.' Ian prevailed. Sher, in awe of Ian and a little more, observed of him rehearsing Vanya, 'Ian sometimes finds it hard to dig himself' and remarked that Sean got impatient with him as he changed everything: 'For God's sake, he says, just do the same thing twice in a row.' Mathias proved his mettle in reining Ian in, and the production and performances became a moving and memorable revelation for Ian. He confessed he cried on stage as never before. Yet again, here lay contradiction. Mark Barratt, closing his book on McKellen, sums up from a moment in this production how he retains something of the old-fashioned amateur: '[T]he actor who didn't go to drama school, the actor who brushes past Antony Sher who is genuinely breathless and sweating in the wings of the Cottesloe Theatre, ready for his first entrance as Astrov, who must look as if he's galloped miles across country. "Oh darling," drawls McKellen, "you're such a

Method actor, there is an easier way, y'know." And he dabs a little spit from tongue to forehead – "Like so!"'

Yet there was nothing of the amateur evident in the performance, although the shambling amiable approach is to the fore when he mumbles about grief and rage. As soon as he sees Janet McTeer's Yelena he is smitten: when she glides past him he, as Benedict Nightingale writes, 'absurdly combs his moustache, grinning dopily after her. Then the emotional corpse is twitching and forlornly asking questions and all too successfully resuscitating himself.'

When he sees the landowner Sebryakov (Eric Porter) who has disappointed him over the sale of their property, he collapses breathlessly and totters with rage: 'You've ruined my hopes!' 'There's a would-be killer inside the rumpled green corduroy,' Nightingale goes on, and then, far worse, underlines 'the desolate resignation that ends by disarming and unmanning him'.

The portrait of defeat is all the more moving for its refusal to pull at the audience's collective heartstrings, the sorry tale of a man significant only for his insignificance. As Nightingale concludes, Ian and Sher's Astrov were the 'victim of Russia and himself. They left us feeling there's exceptional interest in what are nevertheless unexceptional lives.' Mathias found his explosion and release of anger the truly remarkable feature of Ian's performance.

With the success of *Vanya*, and its well-deserved awards, Sean proved Ian's choice of him fitted in well with Ian's character, indicating his powers over Ian lay in not always letting him have his way. Ian was delighted with the acclaim showered upon Sean's direction.

25

New Labour Interlude

'In his warm embrace? Oh no, that's just his arms. If you
want to know if he loves you so, it's in his kiss.'

'The Shoop Shoop Song', Cher

The hallowed door of Number 10 opened in July 1997 to a
string of cultural celebrities such as Whitehall had never seen
before. Alienated, disillusioned voters tired of the political class
had elected Tony Blair, a young and idealistic cultural supremo
with a brave new world feel of 'putting the people first'. He set
out his investiture stamp of show business values with a dazzling
array of names: Ralph Fiennes, Lenny Henry, Tony Robinson,
Helen Mirren, Harry Enfield and Eddie Izzard were but a few
of the acting luminaries there, and the range of characters included newspaper editors such as Piers Morgan, writers such as
Margaret Forster, Margaret Drabble and her husband Michael
Holroyd, designers (Vivienne Westwood, Caroline Charles)
and, naturally, the new aristocracy of pop stars led by Oasis's
Noel Gallagher, who declared, 'When the fookin' Prime Minister [sends you an invite], fookin' ell, you've got to go.' And
naturally, of course, there was Sir Ian McKellen.

At the party, themed 'Cool Britannia' – no longer Rule Britannia – Margaret Forster was deeply impressed by Tony Blair,
who made an obscure reference to a book 'I had written about
Carr's biscuits'. She was naively taken in by his 'homework'.
Margaret Drabble, a little more scornfully, attended 'the party

with more curiosity than hope, having voted Lib Dem'. 'I've no idea why we were invited. Not many writers were there (left-wing figures such as Harold Pinter and John Mortimer were notably absent) and a lot of showbiz people whom I didn't recognise. Tony Blair spent a lot of time in an alcove being photographed with Oasis. I didn't know what Oasis was, but he did.'

She did, of course, recognise Ian, her erstwhile contemporary. He had played her lover in *Deutsches Haus* years before at the ADC Theatre, Cambridge, in which he had planted on her many kisses and heartfelt tender words. He had also been her lead in the adaptation of her novel, *The Garrick Years*.

This time Ian had his eye on a different quarry, and was set to make a similar impact. Tony came over to McKellen, the fellow master thespian. Ian – very unexpectedly – said to him, 'May I kiss you, Prime Minister?'

McKellen, master of the grand gesture, pulled out of the hat the most memorable moment of the party.

The Prime Minister, of course, eyes flashing enthusiastically, inclined a cheek at once and then, to unbelieving onlookers, Ian leant towards him, and delivered a lengthy smacking kiss on the lips.

Tony probably did not anticipate what he was in for, but as John Tydeman, Ian's oldest Cambridge friend, explains, 'Ian's a cuddler, a hugger and a kisser – and it's always on the lips, whether gay or not.'

When is a kiss not just a kiss? Ian had given Tony his own Tony Award, his seal of approval, generous, unconditional, big and open-hearted. We should remember Blair at this point had only been premier for three months. The comment of the Bishop of Carlisle in Shakespeare's *Richard II*, after the big celebration ('A woeful pageant have we here beheld / The woe's to come') still had some time to play itself out.

We should beware reading too much into it, for only several years later, shortly after *The Fellowship of the Ring*, the first film of the *Lord of the Rings* trilogy, was finished, we find from Ian, interviewed in the *Radio Times*, that the love-in with Tony had been abruptly broken off. He accused Blair's government of betraying the homosexual rights agenda, condemning it as being no better at tackling gay issues than John Major's was, describing it as 'woefully ignorant about gay people and their problems, as most politicians at the time . . . I don't detect the present Government is any more willing than he was to move things ahead. It's still legal to sack someone for being gay, which is appalling.'

Asked about the irony of his acceptance of a knighthood from Margaret Thatcher, he was quick to answer, 'I'll always be glad I was offered it after I'd come out – and Maggie knew she was giving it to an openly gay man, not a species she is renowned for favouring.'

A 'Labour Party source' refuted Ian's surprising charge, but Blair had clearly caught the McKellen kissing bug, going on to kiss Gaddafi and, surprisingly even in 2017, Jean-Claude Juncker, President of the EU, in a fulsome embrace.

Much later, Ian moved on to profess allegiance to Jeremy Corbyn in rather eyebrow-raising terms, but then admitting a preference to be Alastair Campbell rather than Corbyn. Shades of Iago, perhaps?

26

Hollywood God Hubris

'If a camera had drooled over a woman's body the way it drools over Fraser's, there would have been protests!'

Evening Standard, 10 March 1999

A career in films still eluded McKellen until the late 1990s when his sixtieth birthday approached. Richard III aside, there was, in spite of middling-to-good roles in *Cold Comfort Farm*, *Restoration*, *And the Band Played On* and other films, still nothing truly remarkable to be discerned except an apprentice film actor keen to improve his skills.

In 1995 the Hollywood director Bryan Singer, a New York orphan raised in a Jewish household, and a critically trained cinema director at the University of South California, had seen the advances made by McKellen's modern Richard III, portrayed as the crypto Nazi-fascist. He was impressed. A second stab was in the offing for Singer to make Stephen King's novella *Apt Pupil*. Singer called *Apt Pupil* 'a very dark subject matter and it was something that came from passion'. Set in the 1980s in California, a high-school student called Todd Bowden finds a Nazi war criminal living near him under the pseudonym Kurt Dussander. Obsessed as he is with Nazism and the Holocaust, he engages Dussander to share stories in a downward-spiralling study in cruelty. Seeing McKellen play the old man Amos Starkadder in John Schlesinger's *Cold Comfort Farm* as a convincing crypto-Nazi, Singer overcame his first objection to Ian as the forty-five-year-old Dussander, for originally he had a German in mind. Said Ian, 'I felt if I could combine his complexity, his colourfulness, to the stoic German character it would create a character that, although evil, would garner more sympathy and would be more enjoyable for the audience to watch.'

He brought, as well, a chilling plausibility, an enriching over-lay of old-man mannerisms with shades of the earlier Justice Shallow. Critics detected a gay subtext in *Apt Pupil*, as well as finding unconvincing the central plot that the fourteen-year-old pupil should succeed in finding Dussander when nationwide Nazi hunting had failed. Ian's sympathetic portrayal was criti-cised for blurring the morality of the message, in what Caroline Picart and David Frank described as a dangerous 'subterranean way'.

At a coarser level, in *Apt Pupil* ambiguity pervaded the mutual manipulation. 'You're fucking me,' says Todd, to which Dussander answers, 'We're fucking each other.' On his role as Dussander, McKellen commented, 'I concentrated not on the man who did monstrous things, but the man who did perfectly ordinary things, like go shopping in southern California in a polyester suit.' The film cost fourteen million and earned only nine.

Rumours and even allegations, dismissed in lawsuits, aligned Bryan Singer to the less savoury aspects of Hollywood life. A shower sequence which included naked fourteen- to seventeen-year-old college students engendered a civil suit by one of the extras, alleging the film bullied and harassed them into strip-ping naked, but the lawsuit was dropped. Ian never mentioned that anything untoward was going on, if such it had. (With the scandals and allegations centring on Hollywood, Harvey Weinstein and Kevin Spacey in late 2017, new accusations of sexual misconduct, added to the old, were levelled against Singer, including one of rape, while he was directing *Bohemian Rhapsody*, the biopic of Freddie Mercury. The University of Southern California, to whom he donated five million dollars, repudiated his patronage. In 2019 his name was removed from the film's BAFTA nomination for Outstanding British Film.)

There was a certain brazen naivety about McKellen's quite nakedly stated ambition to win an Oscar with the next Hollywood film of his to be released just after *Apt Pupil* in 1998. Simon Callow pointed out to me in 2018 that McKellen had gone 'to hang out in Hollywood in the late 1980s for six months, just playing small parts and learning how the system works. Then he hit gold.' Callow had a novel with him when they had supper one day in 1998 and said, 'I really want to make this into a film.' 'I've just made it,' said McKellen.

This was *Gods and Monsters*, added Callow, a 'brilliant imagining' of the circumstances of the death of the director James Whale. My own response on a recent viewing was more muted. I found it sometimes slow-moving, even desultory in its account of the erstwhile *Frankenstein*'s director's last days. Forced to retire because of a homosexual scandal, he committed suicide by drowning himself in his own swimming pool. There is an element of *Death in Venice* romanticism in Whale's sexual fixation on his hunky young gardener. 'Excuse me, are you famous?' 'I had my time in the sun,' is the measured McKellen/Whale reply. Ian empathises deeply and is well immersed in the self-regarding hero's soul during the very short twenty-four days of shooting, as he deconstructs his prey's shaky heterosexuality by undermining faith in his rigid conformism. The filming lingers on McKellen licking his lips while tempting the gardener to reveal his naked body, which might suggest self-indulgence. But it is more than this, as McKellen conveys feelingly Whale's anguish as the gay Englishman who suffered trauma in the First World War trenches, and then fell in love with California. By turns he is self-pitying, blatantly manipulative, wittily detached and funny, switching to quivering fury while pinpointing all the variations on Whale's sexuality.

It won rapturous plaudits for openness and honesty. Critics hailed these strengths. Ian's presence is always convincing.

Above all, for himself, he had mastered the way he had scaled down performance for the intimate eye of the camera.

But to what end? What exactly was the point of showing this poor old man's demoralised narcissism (caught between sexual desire and self-pity), as he lived out his fantasy? The point perhaps lay in that controlled display of Whale's sexual appetite, Ian believing he could carry it to the highest realm of winning an Oscar. The glittering-prize aspiration was much evident. His knighthood made him an instant target for US interviewers wherever he went, but in one article that promoted Nick Nolte's claims to win the Oscar for Best Actor, he worked off his anger at the rigging:

'Now, my people are going to have to get something placed about me to counter it,' said the rival nominee slightly with tongue-in-cheek, like a weary Godfather arranging a retaliatory hit, except this don was wearing leather trousers. 'This, I am afraid, is how it works.'

McKellen flew to New York like a political candidate to campaign for his Oscar. He appeared on *Good Morning America* (agenda-setting), David Letterman (jokey), the *Charlie Rose Show* on PBS (intellectual, supposedly), the *Daily Show* on Comedy Central (hip) and several Academy Award specials. He was now considered to be in pole position. Andrew Billen wrote in the *Evening Standard*, 'Everyone likes prizes but I had presumed McKellen would not let his liking show so obviously. He is a Serious Classical Actor, a refined voice in the cause of gay liberation and certainly no ambitious ingénue, indeed, part of his belated cinematic success may be due to the screen's liking for the particular puckers of his fifty-nine-year old face.'

'I think it is rather the reverse,' McKellen countered. 'People think differently about me. I'm usually known by the press outside England as Ian McKellen the stage actor or Ian McKellen the Shakespearean actor, or of late, worryingly, Ian McKellen the veteran actor. But now I think, for a few months at least, I will perhaps be labelled a movie actor as well.'

Here, McKellen was delivering a first, for previous gay actors who had won Oscars, such as Charles Laughton for *The Private Life of Henry VIII*, going back to the 1930s, a different time, had not made their sexuality an integral part of their public personality. Here he was, proclaiming public victimhood, and even saying beforehand that he would not get an Oscar because he was gay. Who could not then approve of his making this film? His life was an open book, later shown to the world on his accessible website. He had not had a steady partner for ten years and was apparently living a celibate life. A reporter in Hollywood listed his rivals, putting the question – could he, as the first openly gay actor, win? 'There's Edward Norton, up for best actor for his performance in *American History X*, telling me yesterday he wouldn't have gone into acting if he hadn't seen Ian McKellen, fellow Best Actor nominee for *Gods and Monsters*, on a school trip to the theatre.'

Ian took Sean along with him to the ceremony, still the leading light in his court of supporters. Delighted as he had been with the nomination, Ian could not get over his anger and disappointment when he failed to win, and Roberto Benigni won the Oscar for *Life is Beautiful*. He, Mathias and friends withdrew to lick their wounds, shut themselves away after the ceremony, and refused to talk to the press. Even the promoters of *Gods and Monsters* were against him winning the Oscar, he claimed: he had been forced to lose the opportunity to denounce homophobia in the movie business (speech already written and committed to memory). Aghast at the prospect of an Ian rant, the promoters were keen to play down the theme, and they dropped Stonewall as the beneficiary of the film's London premiere.

Redirected aggression and anger, or transference (even scapegoating) might be explained as McKellen's next very public move after the Hollywood fiasco. Or just being a chameleon actor? Pleading a return to his old socialist principles and his forebears who were preachers, missionaries and pacifists, he turned his back on London and the National Theatre, proclaiming, 'I'm going back to rep with local audiences and a community of actors . . . it is possible I may not be seen on the London stage again.'

This emotional reaction came from his own sense of rejection; maybe, if we see theatre as McKellen's family, it was like turning against your spouse or the person closest to you. It took the form of asserting his strongly puritan as well as his humble side. His grandparents, we should bear in mind, came home from their honeymoon and got down on their knees on the bare flagstones in the kitchen to ask God to bless the house.

The West Yorkshire Playhouse in Leeds, where he now set up his rival camp-in-exile, was hardly a backwater, and there was not going to be any Long March of Chairman Mao to return to power. Richard Eyre shook his head in dismay: he thought it was fantastically sentimental. How could McKellen imagine the Leeds bourgeoisie was hugely different from the London bourgeoisie? Why did he have to dump on London in order to justify his emigration? Was it such a massive act of martyrdom to go to Leeds? Peter Hall was more blunt – and entirely prophetic: '[The media] knows, he knows, and I know that he will not appear on the London stage again until he appears on the London stage again.' McKellen arrived in Leeds in September 1998 and appeared in *The Seagull*, *Present Laughter* and *The Tempest*, leaving at the end of the following February.

Subtly, by stealth, a new form of 'artistic licence' had come to be accepted in the visual-dominated world. This licence, which always had an imposing, often riveting, picture to go with it (and McKellen's sixty-year-old face was now richly weathered with the particular puckers for all seasons) could now be deemed 'luvvie licence' or 'celebrity speak' or even 'limelight lying'. People in the public eye could, for outrage or reaction, or because they craved continual attention, say just about anything, as long as it conformed to the soundbite, and the known, often

narrow, narrative of their lives. (An opposite tactic to cope with
avid press interest was Michael Gambon's. He avoided interviews or refused to take them seriously. 'You will gather,' wrote
a *Guardian* journalist in 2004, 'Sir Michael Gambon is not invariably and entirely truthful.')

Even so, there was a new inner uncertainty the many-sided
McKellen suffered. Amanda Mitchison in *The Times* lifted the
lid on this, exploring the positive tetchiness of Serena. When
he came in to see her in a break from rehearsal in Leeds, where
he was to open in *The Seagull* (and playing Dr Dorn, a minor
role), she found him a lithe figure in dark green shirt and black
leather trousers who restlessly, while sitting opposite her, curled
up with legs under him, stretched out, perched forward, rocked
backwards and forwards on the back legs of the chair. The
hands were restless too – passing through his hair, stroking the
table in front, or cupped over his knees. The labile face – in
his paroxysm of discontent and power play in the eyes with
a glittering stare – gave way to bored, sulky lowering to the
room's corner, chin up, eyes half shut, as if spoiling for a row.
And then there was the dazzling smile to wash over and win the
journalist. 'Asked the obvious questions he fixed a bored gaze
on the radiator . . . Then his limbs spread out under the table
like a starfish.'

McKellen was unhappy and Mitchison caught his bitter
mood. He regretted playing old men in *Apt Pupil* and *Gods and
Monsters*. 'I have always had a line in old men. I have always
been interested in the physicality of acting all the way through
the body, the feet, the hands, everything. So, the body giving
way and not responding the way it used to is interesting. But
I would love to act a character in his prime . . . a script came
through the other day and the character was a hundred and
two.' He could now vindicate his explosive moods and temper,
even though these were rare – since 'coming out', of course –
claiming in principle that he was much more in touch with his
temper. 'I'm a very phlegmatic person. I find it very difficult to

be angry. Until I came out, I saw somebody else's point of view, even if I thought in the greater scheme of things they were misguided. They had their reasons.' Yet he would still claim, 'Now I am a little more confident of where I stand, less tolerant than I used to be.'

One is by now wary of such self-pronouncements – and so was Mitchison, who saw just about all he said as 'touchy, chippy, self-conscious actorliness'. She bravely quoted *The Seagull* at him as a comparison, when Trigorin, the famous writer, wallows in self-pity and confesses, 'I feel tetchy and worthless . . . I'll never be anything more than charming and talented. And when I'm dead it'll say on my gravestone, "Here lies Trigorin. He was good – but not as good as Turgenev."'

But McKellen ignored this, escaping into an intense rendition of some of Dr Dorn. Once an actor . . . He flipped to the other side of the coin, pronouncing himself happy with some aspects of Leeds because it was the first time his theatre ever pulled an audience out of the local pubs. When they advertised *Shakers*, John Godber and Jane Thornton's play about cocktail waitresses, with a poster of thighs and suspenders, 'Every time one of the characters said "f***" the building shook with laughter.'

As Hall had prophesied, soon after winning acclaim as Prospero and appearing as Dorn, and in *Present Laughter*, he was back in New York at the Broadhurst, and at London's Lyric Theatre, in Strindberg's *Dance of Death*. The age he lived in adored the celebrity actor McKellen, while all he did and said kept his openness forever in the public eye. Already something else was in the air, and a great transformative moment in McKellen's life and career powered, even hurtled, its way towards him.

First and foremost McKellen is known the world over and owes his exceptional fame to his roles in the *X-Men* films and *The Lord of the Rings*, while all media attention, in whatever form it takes, kicks off with mention of Magneto and Gandalf. The resounding overture or run-up to playing Gandalf in *The Lord of the Rings* was the first *X-Men* film in 2000, in which he plays Magneto.

The X-Men are a small group of mutants with superhuman powers taking various forms, which put them at odds with normal humans. The tension in the films lies between those who want to live peaceably among humans and those who want to destroy them. Their mutations had been caused by radiation from atomic blasts. (Originally Magneto's mutation was caused by the circuitry of an electro-magnetic power, and he is the mutant controller of the world's electrical power.) Two of them, Logan (Hugh Jackman) and Rogue (Anna Paquin), spark off the warring conflict between opposite approaches to the acceptance of mutant kind: peaceful co-existence, as the amiable, godlike yet wheelchair-bound Professor Charles Xavier (Patrick Stewart) advocates, or the militant Brotherhood of Mutants, led by Magneto (McKellen), which fights for survival and domination. Xavier, founder of a school for mutants, is the authority on genetic mutation and a mind-reader. At first an accomplice, friend and fellow conspirator and then an enemy to Magneto, he was the first to be cast, as Stewart's success as Captain Picard in *Star Trek* had catapulted him into fame after two decades as a leading Royal Shakespeare Company player. Their scenes together of verbal jousting are the best in the film.

McKellen in his documentary *Playing the Part* (2017) says he felt he'd found complete success after winning a Tony award, a Golden Globe, a Screen Actors Guild award, and an Oscar lead actor nomination for his performance in 1998's *Gods and Monsters* – the first in decades for an openly gay actor. A quick perusal of the Marvel comics, however, caught his fancy.

McKellen's first impression was that he wouldn't be good as Magneto, for: 'If you look at the comics, Magneto is usually drawn from a low vantage point, his legs wide apart, a superhuman body of muscles and power ... then there's me, Ian McKellen.' He asked the production team to come up with a false muscle suit to beef up his thighs, calves and pecs a bit because 'becoming a cartoon character isn't easy,' he said. But what excited McKellen finally to embody Magneto was the inner character of the superhero: he was very unusual, the exception to the rule when it came to superheroes. 'These stories mean something, and that's what separates *X-Men* from the other comics. Superman, the Hulk, Spider-Man, even James Bond, they're all the same people – wimps who change out of clothes and become superheroes, discovering their inner light. That's not Magneto. He's political, a warrior, clear-sighted, pained, anguished, determined.'

He also saw Xavier and Magneto as related to his activism. Both wanted a world where they existed without fear, and while McKellen considered Xavier as the gentler, caring Martin Luther King Jr, he aligned Magneto with Malcolm X, ready to fight to the bitter end. The Fox film company, too, when the idea was first submitted to them, responded favourably because it took seriously the comparison between the pair. Further historical relevance came from the Roman Emperor Constantine's conversion to Christianity ending the persecution of early Christians; this analogy was underlined in a deleted scene in which the character of Storm teaches history. Senator Joseph McCarthy's witch-hunting of communists was also brought into the mix.

After being in development for over fifteen years, with a final budget of $75 million and Bryan Singer as director, filming – mainly in Toronto – began in late September 1999, continuing until early March 2000.

Magneto was a startling departure from McKellen's work in the theatre, and not in any way a study of complex human behaviour or personality. *X-Men* established psychology and types of character briefly and effectively, but not in any depth. The sense of depth comes from suggestion or suggestibility picked up by the viewer.

The dialogue is very simple: one sentence line, with monosyllables. The mutants have allegorical names like medieval mystery play characters, such as Rogue, Storm, Mystique, Dazzler, Angel. 'Our cause will be theirs,' they say. They are jealous, angry, violent, intellectually aware of causes and preaching. The point made over and again is that the mutants 'are incapable of human contact', although they would like it. The hands stagger and repel as a pretty non-mutant woman tries to touch and embrace Logan's face. They could be disguised homosexuals in an allegorical tale, alienated from society, or they could equally be Conservative politicians sent away to boarding school at the age of seven, emotionally cold and unable to make contact with ordinary feelings and people. Brian Cox, who was in *X-Men 2*, the sequel, found Bryan Singer 'one of the most gifted directors I've come across', but that he was somewhat confused in the way he handled actors. One evening in Vancouver he telephoned Cox saying, 'There was a hell-to-do today. Just as well you were not there!'

Singer had taken painkillers and lost the plot, gone ballistic, summoned the cast and lambasted everyone, especially Patrick Stewart whose career, Singer boasted, had enjoyed a new lease of life from *X-Men*, having insulted him earlier as a *Star Trek* hack. Ian, says Cox, kept out of it, having 'an instinct for avoiding trouble'.

The *X-Men* films introduced Ian to a whole new generation of actors who appeared with him. When he was filming in Canada in 2002, Ian told one, Alan Cumming, who was gay, that he wanted to visit Vancouver's nudist Wreck Beach.

'These girls came up and said, "Are you Ian McKellen?" and they gave him a big thumbs-up.' Cumming was on Graham Norton's chat show transmitted in North America when he mentioned this. Next day, Cumming's phone rang and when he heard McKellen's voice he went, 'Shit.' It was like, 'Oh, hi, Ian, are you in town?'

McKellen replied, 'Yes, darling. I was watching television last night. I saw you talking about my penis . . .' So this was a glimpse of time off from the world of mutants: 'Booming along

Wreck Beach with a male companion, biting into a hot dog and letting it all hang out.'

In *X-Men*, Ian's face is revealed in its craggy ordinariness, and his strikingly and upright camp posture is pitted against Stewart's sedentary powers to provide riveting verbal and visual interchange. There's much vulnerability of human flesh in the violence: appealing, lively faces, naked chests, or forearms, wrists, hands, feet: it's pure fantasy, with all the visceral thrills, if such they are, of *Casualty*. The character of Mystique (Rebecca Romijn, the flexible, sinuous female, a sexy blue, nude number suggesting fish scales) adds a Dior chic to the proceedings. The defence might be made that it is all rather a hotch-potch: but no one dies. After all, they are comic-strip characters; they have to go on living till next week, and fighting one another to establish who is top mutant when they are not fighting normal humans.

Destroying 'normal' humanity is the aim of the Mutant Brotherhood. Magneto preaches, for example: 'In 1949 . . . America used to be the land of tolerance, peace, etc. . . .' and now we have Bush, it is implied. Where have 'the snows of yesteryear' gone? Ian and Patrick have both claimed the importance of the historic parallels and political commitment of *X-Men*. 'The producers considered it is an allegory, that is, to raise money first of all for black civil rights in America. But I rather linked it to the struggle for gay rights,' Ian told David Thompson, who was making a film about him, 'that each civil rights movement splits between the integrationists and the separatists, the proponents of non-violence versus violent activism (Malcolm X). Any member of a minority facing discrimination can relate to the mutants' dilemma.'

Ian claimed that 'Shakespeare's heroes were thinkers and so is Magneto. When Mystique asks me, "Are you a god?" I answer, "Bringer of light, wisdom and understanding." But one danger of allegory is that it can so easily become self-important posturing; indeed it may be better to convey a political message not with allegory but with direct documentary. Magneto is a pure narcissist, or so Ian plays him, aware of power, self-satisfied, without self-doubt. He is such a contrast to Gandalf, whom McKellen was to play next, and who is not an allegory for anything, but always himself, full of self-doubt and questioning wisdom. The central character, or characters, in a great story is just a great character, like Badger in *The Wind in the Willows*. I counted how many times the word 'power' is used in the first film: dozens. The mutants want power to the degree that they are obsessed by it, either to protect themselves from destruction, or to control and destroy others.

There is much to engage the audience in *X-Men*, such as the startling exchanges between McKellen and Stewart, and Xavier's school for mutants is intriguing. It is there they learn 'Anonymity is the first defence against the world.' Ian and Patrick are always mesmerising in their rapport, but I found Logan (the central character, meant to be 'Everyman') two-dimensional and frankly a bore. Likewise, the endless fighting and aleatory bodies, with their mutating flesh splitting up, transforming or disowning itself, are repetitive and off-putting. *X-Men*'s attraction would seem too often to be primarily that of endless permutations of violence, with the liberal, do-gooding element just a veneer.

You could say the heaven/hell dichotomy is a very twenty-first-century axis, and certainly met the approval of the American reviews: 'Icily commanding McKellen endorsed Magneto's innate burnished classiness [which] helps in making the plot a cut above comic-book average' (*Denver Post*); 'When [Stuart and McKellen] go golden throat to golden throat, it is like watching members of another species' (*New York Times*). The first *X-Men* earned over $296 million worldwide and was followed by sequels, prequels and spin-offs, giving a new boost to superhero films over the following decades.

THREE

Casting Final Spells

'Dangerous!' cried Gandalf. 'And so am I, very dangerous:
more dangerous than anything you will ever meet.'
                    J. R. R. Tolkien, *The Lord of the Rings*

27

Your Double Goes Before You

'Gandalf is a door-opener'

Ian McKellen, *2017*

McKellen owes an extraordinary debt to Ronald – or J. R. R. – Tolkien. With Shakespeare's bust on display in his riverside home, he rhapsodises often over the bard's greatness, and what everyone owes him, and he is truthful and eloquent about Shakespeare the man. He lavishes praise on other writers from Chekhov to Martin Sherman, yet when he entertains any number of guests with unbounded generosity in restaurants, at the end of the lunch or dinner party he rises to his feet, looks around benignly grinning at everyone, and addresses the company with the words, 'Gandalf pays!'

At the very age when Margery's illness had been casting and deepening that lasting shadow over her son's life in Bolton, an Oxford professor of medieval literature was putting the final touches to his epic depiction of the timeless wizard. This was destined, more than anything else, to take the Bolton School boy into unimagined realms of fame and gold, far beyond any conceivable ambition he or his family might have had.

The parallels between Ian's life and that of Gandalf's creator are extraordinary. Humphrey Carpenter, a writer who lived in Oxford, met J. R. R. Tolkien in 1967, calling on him at Sandfield Road in Headington, his ordinary suburban home, which W. H. Auden once called 'hideous'. In his biography of Tolkien,

Carpenter's first-hand description of the creator of Ian's most famous role has a striking similarity to McKellen. He found Tolkien had what we can identify as the same strange voice, deep but not without resonance, entirely English but with some quality he could not quite put his finger on, as if he had come from another age or civilisation . . . '[While] he does not speak clearly . . . He speaks in complex sentences.' This description eerily fits Gandalf and Ian McKellen, as well as Tolkien. Perhaps by his seventy-sixth year, when Carpenter visited Tolkien, he had grown into this unearthly figure. Carpenter was clearly out of his depth when he talked to him, for he believed some strange spirit had 'taken on the guise of an elderly professor'. He had completed *The Lord of the Rings* nearly twenty years before.

There is much more than the voice. Tolkien was born on 3 January 1892, and a month later, in Bloemfontein Cathedral, South Africa, christened John Ronald Reuel. He once said he sometimes did not feel this to be his real name. At the age of three, Tolkien suffered a bout of rheumatic fever in Pretoria. Ian McKellen had also been three when he caught diphtheria, which some claim resulted in the highly idiosyncratic tone of voice that so colours his performances.

Arthur, Tolkien's father, a bank manager, suffered a severe haemorrhage and died when he was four years old, during a time when he and his mother were visiting Birmingham (where both parental families had homes). Mabel, his mother, who had no great love of South Africa, brought Ronald and his brother Hilary up in Birmingham, and it was here his now widowed mother, in the course of her devout Catholic practice, befriended Father Francis Morgan, an Oratory teacher, who became protector and mentor to her two sons. In 1904 when Ronald was twelve, Mabel was diagnosed with diabetes and died the same year. Tolkien felt his 'own dear mother was a martyr indeed, and it is not to everybody that God grants so easy a way to his great gifts as he did to Hilary and myself, giving us a mother who killed herself with labour and trouble to ensure us keeping the faith.' In 1949 when Ian was ten, his mother Margery had been taken into hospital with breast cancer. She died in 1951. Ian was twelve, exactly the same age as Tolkien when his mother died.

Ronald was a cheerful, almost irrepressible person with a zest for life. He loved good talk and physical activity like the Hobbits he created. He had a deep sense of humour and a great capacity for making friends. But from now on there developed a second side, more private but predominant in his diaries and letters. This side was capable of bouts of profound despair. More precisely, and more closely related to his mother's death, when he was in the mood he had a deep sense of impending loss. Nothing was safe. Nothing would last. No battle could be won for ever.

Father Morgan became Tolkien's sole guardian, a kind and generous benefactor. Ian's father Denis, who as a pianist had some inclination of an artist, was the borough engineer of Bolton, and to his son had been a remote, unapproachable figure. Ian had no place to channel his grief or even share it, although he had been very close to his mother. Denis and his son had little rapport, and Ian, mourning in an unexpressed and even secret way, had grown somewhat lonely and into himself.

While Ronald channelled that emotion of loss into religion, which provided an outlet, Ian's emotion had become less specific, more widespread and directed more towards glamour and entertainment than liturgy and language, the spoken versus the written word. Carpenter claims his mother's death made Tolkien into two people and that his faith took the place in his affections that Mabel had previously occupied. This may be particularly pertinent to McKellen and may even be put forward as an accurate description of his personality. Two people to start with in life. In McKellen's case the theatre substituted for religion.

A romantic disposition towards women and especially

towards Edith Bratt, his first girlfriend, daughter of a single mother, whom Ronald met when he was sixteen and she nineteen, remained with Tolkien all his life. Their love survived early years of separation, while Edith, 'remarkably pretty, small and slim', remained his ideal, his inspiration for the female characters in *The Lord of the Rings*. Father Morgan forbade Ronald to write to her, or to see her until she was twenty-one. He gave in finally and married them in 1916. From the start, it was not an easy marriage, and although blessed with four children, Tolkien found domestic concerns rather irritating and trivial.

Yet 'I feel on my own, a bit of an orphan,' McKellen confessed on the BBC programme *Who Do You Think You Are?* This was equally true of Tolkien, although dragons and mythological beings were for him what fictional characters were for Ian.

If the similarity of background between McKellen and Tolkien in some ways prepared him for Gandalf, the role still almost never happened for him. Dozens of actors were considered, while Christopher Plummer and Sean Connery, better known film stars, were offered the part before him. Richard Harris was another early possibility but declined, although Ian said he read for the part. Plummer said, of going on the lengthy filming schedule proposed in New Zealand, 'I thought there were other countries I'd like to visit before I croak.' He later regretted turning it down. That's why, he said in jest, 'I hate that son of a bitch Ian McKellen!'

Connery revealed only recently his refusal to do it came down to the fact he 'never understood the script'. He added, 'I read the book. I read the script. I saw the movies. Ian McKellen, I believe, is marvellous in it.' Connery was to be paid six million dollars and, or so it was reported, 25 per cent of the gross, which finally came near to six billion. In 2005, again Connery told the *New Zealand Herald*: 'Yeah, well, I never understood it . . . I saw the movie. I still didn't understand it. I would be interested in doing something that I didn't fully understand, but not for eighteen months.'

Even before the casting of Gandalf, there was a bizarre circumstance affecting whether or not McKellen could do it. I have quoted as an epigraph Ian's remark that no actor was ever first choice, but in fact he actually was the director John Woo's first choice for the role of Swanbeck in *Mission: Impossible 2* (the 2000 film). He turned it down because he was not shown the script first. If he had persisted and accepted to play Swanbeck, which Anthony Hopkins then played, he would never have been Gandalf.

Ian claims he never read *The Lord of the Rings* before he signed up for it. For Gandalf he was offered four million pounds. But it was more likely that in his sensible practical way, he considered the role in script form more relevant to his taking part. Asked about why he was offered the role, he says that he was pretty certain Peter Jackson had offered it to Sean Connery and even Anthony Hopkins before offering it to him. He added that, personally, his first choice would have been Paul Scofield, who was in his late seventies. How each actor was chosen is the first of many epic stories surrounding the making of *The Lord of the Rings*. Ian Holm became Bilbo, in part because Jackson had heard him portray Frodo in the BBC radio adaptation; Christopher Lee was cast as Saruman as a result of reading for Gandalf; Elijah Wood, to prove his claim to play Frodo, produced a video of himself dressed as a hobbit in Hollywood Hills woodland locale. The model-turned-actress Liv Tyler was Arwen, for which her tall, long-limbed grace, flawless skin and dazzling blue eyes were a perfect match. She calls this the result of the decision of Jackson and the writer that 'there wasn't nearly enough female energy' in Tolkien's books, indeed 'the only female energy came from the big Black Spider that kills everybody . . .' So Arwen became the love interest, the blockbuster *sine qua non*. Ian, never one to drop the idea, suggested impishly there might be some love interest for Gandalf (with, say, the dwarf Gimli).

This rejection of roles was duplicated with other characters. Daniel Day-Lewis was offered Aragorn but turned it down. Timothy Spall at one stage was due to be Gimli the dwarf; David Bowie wanted to play the elf Lord Elrond, but this never happened. Then Stuart Townsend was relieved of his part after two weeks of shooting as Aragorn – he was considered too young by Jackson – and replaced by Viggo Mortensen. But 'they say' McKellen was 'lured' – the word Brian Appleyard used – into *The Lord of the Rings* by the arrival at his home in Limehouse of Jackson with Fran, his wife, who had flown to London to meet and choose the cast.

'He's not crazed,' Ian told Appleyard, 'he's just eccentric. He only has two shirts, he doesn't wear shoes, he only wears shorts, he doesn't shave, he doesn't cut his hair. And he's married to this beautiful Goth who did the screenplay. They're New Zealanders – how else can you explain them?'

The preparatory work should never be underestimated: creating the films took eight years, with only one year to create the final version of each film.

Ian found Jackson adamant that he was not going to interfere with Tolkien and would eschew all fairy tale and pantomime. The image of Gandalf, inspired by the drawings of John Howe, was crystal clear in Jackson's mind.

There is a tradition in Hollywood of distinguished British actors playing wise old mentors with supernatural powers. Olivier had been Zeus in *Clash of the Titans*, while earlier James Mason was the benign, omnipotent fixer in *Heaven Can Wait*. Alec Guinness's Obi-Wan Kenobi in *Star Wars* was perhaps the closest parallel to McKellen taking on Gandalf, and of course Richard Harris would be Dumbledore in two Harry Potter films.

Jackson had no qualms when he settled on McKellen (and had the immediate endorsement of Ian's Magneto in *X-Men* to inspire confidence), perceiving straight away that Ian was able to get under the skin of a character and cease to exist as Ian McKellen. Right from the start, with his prime intention of bringing the characters in the book to life, Jackson and Fran considered it of paramount importance that no one character should come to dominate completely over the others. So perhaps it was just as well Gandalf was not a stage role for Ian, or the balance might have been upset.

How should we describe Gandalf? '[He] is not, of course, a human being (Man or Hobbit),' Tolkien points out. 'There are naturally no precise modern terms to say what he was. I [would] venture to say he was an incarnate "angel" – strictly an angelos, that is, with the other Istari, wizards, "those who know," an emissary from the Lords of the West, sent to Middle-earth, as the great crisis of Sauron loomed on the horizon.'

This was the intention the Jacksons had in their adaptation. They did not allow Gandalf to embody completely the author's internally consistent, authoritative and controlling power. Instead they set out to allow Tolkien's integrity and coherence, and sometimes his ambivalence, to come into focus slowly, as guided by the storytelling demands, and the needs of the other characters.

This had been something of a problem for Tolkien, too, for both in *The Hobbit* and *The Lord of the Rings* he sends Gandalf away from the main action and events, and in this way enhances the tension and immediacy of the drama, as well as the expectation and suspense of when he would return and intercede, either with success or failure. His attraction (and this underlines the parallel with, and closeness to, Ian himself) is his commanding distinctness. At the same time he is elusive in his core nature. Above all he is an enigma, insofar as we never quite get to the heart of his mystery, which is what Tolkien intended. There was a lot that made him a tempting role for Ian.

*

Before McKellen arrived in New Zealand, Gandalf had already been filmed trekking across country, the task undertaken by Michael Elsworth, the first of Ian's two doubles. Ian's absence, still filming *X-Men* in Toronto, was causing headaches, prompting the production team to rejig the shooting and push him further along into the shoot. They were throwing around the figure of one million dollars a day if there was any further delay.

In keeping with Gandalf's long periods of absence during *The Lord of the Rings*, it was perhaps not surprising that Ian was not there for the first three months of shooting. He arrived on 25 January 2000 for his first day on location, an hour's flight north of the Three Foot Six studios in Wellington. He has an eye for attractive landscape, and relished his arrival and the surroundings, finding Hobbiton looked settled-in and cosy, 'surrounded by green low peaks and gentle valleys . . . The lone poplars on the horizon look as if placed by the art department but . . . You can never be sure. The smoke rising from the domesticated holes where the hobbits live is provided by an oil-burning machine.'

At once on Ian's part there was complete and enjoyable submission, of an unconditional, and even celebratory nature, as he acknowledged how happy he was. Without as yet, it seems, or so he says, ever opening the book, he had heard Tolkien reading it and could say, 'Tolkien rules the enterprise!' It meant make-up and costume artists immersing themselves in the novel for Ian's appearance, trimming long and cumbersome beards for the heroic Gandalf the Grey and revealing hidden cheek folds.

He found the outward form of the wizard's beard and pointed hat was not all that difficult when he was surrounded by a team of people trying beards, wigs and noses of various lengths. After a day-and-a-half of this he dozed off while they were working. When he woke, he suddenly saw Gandalf staring back at him. 'When I opened my eyes again there were some eyes twinkling back at me, and they didn't seem to be mine – they seemed to be Gandalf's!'

Once the appearance was fixed he could inhabit and infuse Tolkien's characterisation with personal traits, tics, shades of emotion, irascibility, forgetfulness, tiredness to make him a rounded human being (if Tolkien's wizard can ever be called that).

In the Bag End scenes when Gandalf meets Bilbo and Frodo at home, he bumped his head on the rafters, complaining Tolkien did not take Gandalf's height into consideration. There was a lot of 'scale doubling' going on, matching sizes of the actors with the scenery, with Bilbo and Frodo, the stunt double and stand-in played by Kiran Shah, to be in hobbit proportion to Gandalf. There was, likewise, a big Bag End duplicating everything in the small set, so here for the scale Gandalf had a seven-foot-four-inch substitute, whose name was Paul Webster.

Ian was joined by veteran Ian Holm as Bilbo Baggins. Both were experienced over the years with every kind of theatrical mishap and malfunction, yet both had remained down-to-earth. McKellen responded eagerly and warmly, like a child, to familiar surroundings. The kitchen table where Frodo pours the tea reminded him of the family kitchen of his childhood. Yet there was a difference, because Bag End felt to him 'like a hole in the ground. Why are subterranean books popular with children?'

Jackson wanted to have the two Ians interacting on screen together so he put Gandalf closer to the camera, with the result Bilbo could be shrunk and the two of them could see each other's eyes. Jackson says, 'Bilbo's [eyes] twinkle and pierce through you – he is so observant and yet he looks at you as the character.' Each time the camera rolls Bilbo is present. 'Ian [Holm] never repeats himself, he is different in each take and yet always in character. It is a daring approach to film acting, dicing with spontaneity.'

Jackson had a different approach, too, for each actor and,

as a close colleague reflects, rolled with the punches and was flexible. Early on, Holm had told him, 'I ought to warn you that I like to try different things on each take, so if you let me do three or four takes, I'll give you a variety of different readings; and then if I haven't given you something that you like, just let me know what it is you're looking for and I'll try to give it to you.'

Jackson sensed McKellen was in awe of Holm's ability, 'as well as being slightly fazed by playing opposite a character who, on the face of it, seemed to be quite erratic'. Sure enough, one day McKellen pulled Jackson to one side and asked, 'Do you like what Ian does?'

'It's great,' he answered.

'I could never do it . . . I have to decide what the scene is about and then try to achieve that to the very best of my ability.' Jackson endorsed and relished both Ians working in a very different way. He treasured the early scenes with Ian and Elijah Wood in which Frodo rushes in through the door, calling 'Bilbo!', then realises he has gone. With its shadows and flickering candles this was a 'wonderfully moody scene' with which to begin: Gandalf gazing into the fire, smoking his pipe and muttering Gollum's word 'Precious'; the Ring lying on the floor in the hallway. The scene, too, where Frodo sees the letters glowing on the Ring and asks what it means to Gandalf who recites the Ring-rhyme, was, says Jackson, 'wonderful Gothic, creepy stuff from Ian, who was now really nailing Gandalf and bringing great strength to the character'.

Ian completely surrendered to and found ease in Jackson's authority. He was aware of the curtailment of Gandalf's power, but he abdicated from his questioning and searching that had so characterised many of his stage roles, and the involvement, even entanglement, with directors. For example, in *The Two Towers*, the second film, before Gandalf's disappearance, seemingly lost to the Hobbits for good, which marks the end of Gandalf the Grey, the screen version establishes a subtle diminution of his powers and stature in favour of building up other characters. In the key scene of opening the door in the journey through Moria, where solving the riddle, which he does in the book with a hint from Merry, it is Frodo who solves it by divining, in a way the wizard has not, that the inscription constitutes the riddle. But as Ian claimed he had not read the book he might well have not been aware of these changes.

Ian found Gandalf's increased vulnerability a joy and gift, for it deepened and enhanced the weight of Frodo's personal journey with Gandalf's loss or disappearance made into the personal route of Frodo's own decision, heightening his anguish towards the end. Ian loved the fairground, itinerant nature of Gandalf the Grey, so much so that, as Jackson pointed out, 'you can easily imagine he sleeps under a hedgerow and then rides on the next day. He has this wonderful, earthy quality to him.' But the moment of confrontation with the Balrog caused Ian difficulties and some stress as he struggled to find a way to respond as Gandalf. At first he got angry and frustrated: when someone asked, 'Can you tell us what the Balrog looks like?' 'Yes, it's a furry rubber ball!' he answered. He meant the tennis ball on a stick which they had set up to give him an eye-line. The Balrog existed only as conceptual art, so Ian had only a weak idea of what this monster looked like. Jackson felt it was tough on him: 'he got a bit crotchety about having to do this powerhouse performance to absolutely nothing.' Definitively, Ian had met his many-sided match in his director.

'There were never tantrums. That's not the Kiwi way. You discuss your point and you come to an agreement; you are doing it together,' avowed Ian with approval. Jackson was like Ian himself, able to be involved in so many different things with inexhaustible energy. He was patient, he was modest and without pretension. He always made the day ahead enjoyable. His talents and gifts were there from the beginning, fully formed, says McKellen, while the bonus was his sense of humour.

*

There was a central paradox, even irony, in Ian filming in *The Lord of the Rings*. The spiritual power and conviction that Ian embodies in playing Gandalf came, while never explicit, from Tolkien's beliefs.

'Some have puzzled over the relation between Tolkien's stories and his Christianity and have found it difficult to understand how a devout Roman Catholic could write with such conviction about a world where God is not worshipped,' proposed Humphrey Carpenter in his biography of Tolkien. 'But there is no mystery . . . Tolkien's universe is ruled over by God . . . Everything in the end is subject to God . . . He wanted the mythological and legendary stories to express his own moral view of the universe; and as a Christian he could not place this view in a cosmos without the God that he worshipped.' But as he had to place his stories 'realistically' in the known world, 'To make this explicit[ly] Christian, would deprive them of their imaginative colour . . . So while God is present in Tolkien's universe, he remains unseen.' He observes the same was true of Shakespeare. Like many creators in art, music and literature, Tolkien believed he was doing much more than inventing a story. In making myths he was being a sub-creator under God, whom he considered the prime creator, and while he may pervert his own thoughts into lies, they come from God, and it is from God that he gets his ultimate ideals.

'Not merely the abstract thoughts of man but also his imaginative inventions must originate from God, and must in consequence reflect something of eternal truth,' wrote Carpenter, who like McKellen was a lifelong atheist.

Tolkien's religion, not always a source of consolation to him, was 'one of the strongest and deepest elements in his personality', according to Carpenter. None of this is explicit and seen, and in the part, for example, when Gandalf the Grey returns, and becomes much more strong as Gandalf the White, he is now the archetypal Hollywood hero resourcefully fighting off orcs, then is rescued (with Bilbo) by the birds. Yet there is still something more than just heroism, and his power always comes from something greater than himself, similar in some ways to 'The Force' (which Guinness so perfectly embodies in Obi-Wan Kenobi in *Star Wars*). It is at heart a religious commitment.

McKellen rented a house close to Peter Jackson's family home in Wellington. He spent the rest of 2000 in unadulterated pleasure and enjoyment. Doing what he most loved without a break was completely revitalising, utterly productive of happiness. He took the film very seriously, approving of the way it deals with the adult theme of loss of innocence, love of country (yes, even for an unpatriotic pacifist) and companionship. He appreciated that Tolkien was not just writing a fantasy story, but truly a myth, and that this story about the mixed-race group that went off to defeat all the evil in the world might just be the story everyone wanted.

Christopher Lee played Saruman, the antagonist to Gandalf. Lee, seventy-eight years old during the filming, was another phenomenon of this miraculous enterprise. When Lee spoke as Saruman, all Ian could see and hear was Saruman, and he confessed that when Lee rounded off a speech with a snarl, to be within four feet of it was unsettling. He felt relieved he was not wearing his fangs. Off set Ian liked making Lee, fifteen years his senior, and a veteran of over two hundred films, laugh with theatrical chestnuts, such as when Noël Coward reads a poster: 'Michael Redgrave and Dirk Bogarde in *The Sea Shall Not Have Them*. I don't see why not. Everyone else has.' On their first day of filming in the Isengard gardens Saruman and Gandalf exchanged words that were later dropped. Gandalf has spied a couple of orcs scuttling among the trees. Astonished, Gandalf has the line: 'Orcs, servants of the Enemy in Isengard.'

Saruman replies, 'Not his servants – mine.' It indicated that, at this point, 'Saruman the White' – in other words, not his evil double – was not what he seems.

'Orcs – and so far from Auckland,' cheeky Ian revised his line.

When in flooded Isengaard they came to shoot Saruman dead, 'We laid Christopher on top of this great barbed wheel' Jackson said, 'and attached the end of a spike, covered in blood, as though it was sticking out of his chest. I then tracked the camera over the top of him to simulate the turning of the wheel. Christopher was in a good mood: I don't think, at that stage, he'd dwelt much on the ramifications of being shown in such an obvious dead pose.'

Lee, intrepid villain to the end, knew Tolkien's text better than everyone else. Not only had he read it when it first came out, but he had reread all three books yearly ever since. He was the only cast member to have met Tolkien, in a pub in Oxford (the Victoria Arms) where he was once having a beer with friends when Tolkien walked in. One of Lee's friends knew him 'and he very kindly came over to us'. Lee admitted in the end he did find the film very hard work. He lived to the age of ninety-three and died in 2005.

There are, and will always be, critics who say *The Lord of the Rings* films should never have been made. Arguments have been raised, or raged, on both sides, in all the media. A contrary view was that of Salman Rushdie who pronounced Jackson's picture an improvement on its source material, if only because Jackson's film language was 'subtler, more sophisticated and certainly more contemporary than the stilted, deliberate archaisms of J. R. R. Tolkien's descriptive prose and, even more problematically, of his dialogue.' In his *Summa Jacksonica* David Bratman fiercely disagreed, contrasting Sméagol's agony in the book *The Two Towers* 'moving and better written than the filming; how much more sense it makes when his two personalities reflect that he is in two minds about this than in the film. "Leave now and never come back ⸳ . . . leave now and never come back . . . leave now and never come back," says Film-Sméagol. What subtle, sophisticated dialogue, eh, Mr Rushdie?'

A much-raised comparison was between the Arwen of Tolkien, the serene and beautiful image of feminine passivity, created perhaps in reaction to his own difficult marriage to Edith, and Liv Tyler's Arwen.

Jackson stepped in positively here, as he saw an Arwen storyline did not exist in the books beyond the concept of an immortal Elf loving a mortal Man. 'We wanted to create a story for Arwen – and we just thought, well, you know, why don't we crank up the tension by having Arwen sort of ordered to take the ship as well. There's no way you can create a greater conflict between Aragorn and Arwen than to have them permanently separated.'

Since the books were written, an unromantic reality had taken over in the depiction of female role models and heroines. The pattern of obedient passivity was left behind. Tolkien's Arwen, modelled more on the Greek Psyche archetype, became a modern woman, or rather superwoman, as one feminist described it: one of 'Jackson's pumped-up, butt-kicking fearless heroines, masters of machinery, battle technique, physical hardship and emotional adversity – also able to nurture a child and experience romantic attachment.' Yet Liv Tyler's portrayal of Arwen never loses its romantic appeal as one sees in the scenes she plays with Ian: her appeal to him is potent.

Tolkien, who sold the film rights for £10,000 in 1969, did not object to a film or theatrical adaptation. Even though he was always being charged as unworldly, he saw the failure of poor films lay in their exaggeration and in the intrusion of 'unwarranted material owing to not perceiving where the core of the original lies . . . One of [the film-maker's] chief faults is his tendency to anticipate scenes or devices used later, thereby flattening the tale out . . . He has cut the parts of the story upon which its characteristic and peculiar tone principally depends, showing a preference for fights.' Jackson didn't flatten out that characteristic and peculiar tone, even though when he came later to make *The Hobbit* the 'preference' was decidedly for fights!

Defying five demons when Gandalf the Grey became Gandalf the White was, for Ian, like shouting on the battlefield as Coriolanus or Richard III and therefore familiar and straightforward, although not so complicated and challenging. Between Gandalf the Grey in the first half and Gandalf the White in the second, Ian was never in doubt which Gandalf he preferred. The more complicated Gandalf the Grey had 'enormous strength, resilience, intelligence and determination, passion and generosity. He was also very human, very frail, in the sense that he liked to drink, he liked to smoke, he liked to laugh, he liked to play. He was also human in the sense that he was worried he wasn't doing the job properly – that he'd somehow let Middle-earth down by not anticipating Sauron's revival. He had to really organise himself. That was a fascinating character to play.'

Tolkien wrote *The Lord of the Rings* from 1937 to 1950, and there's quite a lot of commentary that draws parallels between the world-war situation, and Hitler's evil, with the Dark Forces, the hordes of orcs and especially the evil figures of Saruman and Sauron. Much, too, is made of the interchangeability of forces in Gandalf himself, who sometimes appears as Sauron, while Sauron also changes his appearance to that of Gandalf. In other words, Gandalf, too, is a man of disguises, like an actor.

There is an extraordinary confrontation in *The Two Towers*, when Gandalf and Théoden, having defeated the overwhelming forces of orcs and their allies, seek out Saruman in his tower. 'Have we ridden to victory,' asks Éomer, 'only to stand at last amazed by an old liar with honey on his forked tongue? So would the trapped wolf speak to the hounds.'

The whole import or drift of this vivid scene is that Gandalf, supported by the wavering Riders, stands up to the wily

Saruman, who argues with all the charm and plausibility of a great hero and saviour (just as Hitler did, in order to achieve domination of Europe) – 'You are a liar, Saruman, and a corrupter of men's hearts' – but is prepared in the end in *The Two Towers* to stand up to him with force.

Matthew Parris has said McKellen is, to exaggerate his comment slightly, a commanding officer in the closet. But surely it's Gandalf, in these years since he has played that part, who is at heart closest to who he is. You can see some of the 'extraordinary goodness which is clear to anybody who meets him, but which isn't always apparent on stage', Brian Cox has said. McKellen identified wholly with Gandalf and said, 'I am quite happy to be thought of as Gandalf.'

28

A Footfall of Memory Interlude

Because everything on *The Lord of the Rings* was made in New Zealand, so far from Hollywood, from the special effects to the costumes and props, 'It just felt like such an organic, amazing thing,' says Liv Tyler. She was with the second unit, but Peter and everyone else were on top of the mountain, and they got stuck in a blizzard. 'There were all these huge disasters that everybody had to go through, and we all had to be rescued. It was pretty amazing . . . New Zealand is very beautiful.' New Zealand gave Ian the chance to pursue his favourite hobby, which was looking at countryside and especially mountains.

Late one night after the day's filming, he was sitting in a park on a bench when a young man came up to him and sat down. They lit cigarettes. Ian still smoked enthusiastically and gave up, he says, in July 2002, after the main filming was over. Like many of his generation, when seventy-four, he revealed, 'I had my first cigarette (filched from my father's jacket in the wardrobe) before I ever drank alcohol or managed an orgasm.' He points out that Gielgud died at ninety-six after 'a lifetime of Turkish cigarettes', although in fact they were liquorice-papered Gauloises noires. 'Perhaps there's some special kippering effect on the lungs that saves great actors.'

The young New Zealander's name was Nick Cuthell; he was a painter or art student, strikingly handsome with long, flowing black locks, and he was intelligent and much liked. Cuthell is a good painter. His painting of Queen Elizabeth II hangs in the New Zealand Parliament.

They hit it off at once. How deep and committed it became on both sides is unclear, and whether or not it was anything more than a platonic attachment remains debatable. Ian claimed later, 'having brought the twenty-two-year-old back with him' in early 2001 to London, that he was 'rewarded with a relationship of a year's standing'.

Cuthell reaped the kudos and attention of being seen on Ian's arm. When Ian attended the Academy Awards ceremony and failed, although nominated, to win the Oscar for Best Supporting Actor, ABC Television filmed McKellen holding Nick's hand. Later, at 3 a.m. in the Veranda Room, Ian was seen joyfully dancing with Nick. Some comments were less kind. 'McKellen's arm candy, twenty-two-year-old Nick Cuthell, raised eyebrows when he accompanied the *Lord of the Rings* star to the Academy Awards ceremony. Alas, according to claims in the US, the relationship is not as solid as it first appeared. For when he is not with Sir Ian, sixty-two, Cuthell is reported to be found in watering holes propositioning women, allegedly telling them that he is only dating McKellen "for the lifestyle."'

A 'toiler for Sir Ian', i.e. press agent, countered that 'Nick is in a loving, committed relationship with Ian,' and scotched reports that Cuthell had admitted having a girlfriend in New Zealand. 'Women are always throwing themselves at him. Maybe he said that to resist the attention.'

What actually happened between them might be of interest to the prurient, and seized on by the tabloids, but as Ian seemed more ready to be probed by Bryan Appleyard than by any other interviewer, he said frankly almost a year later after he had just ended the Cuthell affair, that Cuthell was his 'legacy' of filming in New Zealand. He had met him in the street in New Zealand and 'brought him back. But that's unfortunately come to an end. It was another attempt to get in contact with real life. It didn't continue and there are reasons why it shouldn't.'

Not for the first time he said he was not unhappy living on his own. 'I don't feel a failure. Living on your own is an appropriate thing for a human being to do.' He claims his work might 'get in the way of doing something else that is nothing to do with work, which might give me as much satisfaction as work. Maybe something like working at a relationship.'

But then he did have many relationships with lifelong friends so perhaps here he was being unduly harsh on himself. And one happy consequence of his relationship with Cuthell is that much later, when he, Evgeny Lebedev and Sean Mathias bought The Grapes, Ian commissioned the Kiwi artist's painting of Dickens with the three owners to adorn the front bar.

29

Saturnalia Time

'Imagination,' said Napoleon, 'rules the world.' *The Lord of the Rings* was ruled by a man whose exuberant imagination had such breadth. The impact of the trilogy in turn came to rule for some years the entertainment and media industry, spreading its influence far and wide through frequent repeats and its haunting musical score. And, importantly, it was not the creation of a committee, a consensus group, a caucus or splinter mob, or that of a petition or mass demonstration, but of one man and his wife.

To record the technical adjustments to the make-believe launches anyone trying to write an account into realms and reams of the improbable. McKellen recalled the extraordinary facts, such as the Three Point Six studios in an old paint factory with no heating, no air-conditioning, no sound-proofing, right next to Wellington airport. 'Every take was preceded by a conversation between the assistant director and air traffic control, letting us know we had three minutes to get the shot. Every word of the film has been dubbed, though you'd never know.' He kept asking, 'Do these Kiwis really know what they're doing?' How easy it was to 'underestimate someone who doesn't wear shoes and who's only got two shirts and they're both the same colour, and never cuts his hair. Peter Jackson doesn't look like a major director who can organise vast troops. He looks like a . . . hobbit . . .' Ian's brief and terse comment was, 'I never once saw Peter tired.'

The pace was relentless, but the equanimity and control

never flagged, although one day, on the Rivendell set, waiting for the lights to be set up, Jackson lay down on Frodo's bed, and fell for a couple of hours into a deep sleep. Here was a different kind of heroic saga: the film-maker's. Each night he was supposed to be watching the dailies, but with three units shooting it was not an easy task. They would finish at 6.30 and, an hour later, he'd be in the cinema at Weta Workshop, running up to three hours of footage. So every night, before he could go home to bed, he would be watching something that 'ran for the equivalent length of *Ben-Hur* or *Gone With the Wind* – or one of *The Lord of the Rings* films!' After the day's stress on set the nights were also full of stress. He had a recurring dream. 'I'm lying there, incredibly tired and sleepy, and I drowsily wake up – in my dream – and find that the film crew have come in to my bedroom and are standing around the bed, demanding instructions about what to shoot and how to shoot it. That's when I always realise with horror that I don't know what to say to them – that I don't actually know what scene we are filming!'

In the final month of 2000, Ian was so drained he fell into depression because he felt he had to fall back on conventional shooting. A colleague, Philippa Boyens, observes he could 'get quite dark', complaining how tiredness was making his imagination literally seize up. He kept his problems to himself, and always had Fran by his side: 'If I had a partner who wasn't involved or didn't understand then I really would derail and very quickly . . . It's only because Fran and I know the pressures we're both under that we're able to keep on top of them.'

Fran, for her part, says, 'It's about understanding and about problem solving.' A colleague of hers says, 'Fran lobbied to bring in extra help as the sheer volume kept mounting up.' Key workers on the film attested to 'the seamless line between the two, and their single commingled unified vision'.

It grew horribly frantic as Christmas 2000 loomed. They had made it to the final day of principal photography. On the morning of the last day Jackson shot the Council of War scene. They staged in the hall at Minas Tirith the debate between Gandalf and Aragorn (in the book it takes place in a tent). In the afternoon Jackson shot Aragorn in the hall putting on his armour and strapping on his sword before going out to confront Sauron. (In the end the scene was never used. They could all have gone home a bit earlier.) They 'were shooting some really serious dramatic scenes, but it was a fun day,' said Jackson. 'Everybody was in a good mood. Someone had brought in a feather boa and, all day long, we had guest clapper-boarder operators – the only proviso being that they had to wear the feather boa while doing it . . . We wrapped up about five o'clock, but word came through that Fran was still shooting (with the unit two) so we drove across to her, snuck onto the set and the champagne finally came out about six o'clock!'

There was a big party in Shed 21, one of the original wharf buildings on Wellington harbour, with limousines, two thousand invited guests, the mayor and other illuminati. To the by now exhausted, Jackson, this was just a symbolic event. More years were yet to come, editing additional footage, and reshooting scenes, with the whole unending razzmatazz of promotion. The 274 days had come to an end. Ian described the film as being shot just like a home movie but even so, the statistics were staggering. As Mark Barratt reports, two thousand film crew, in five studios with twenty-one cameras, shot 4.5 million feet of film and ran three hundred and thirty vehicles on thirty kilometres of newly made roads. The props numbered forty-eight thousand. Helm's Deep, 'scene of one of the climactic battles, just one of three hundred and fifty sets, 'was as large as a city block'. Many sets, such as the ancient wood and stone Prancing Pony Inn and the gates of Minas Tirith with its sculptures, were fashioned from polystyrene and sprayed. They planted Hobbiton with flowers and crops a year ahead to establish themselves. But the oak tree under which Bilbo Baggins has his birthday party was 'artificial. Standing in concrete and supported with wire guy ropes, the enormous structure was covered with a quarter of a million hand-painted leaves and acorns.'

The film production had become one of New Zealand's major employers, but McKellen was right, the whole enterprise still had the air of a cottage industry. Members, mostly ladies of a certain age, of the Wellington Knitting Club knitted armour for fifteen thousand extras out of string. In contrast to this they logged every single frame they had shot 'into a computer for digital manipulation in post-production . . . [so] the green grass of the Shire could be made just a little greener and all the colour could be drained from the landscape of Mordor.'

'I think now that the camera is a very small theatre, with the audience very, very close – and very friendly, too,' Ian confessed about his experience shooting the three parts of *The Lord of the Rings*. But this was only half the battle. They had to let slip the dogs of Promotion.

On 13 January 2001, the day before the launch, prior to the fifty-fourth Cannes Film Festival in June, New Line Cinema screened a special trailer from all three films to excite fans with a first glimpse of the highlights at Château Castellaras in Provence. There were dumbstruck but somewhat basic re-actions from the fans amid the euphoria: 'Then I saw Balrog . . .I've seen the Thing of Shadow and Fire as it breaks through a wall. My God.'

Dating back to Roman times, Château Castellaras had a chequered history, and was mostly in ruins until imaginatively restored by Jacques Couëlle, a twenty-six-year-old architect tycoon who made a worldwide fortune by inventing an earring clip and taking out a patent. It had been the setting for Gérard Philipe's *Fanfan la Tulipe* – who could ever forget Fanfan's dream of a disrobed Gina Lollobrigida bathing in its fountain? One of its owners was Duško Popov, claimed by some as the original for 007. Now it became a roaming ground for Tolkien's world – and with easy access from Nice airport.

The cast turned out in force. The château. decorated to create the spirit and essence of Middle-earth, had Gondorian banners and pennants fluttering overhead at the entrance to the hall, where horse-head beam-ends, tapestries, braziers and Théoden's throne replicated the Golden Hall at Edoras. Gandalf's staff, Galadriel's vial, elves' swords and dwarves' axes were laid out on display. Bilbo's Bag End had been built for guests to crouch in, while seven-foot barmen made them reach up like hobbits for tankards of ale. A giant poly-styrene cave troll stood in the grounds. All members of the Fellowship of the Ring had been tattooed with matching souvenir symbols on the arm, and when asked what this stood for Ian answered cryptically, 'This means you're in the Fellowship.'

He and Christopher Lee exchanged wizard-lore as Gandalf and Saruman. The Hobbit actors raced around like children, while John Rhys-Davies (Gimli) told everyone it would be bigger than *Star Wars*. What a great reunion for everyone after shooting, and for Elijah Wood a 'bizarre' invasion of France for a Rings vacation!

Once ignited, the anticipation spread over the following months with the two legends coming to life, the actual history of the shooting, and the first film, *The Fellowship of the Ring*. New Zealand's newspapers had a story every day; the wider press sheepishly followed, while film and entertainment magazines ran special supplements. Tolkien's publishers campaigned to sell copies of the book with the publicity pitch 'Read it before you see it.' The BBC transmitted the original radio dramatisation with Ian Holm. Ralph Bakshi's earlier animated version came out on DVD with an account of how it was made. And then there were New Line's official tie-in books.

Towards the end of 2001 the film was 'locked down'. For Jackson, that instinct that says, 'You know what? The film's done!' had arrived. 'You keep on going until that moment when you get that gut feeling . . . the movie has found its shape and it's time to leave it alone'. Jackson and Fran could breathe with relief.

Remorseless Ian was straight away back on the Olivier emulation track in September 2000, rehearsing with Helen Mirren the two-handed marital bloodbath of Strindberg's *Dance of Death*, directed by Sean Mathias. Apparently, he told Mathias, he had seen Olivier, when performing this, throw a cat out of the window, though Mathias said it never happened. He rather relished the timing of this Broadway offer, saying with tongue in cheek, 'I've always thought that was the most glamorous thing an actor could do, starring in a play when his new film is coming out. What more could an actor want?'

He had a mind here to improvise and move about, feeling his way on stage as he had in the National Theatre *Cherry Orchard*, directed by Mike Alfreds, but with Mirren this had not washed. She did not respond to this approach. 'Tricky,' Sean Mathias had called it. 'Mirren doesn't like to do too much working out; it sort of kills it for her. She didn't enjoy the method. I think she found him self-serving.'

To which Richard Eyre's perception adds weight: 'Meaning is everything to Ian ... He's fantastically intolerant of other actors if they just come on and generalise. I've seen him actually shake an actor to try and get the actor to be specific. He's intensely demanding. I can think of one production in which he was so irritated by the inadequacies of an actor that he would physically move him across the stage.' It was good he did not try to shake Helen Mirren. Well, here was the rub, ably expressed by Eyre: 'The difficulty for a director is squaring the circle between Ian's all-consuming working method, and other actors, some of whom prefer to approach through instinct. The hardest thing for him to curb is his instinct to draw all the energy of the event to himself.'

A week after the 9/11 Twin Towers devastation, they opened *Dance of Death* to a mixed critical reception. Soon he didn't feel that he had done the play justice, and was rather ashamed of his performance, he told Benedict Nightingale, because it was far too big. Later, stickler that he was for self-improvement, he did not want to let it stop there, and brought *Dance of Death* to London to the Lyric, Shaftesbury Avenue, with Frances de la Tour replacing Helen Mirren.

Back on home soil with a new Alice to lacerate, more comic and malleable than Mirren, he could have things more his way and he toned down. He felt more relaxed with de la Tour and with the role in New York under his belt. Both performance and production turned into more of an intimate conversation piece than tooth-and-claw conflict. As someone becomes unsure, his or her own performance comes more to the fore than his relationship with the other characters. With a sense of security he can relate and connect. In one mea culpa confession, discussing earlier roles and bad habits, he explained that he had grown out of that insecurity: 'It's Ian McKellen running alongside the character, commenting as they go arm in arm, "Get this! Got it?" Being the messenger. Now I'm the message. The character I now start with is me. The one quality I've got now – I suppose I've been working towards it all my life – is confidence. No greater gift to be given to an actor.'

On 10 December 2001 he boarded a Concorde to be at the Odeon, Leicester Square, for the appropriately English world premiere of *The Fellowship of the Ring*. True to form, cutting through all the hype and extravagance of this memorable occasion, Peter Jackson arrived under-dressed in shirt-sleeves muttering to a reporter how all-consuming and exhausting a passage it had been and almost driven him insane. Ian sat in the circle with his cousin's children, whom he had brought to the premiere, confessing slight shock at his screen image as he had no desire to think it was him. He suddenly forgot it was and found it all moving, which was 'highly unusual'. He forgot insecurity for a moment and ruminated, with his undercutting and endearing Lancashire wit and self-deprecatory shrugs of the shoulders in between sentences: 'I was aware it might make a big impact.'

Sadly for Ian the Oscar never came that year, or the next; or the one after for *The Return of the King*, the final film and considered, at least from the box-office view, the biggest and best. Hollywood visits came and went, but the ultimate laurel evaded him. Oscar-nominated for supporting actor – as he was for *The Fellowship of the Ring* – would he have to settle for that? The media quotes this supporting-role accolade every time, but it was not enough, it did not quite fit the McKellen profile. Harvey Weinstein's companies had five hundred Oscar nominations. Ian grumbles on forever about it, ten years, fifteen years later. The theme keeps coming: 'There's never been an openly gay actor who won an Oscar.' When it is pointed out 82 per cent of Oscars go to 'straight' actors – this is Ian's statistic – 'You shouldn't look to Hollywood for social advancement.'

Success, yes, with the enormous financial rewards, and the occasional brush with royalty. He found a slight but strange affinity with a fellow cigarette smoker, Princess Margaret, when he met her. He felt 'sorry for her, even though [she is] a hopeless bigot, anti-Semite and the rest – quite a homophobe. But still . . . she was rather pleasant.'

According to Euan Ferguson of the *Observer*, to whom Ian recounted this episode, she took Ian into the garden at Kensington Palace. She pointed ahead to an archway, and whispered to him, 'That's my escape.' Between the trees, a little archway, grass beyond, and it was a secret door where she could nip out to be alone in the park. Nice.

'And then, you know, I looked again. And it was a mirror. No escape. And she knew it. Says it all, really.'

The embrace of merchandising, this did not quite fit either. Challenged by the *Sunday Times* over the selling from his website T-shirts decorated with his drawings of himself as Gandalf and Magneto, this was said to be all very 'schlocky'. 'I think my schlock is rather superior,' he parried with a camp flare of the nostrils.

Magneto and Gandalf are two of the seminal icons of the twenty-first century for anybody into comic strips or fantasy literature. With Gandalf dolls sold in the supermarket in his image, his face on New Zealand postage stamps (he asked specially that it be used for international postage: 'It's not the stamp that's used the most,' he said, 'it's the stamp that travels the most'), his image painted on the fuselages of Air New Zealand airliners, or with slogans: 'Gandalf for President' – McKellen feels quite happy with all that. When asked, 'What would the wizard have been like if played by Mr Connery?' – as if the question was not already self-answered, Ian defined the role so much – Jackson answered that he couldn't imagine anyone else.

Undoubtedly too there is a mystical side to McKellen's self-enhancement with Gandalf. The character refuelled in an extraordinary way the inner sense of his own being, so that he would never run out of energy. Interacting continually with others as the embodiment of Tolkien's character was a transfiguration that would never wear off. In the highly unusual way his life and role-playing had evolved, it would seem, in those first years of the new century, this self-enhancing adventure reached its peak. He was as near as he would ever be to becoming 'an immortal', a cinema god as well as a wizard. Long ago, in his performance as Richard II, Harold Hobson had pointed to 'the ineffable presence of God himself', and here he was almost set in stone as the ineffable personification of good advice, telling you on BA flights to fasten your seat belts, or appealing everywhere for charitable causes. The one-time Burnley boy sat next to Meryl Streep at the Oscars. Colin Powell called himself 'Your mailman' as he dropped a fan letter from his niece into Ian's lap. Children stopped in the street to stare at him, he had a passport to chat to all ages at schools the world over. At a midnight showing of *The Two Towers* in Vancouver with a packed-out audience, when the loudest, deepest voice he had ever heard boomed out 'Gandalf!' he scampered to the front and eleven hundred people leapt out of their seats and cheered and waved and shrieked.

'It didn't prove anything except that they love Gandalf and *The Lord of the Rings*, but to be at the receiving end. The affection!'

The partying went on and on over the next two years or more as the sequels had their previews, with ultimately the three parts winning the 161 award nominations, which included eleven Oscars among them – on Sunday 29 February 2004 those for Best Film and Best Director. Ian had, in the words of the headline press, 'made it big as the aged Gandalf', but still went on stating his belief till the end that the reason he did not win an Oscar was that at the ceremony he had a speech in his pocket denouncing Hollywood homophobia – and that the reason was political. When *The Return of the King* won its eleven Oscars (only two less than *Titanic* and *Ben Hur*), it was no longer his New Zealand boyfriend who accompanied him but Sean Mathias.

By the end of 2003 the *Lord of the Rings* franchise was on the way to its multi-billion-dollar gross earnings and *The Fellowship of the Ring* was high in the rankings of the best films ever made and was to remain so. The completion of *The Return of the King* was celebrated in Wellington with a city-wide street party and a parade from a parliamentary reception hosted by Prime Minister John Key to the cinema for the first screening. A hundred thousand fans were out on the streets. Outriders of Gondorians and Ringwraiths followed by gangs of orcs and troops of hobbit folk preceded an open-top motorcade carrying the stars and the film-makers, past cheering throngs and through a tickertape blizzard. Jackson described the experience as feeling they were 'the first people to land on the moon or something', and he looked, as Reuters told the world, 'like a victorious general at the front of his army'.

What the reporter overlooked was that, with video camera

in hand, Jackson – ever the film-maker – had his own director's-eye record. Later the following year, in Hollywood when
Jackson won the Oscar for Best Director, he expressed how this
had taken the pressure off him, paying tribute to film-makers
who never ever won an Academy Award – 'incredible directors
like Hitchcock and Kubrick . . . what it must be like to have had
their careers and to have had that body of work behind you and
not to have won an Oscar. So, having now won means I never
have to do it again!'

That pressure was there, and still would remain, on McKellen.

What of the two families behind the success of the *Lord of
the Rings* trilogy which by 2018 was reckoned to have made well
in excess of $3 billion? The Tolkien family began suing New
Line Cinema for $150 million, claiming they had not received
'even one penny' from the films. Christopher Tolkien, the author's eldest son, with Priscilla his sister, accused in their Los
Angeles lawsuit the film-makers of 'insatiable greed', engaging
and 'engorging' themselves in the 'infamous practice of creative
Hollywood accounting'.

The Tolkien estate, even so, had received royalties, for according to the *Daily Telegraph* Tolkien had sold the film rights in
1969, receiving £10,000 and a percentage, while in 2007 it had
distributed £1 million to charity and to furthering the works
of Tolkien, including a donation of £450,000 to the Bodleian
Library, Oxford, for an archive. With plans afoot for the three-
part prequel of *The Hobbit*, also to be filmed in New Zealand,
lawyers for the estate were now claiming 7.5 per cent of gross
revenues after deduction of certain costs. Fearing loss of rights
to make *The Hobbit*, New Line finally paid up $133 million.

As the success of *The Lord of the Rings* took off for Ian, the older
members of his blood family gradually left him. Just prior to the
release of *The Return of the King*, his sister Jean, who had been
fighting cancer of the eyes for eighteen months, suffered a stroke
and died. She had been a schoolteacher all her adulthood, and

had four grandchildren from her two children. Unhappily for Ian he was in New Zealand and unable to return for the funeral. When he was back he organised a private show in her memory in the village of Nayland on the Essex–Suffolk border where she had been one of the Nayland village players.

Ian had never talked much about her, and it would seem the McKellen family reticence and observing of privacy ruled here. After his coming out in 1988 he had told Jean he was gay. She answered, according to the *Evening Standard*, 'I wish you had told me earlier because I have a gay friend who is going through a lot of problems. I would have loved to talk to you about it and I couldn't. I didn't feel you wanted to.' She had been a devoted sister and a keen amateur actress to the very end.

Her death was followed a year later when Gladys, his step-mother with whom, he revealed somewhat unexpectedly, he had endured a strained relationship in earlier days before he came out, when she had clearly known he was gay, but not told his father – passed away at the age of one hundred.

They had grown closer with her increasing age, and he had visited frequently, but when dementia set in, less so. He was just about to play King Lear: he had seen her decline and applauded her spirit: '– my God! – and her raging against a life she didn't enjoy . . . That's quite useful if you're playing Lear because he makes so many mistakes, behaves so badly, he upsets so many.' His stepmother behaved badly, but 'only because she was old and didn't understand what was going on always . . . She had an absolute unshakeable belief over the last 10 years of her life that I was only going to visit her because I was having an affair with her cleaner, who's a woman. She had confused her resent-ment about being dependent on the cleaner and on me and saw us as the same person. Right up to very close to her death she still had this belief and she was absolutely horrible to me. She wasn't mad. So when people write about King Lear and Lear's madness, I'm just aware that he's all too human.' McKellen also spun this story for John Lahr in the *New Yorker*. But, Ian told

Lahr, the cleaner wasn't even attractive. 'She had an ass like the back-end of two lorries.' His stepmother persisted, until he burst out, 'Gladys, for heaven's sake, I'm gay!'

As close as a family loss, if not more so, was the death some years later of an old and dear friend, Roger Hammond, to whom he spoke almost every day. Hammond was famously rotund, and had become ever more so since being a bit ahead of Ian at Emmanuel College, Cambridge. As well as satire and review artiste of the Cambridge undergraduate rep, he had later become the resident TV series cleric in numerous sitcoms, and the avuncular noble or tragi-comic butt. Unusually for that generation, when he left Cambridge he went to RADA, from the basis of which he was for most of his life never out of work, gaining a considerable following for his qualities both in roles and his real life, of kindness, and in a phrase especially true of him, his malleable benevolence. A mine of gossip, good humour and caring concern in friendship when, ever more in his Chestertonian girth, he increasingly found it difficult to mount the long stairs to his flat. On his seventieth birthday, at a party at which Ian says he got drunk, Ian bought Roger a year's subscription to a health and fitness regime. When he, too, went under the dark shadow of cancer, Ian took a hand in generously supporting his old friend, sending him on an extended trip to New Zealand. He was always optimistic and fun. Michael Coveney, among other long-lasting friends, attested to how he contributed rotundity to figures of authority and 'a wry gravitas'. Friends were and would always be an integral part of McKellen's history. He never forgot them, even though Gandalf had now conferred on him a globally recognised image of godlike wisdom and power.

30

Tergiversator

'We are not the personal creators of our truths, but only their exponents who thus make articulate the psychic needs of our day'

C. G. Jung

Career changes from show business to politics have accelerated in the new millennium, with in 2017 the television *Apprentice* host, Donald Trump, becoming US President. By comparison President Ronald Reagan, who had been a Hollywood B-movie star and even a screen villain, had a gruelling and formative rise as union leader and Governor of California. But it was too late for McKellen (who did once consider this, like Glenda Jackson, who became MP for Hampstead and Highgate and was Blair's Junior Transport Minister), to take an active part beyond his commitment to gay equality and preaching tolerance on his visits to schools. He was still the ardent advocate, proud to visit over fifty secondary schools in two years. 'It's wonderful,' he says.

I've met kids who think they're anti-gay and you talk to them and it turns out they don't know much about it, it's not a subject that is talked about. But [to see] a young gay person who, at fourteen knows, and comes out successfully to his parents and family, teachers and friends, it's astonishing. When you hear people saying, 'You shouldn't be talking about homosexuality in schools,' well, if you don't there is going to be another generation of people who are confused, bewildered, suspicious, threatened. These kids aren't threatened by it.

He continued campaigning for Stonewall. He would take offence on behalf of the targets of jibes, an especial instance of this being when John Key, the New Zealand premier, said of David Beckham that he was handsome and a really nice guy, but 'thick as batshit'. When Key told Jamie Mackay, a chat show host, that he would struggle at a charity golf event when wearing a 'gay red top', Ian weighed in, again declaring the Prime Minister should watch his language, and this could only encourage homophobia and reflect badly on New Zealand.

He soon would be embarking on the biggest text of all. The challenge was to outdo not only Olivier's Lear, which perhaps was easy, but all the others who had played Lear, including Glenda Jackson. Still very self-questioning as he discussed his roles and habits, he still didn't really know who he was, and yet again came back to the rationalisation which by now we can see was the openness behind which he hid himself. Eyre might have sounded somewhat foolish when he said of Ian: 'He likes the smell of napalm in the morning,' but it was true – he sees off anything that he perceives as a threat. His desire to keep himself hidden made him sometimes dangerous to other actors when he boils over, but it can inhibit him from freeing himself.

Who 'blinked' first, allowing him to play Lear for the RSC, or having Trevor Nunn, who directed by far his best two performances to date – Macbeth and Iago – in charge? Nunn is certain it was Ian. He asked him four times, finally threatening, 'You've got to do it or I'll never speak to you again.' Nunn, no longer running the RSC, took it to the governors who suggested, 'Why not a world tour?' They threw in *The Seagull* as well, with Ian (as Trigorin) and Frances Barber (as Arkadina) to lead the tour. McKellen decided his time had come to play King Lear.

David Weston, who played the role of Gentleman and understudied McKellen, heard a loud shriek as Frances Barber, cast as Goneril, made her first entrance in rehearsal, and as she and Weston kissed like 'luvvies' he asked her what she was doing playing Goneril to 'Sir Ian McKellen when she is such a bosom pal of Sir Derek Jacobi.' Barber laughed and told him Derek was planning to give his Lear in the future. She was here with his full permission.

They elected to do it first in the Courtyard Theatre in Stratford, a replica of the Other Place, so 'we were getting away from the traditional production with the theme of Lear as a Tsarist, surrounded by Orthodox trappings, assuming Godhead, and it was impossible to rebel against God. 'This was completely new territory,' says Nunn, 'as when Lear mean-spiritedly wants Goneril to have a deformed child, in this production he smokes a cigar.' McKellen had not seen Scofield's original Lear in the legendary Brook production of 1962, but had listened to John Tydeman's 2001 radio production for Paul's eightieth birthday. 'I pinched his wolfish double barking howl on the second two words of "You unnatural hags" when he turns on his daughters before departing for the storm.'

Nunn from the start, as recorded in Weston's wry and highly readable diary of the production, pointed to the similarity between Jacobi and McKellen at their first encounter with their understudy: with a touch of possessiveness McKellen placed a sympathetic hand on Weston's shoulder and told him that he would not be off. 'I remember Derek Jacobi saying the same thing at Chichester in 1995,' Weston writes, 'and then having appendicitis on the opening night. Decide to start learning Lear as soon as possible.'

Lear is regarded as the greatest play by the world's greatest playwright. Here we witness Ian at the pinnacle, embodying the main role for the RSC, followed by a world tour. How did his approach differ from Olivier's? To play a great king like Lear, Olivier believed, you had to be imaginatively convinced that his crown and all it entails is solemnised and conferred to him by God at his coronation. You need this to play it properly. But how would McKellen, who most emphatically did not have the same attachment to spiritual values, approach it? For him, it was about studying royal ritual and his own. It is about sanctioning. How would he demonstrate his belief that kingship is created entirely by the way other people react to you?

He illustrated this with an example from a sit-down dinner he threw for forty on New Year's Eve 1999. One of the entertainments for the evening was to watch the Queen going by boat to the Millennium Dome. He was dismayed to see this unattractive vessel chugging downriver. 'She was on City Cruises! If she hadn't been wearing lime green, one wouldn't have noticed. We wanted proper people rowing her up. I wanted her to do the job superbly.' Here he criticised the Queen for not acting with royal importance, acting like 'royalty', acting as a service industry with a moral purpose. It satisfied the preacher in him that providing thrills for the audience, showing an enormous range of feeling and an instruction or exposition of his forensic detection method, was a service industry. But he would also always try to show it was much more than that.

Confronted with playing Lear, as he did in 2012, Jacobi had a similar point. 'So who is He, the actor? Is He good or is He evil?' He calls all the prying and probing to discover the 'real him' as all rather primitive.

When you play the King you don't play the King, you play the man inside the King because everybody is doing the King for you, bowing and scraping and walking backwards, plus you're the only one who gets to sit down. It is situation that drives and directs character. When friends say you have behaved out of character, I think they are wrong. Anything is possible. Given the circumstances you could murder someone; given another you could selflessly give your life. It is the interaction between people which defines them.

'Don't try to show all the character,' warned Peter Hall in similar vein. Ian set out in the five months of rehearsal striving to do just this. He seemed at the start not at all at ease with where he was going with Lear. Richard Hoggart wrote, in his influential book *The Uses of Literacy*: 'The scholarship boy has been equipped for hurdle-jumping, so he merely thinks of getting on, but somehow not in the world's way . . . He has left his class, at least in spirit, by being in certain ways unusual, and he is still unusual in another class, too tense and over-wound-up.' Unlike his approach earlier to Macbeth, which Michael Grandage praised as the Macbeth for two or three generations – and possibly because there was no equivalent weight of Judi Dench as Lady Macbeth in the cast – he was all at sea.

There was no search or comparison with a present-day figure: how could there be? Lear is Lear, a law unto himself. Nunn saw him as pitiless. He described the play's 'tremendous though unpalatable and unrelenting sense that this tragedy has to stop. Shakespeare is saying "There is no God" whereas the greatest pentameter ever written is "Never, never, never, never, never."'

The meaning was plain. Lear is mastered by passion: 'Wrath leadeth shame on a leash.' The tragedy is that of being misled by flattery, for the flatterer always says and does what will give pleasure, but the friend (in this case the loving daughter Cordelia) does not hesitate to give pain, offer a rebuke or correction. It was an uneasy challenge for Ian, dependent as he was on his court or inner family of actors, as for them he could do no wrong. Led by Sean Mathias, there was David Foxxe, a veteran Canadian actor, and younger acolytes who formed this circle. Sean said in 1994 to the *Telegraph Magazine*: 'Our relationship is different but for the most part better than it has ever been. Ian has been a private and a public ally and there have been times when we've counted on each other for that kind of allegiance. He is very loyal. One of my closest friends in the whole world. In fact he's more than that, he's surrogate family.'

31

Double Standards

'Je suis le champ vil des sublimes combats'

Victor Hugo

Turning now from the sublime to the ridiculous: during the storm scenes of King Lear for the Royal Shakespeare Company in the United Kingdom and its subsequent world tour of 2007, Ian McKellen stripped to the buff 345 times. He had a track record for baring all in *King Lear* as Edgar before he played the eponymous role. Fellow member of the Actors' Company Margery Mason had seriously not approved, and was shocked at him suddenly taking off his clothes in the 'Poor Tom's a cold' scenes. At that time he was celebrated as a schoolgirls' Shakespearean heart-throb. When questioned about the first week's school booking at Wimbledon, McKellen, reported as being thirty-two (in 1974, he was nearly thirty-five), riposted that the nude scene was 'symbolic'. He could not see why hundreds of teenage girls should be upset, for it was in keeping with the production and the setting. The audience took little notice, and reactions were pretty passive, but one night a voice in the Wimbledon audience was heard to utter: 'Ummmmm, nice one, Cyril!' Germaine Greer later in her *Guardian* review of *King Lear* recalled that McKellen had said, 'This was a simple image to counterpoint the impenetrable obscurity of Edgar's language.' Greer took great exception in McKellen's 'bland assumption that Shakespeare's language is impenetrable'.

At the final run-through of the 2007 *Lear* in a Clapham re-hearsal room, Ian first revealed to the cast and director Trevor Nunn (who must be held complicit) his 'member', as Weston refers tactfully to it. Nunn defended it: 'First seeing Poor Tom all his awareness of the "poor forked" animal is justification enough.' Yet it was to assume greater attention than anything else.

McKellen in Clapham first bared all on the line, 'O reason not the need'. His understudy noted his magnificent manhood dangling 'in the dusty Clapham air', while the female heads of department averted their eyes. Weston realised his own place in the pecking order, saying, 'Sir Ian's part is much bigger than mine.'

Rehearsals were not happy, and during their first run-through, in their rehearsal room before opening at the Courtyard, Strat-ford, Ian showed exhaustion and voiced dissatisfaction with himself. At the end of the play when Ian straddled over Romola Garai as the dead Cordelia, he farted loudly and declared, as if commenting on himself, 'This is the first truthful thing I've seen in your performance.'

When Lahr came to see *Lear* at Stratford in 2007 before it came to New York, he recounts how he went out on a McKellen 'post-prandial shindig' for his fellow actors. He described how Francis Barber acted out her version of McKellen and Nunn at work, 'as McKellen leaned against the wall, smiling. "Trevor, I would like more thunder on that line." "I think, Ian, that it's a half line, and you can do it without thunder." "No, but, Trevor, I would like some thunder at—" "Ian, Shakespeare was not a meteorologist." "We're aware of that, Trevor, but I would like—" "I've given you dogs. I've given you thunder. I have given you every sound effect that Shakespeare has told us to give you . . . Please shut up and do the scene." Then, turning to nod in McKellen's direction, Barber went on, "and he says to me, 'He really is a fat-assed bastard!'"

When they began previews in April, Ian went out to the

Dirty Duck, the pub near the theatre in Stratford-upon-Avon, after every performance, apparently because he had to unwind. Weston noticed also Ian's constant changes of the textual inflections, trying himself to keep up with them. It was the full exposure that began to become the theme of the production in the public domain. The *Daily Mirror* picked up on it at the first preview on 7 May. Mentioning Ian's hair dyed a pure white ('Lear the White' as opposed to 'Gandalf the Grey'), it proclaimed that as 'Gandalf waves his wand', pointing at some members of the audience a few older people but mostly teenaged school-trippers, were shocked as they hadn't been warned. Germaine Greer hailed the 'full beauty of this sublime *coup de théâtre*', the display of McKellen's 'impressive genitalia' as 'perverse as anything Trevor Nunn has ever done', replete with inexplicable dumb shows in which the Fool is hanged on stage, 'hoisted aloft . . . feebly jerking as if to suggest his neck has been broken.' Overall, though, Greer dished out what was probably the most scathing review McKellen ever had, finding him 'as irritating as any fractious, befuddled, sclerotic old bugger you've ever met . . . such virtuoso caricature makes sympathy impossible.'

Ian found her article deeply hurtful and perused it for tips and 'anything I can put right'. She had criticised the shaking of his hands, and he admitted she was 'sort of right' – and gave the excuse that he was working in this alien theatre and wanted everybody to see 'a theatrical gesture for a theatrical space'. He 'amends' the wobbly hand. He went on with excuses – his neck impedes the voice when he's angry, and pointed to his own tendency to give them a show: it was all about making effects.

Quick to exploit and yet down-pedal the publicity, the RSC put up a sign outside saying the production contained gunshots, strobe lighting and a 'glimpse' of 'male nudity', echoing Kenneth Clark's distinction between the 'naked' and the 'nude' – its artistic transformation. Spinning out of control, the drama leapt with a bound into high entertainment as the *Guardian* invited readers to post comments and printed nine derogatory reviews out of ten. The perfect cause célèbre was born!

The press was not yet allowed to review because Frances Barber as Goneril had injured herself. The critics, like usurped miniature King Lears, grumbled about their exclusion, until in June Michael Billington was invited to redress the balance, when he saluted 'McKellen's moving, majestic Lear' – but even Michael could not resist – 'uncovers a naked humanity.' He took a swipe at Greer: 'Only those with dirty minds will be dismayed by McKellen's nudity.'

As Gloucester's line 'We have seen the best of our times' went on gathering momentum, the farce could have been written by Aristophanes. That 'the member is the message' became the repeated 'soundbite', the top 'news' story on McKellen.

The press night had been delayed because Frances had to have a knee operation. The controversy heated up. Ian waded in to refute the adverse criticism. The production started to become a litany of mishaps and flat performances, with Trevor giving the cast endless notes. He was personally attacked by critics and then publicly defended by his wife Imogen Stubbs. It clearly still rankles, as he told me in 2018: 'Charles Spencer was maybe mean-spirited when he wrote, "Trevor Nunn is a talented director but an appalling human being."'

Gradually they won some good reviews and the production's sales filled, as it prepared to take off on its year-long world tour. Ian received plaudits for his 'breathtaking performance' when in Newcastle.

In spite of the setbacks McKellen received rapturous ovations, but doubts inevitably seemed to pursue him. In New York he complained, 'It's a fucking hard part. It looks easy, but it's a fucking hard part.' One arresting accolade came from Ben Brantley in the *New York Times*. Although he called the production popcorn, 'heightened costume drama sped along with adventure-style movie music, replete with black-hearted snarling villains', he found that 'one of the marvels of Mr McKellen's performance is its suggestion that a so-called second childhood can be as rich an educational process as the first . . . By tortured degrees . . . this Lear arrives into 'a pained resignation that comes with facing the nothingness into which all men descend.'

In Minneapolis, says Weston in his diary, 'everything falls apart', and showed perhaps this underlying insecurity in Ian's performance. Maybe this fragmented, many-sided Lear, full of effects and poignant personal exposure had all been too much for him. By the final performance in Minneapolis he was roaming like a hungry old wolf, more angry than the cast had seen him before on the tour, using his anger to inject energy into his performance.

Monica Dolan as Regan put on her character's usual sneering manner, but Ian snapped and positively snarled at her, and with his contempt boiling over, 'slightly pushes' her, as Weston put it. Philip Winchester, who played Edmund the bastard, took umbrage, along with others in the cast. They complained to the Equity representative. After the episode Weston went to Ian and found him alone and distraught, and 'he looks at me like a hurt little boy with his eyes: "The whole company is against me. They say I have behaved badly."'

Weston pledged unswerving support, claiming that great actors should be given some leeway. 'I saw what he did. It was just a push. Nobody would be here without Ian.' Culpable or innocent as he may have been (and he was defended hotly by Francis Barber), it was evident that Ian by now had lost his cool and did not quite know what to do to rectify matters. 'It all appears to be falling apart at the seams,' moaned Weston. If only for a moment or two McKellen relinquised the commanding officer's steely control. His perfectibility and his serene sense of having energy and control in reserve had departed.

I am not convinced by Ian's magisterial assessment to John Lahr of his performance on tour: 'In a sense Lear is the apotheosis of McKellen's hard-won authenticity.' Parallel with the ongoing triumph of the performance on tour, his naked display continued to raise its head, notably in Singapore when he was not allowed to reveal what the local press called his 'big boy'. Far East audiences had to be over twenty-one to witness such a treat (not like Surrey schoolgirls). The *Straits Times* went to the heart of the matter: 'McKellen will not shed all here; but due to an agreement between the RSC and SRT [Singapore Repertory Theatre] . . . will wear underpants.' When asked to comment on the local ban on homosexual acts, he said he felt rather guilty calling it, 'a law left over from British rule'. Typical Ian dig!

New York rose to its feet with Ian's tackle restored and with a lot of gay men in the front rows. But by the time they reached Minneapolis and the episode with Regan, the 'saga of Ian's mighty cock' had become somewhat old hat. Local radio called attention to the advice 'Sir Ian's Lear ignoreth: "Have more than thou showest,"' Anne Tennant, a regular of FM107, who usually discussed trends in celebrity plastic surgery, complained: 'He's on the stage thrust . . . right there in the faces of the local blue bloods with famous names who sit in the front row of every opening night. He is probably the greatest Shakespearean actor we've got and he completely derailed the climax of *King Lear* by exposing himself. And not only does he expose himself but when he pulls his shift up, he does a 360.' Ms Tennant went on to admit he was considerably better endowed than anyone she had ever met in her bedroom career. She thought Ian was 'nowhere near' relaxed about it. While 'Lear has lost his sovereignty over not just his kingdom but over his mind, what we had was the sovereignty of Sir Richard.' Sir Richard was not the name she used on the radio station.

Was McKellen making this gesture as Lear to the elements or to the public? In the 1980s aged naked men in the gentlemen's bathing section on the bank of the River Cherwell in Oxford used to flaunt their wares to the view of passing punts. Did Ian see Lear as part of that tradition? Modern Western culture was certainly dominated by considerations and demonstrations at every level of sexuality. Sigmund Freud conceptualised the penis as a means not only to unlock everyone's private history, but also that of the whole human race. For Freud it was 'the powerful, the creative, the intellectual, and the beautiful, as well as the ugly, the irrational, and the beast within us all'.

Ian himself would have issued a massive yet modest disclaimer to this contention, but perhaps it was not hard to see why Lear's full-frontal exposure came to attain an importance that Ian hadn't intended. Was it right to view this as a defining gesture, reinforcing and empowering gay activists and the political side of McKellen's personality? In the social and historical climate of our day, with the general loosening of taboos, its point could not be not lost.

Jacobi, before he played Lear in Michael Grandage's 2012 production, said to Toby Robertson, 'I'm not going to do as Ian did. It was ridiculous. I timed it. Ian peeled off his top and it was such a long time, about a minute, and all this time you were left staring – it was totally ridiculous.' But also what a laugh. 'Oh yes! A very large widdle-waddle,' comments a close friend who has known McKellen all his life. 'It just goes upwards and doesn't extend. It's fat and gusty. He's very fond of it and doesn't mind exposing it!'

The decision to strip naked will long be remembered, remaining as much as any other single act in his life a famous moment. This narrative of the Lear tour exposes the age's double standards (in other words, we are all grown up, aren't we, as not to be put off by a bit of naked cock, on the other hand we can't stop talking about it). Whatever arguments may be put forward in defence or attack, or justified as art, such exposure was an influential display of power and threat.

During its year of performances Lear grew and grew in what was now time-honoured McKellen practice. It reached its peak on the return to London at the New London Theatre. In mid-November Nunn rallied his cast for the final straight and they held a twelve-hour technical rehearsal. He gently coaxed

Monica into adjusting her performance in the first half of the 'reason not the need' scene. He likewise told Romola she must look at him after he wakes up. 'She complies without a murmur and immediately, to my mind, the scene becomes more moving,' observed Weston. Some of the cast baulked at more rehearsal and Nunn lost his temper and asked Jonathan Hyde (Kent) if he wanted to direct the play. Ian remained very quiet during this ruckus. Weston commented, 'I wish the two of them would stand together; it would solve many problems. Trevor stands firm.'

Sean Mathias was still a close and important part of Ian's entourage. Weston reported an earlier episode indicative of Mathias's adverse opinion, when he and his wife had been invited to have a drink on 26 May at the Dirty Duck with Ian after one show. On this night Mathias saw Lear for the first time, and he and Ian stayed so long in the dressing room afterwards that David and his wife decided not to wait. Ian apologised profusely for not turning up, but at the next performance as Lear he was very flat, which Weston believed may well have been due to Mathias giving him notes on his performance, in other words being highly critical of it.

Benedict Nightingale's review more than others picked out when and where McKellen's performance showed the man behind the performance, and how he managed by the end of the run to bring out the whole complex and complicated nature of his being as a match and in accord with what Shakespeare was saying.

This doddering ruler [wrote Nightingale] is cut off from people, children, reality and himself – and will make a journey more extreme and spiritually instructive than Czar Nicholas II's. Here is the McKellen lifelong mantra, extreme and spiritually instructive . . . He promises not to weep, then does so. He promises patience, then rages.

'Its centre is Lear's question: 'Is there any cause in nature that makes these hard hearts?' At the time the white-bearded king is putting a stool on trial in the belief that it's his daughter Goneril. But McKellen delivers the line gently and quietly and lingers over the word 'hearts' in a wondering, interrogative way, as if belatedly discovering that such an organ exists – and exists in him . . . Always you're aware of Lear's contradictions.

Sam Mendes, theatre director and James Bond film director, asks every actor who works for him, 'Who do you do it for?' Applying Mendes's question to McKellen, then speculating on an answer, I think it could be that he was looking in Lear for himself, and not in himself for Lear. Was he then ultimately doing it for himself?

Derek Jacobi and his director Michael Grandage's later approach to *King Lear* at the Donmar Warehouse Theatre was very different from Nunn and McKellen's. They heavily cut the text, simplifying some of the complications and the protracted Gloucester scenes. Orwell had a point when he said it is not a very good play, apart from its greatness of language and spirit, considered just as a play. 'It is too drawn out and has too many characters and subplots.'

'Sir Derek Jacobi's extraordinary turn in the title role of *King Lear* at the Donmar Theatre in London is turning out to be something of an acting master-class,' wrote the *Sunday Telegraph*'s man in the stalls, adding that Jacobi was a lot better in the role than Sir Ian McKellen had been a few years earlier. I cannot imagine this report going down well with Ian. He also reported sportingly that an associate of Sir Ian assured him that 'the actor expects to get along to pay homage, too, within the next week or so'. An 'associate' of Sir Ian? Had he become so grand as to have a spin doctor? An informant tells me that McKellen, when he did go along to see it, was very scathing about it, so the jealous sense of rivalry with Jacobi must have hit him deeply.

It surely became an important part of his motivation to perform Lear again at Chichester in 2017. Later he was to dismiss this 2007 performance of his as 'a wistful presence [so he called it] at the heart of Trevor Nunn's vehemently operatic production for the RSC'.

32

Interlude: The McKellen Banterland

'I love anecdotes. If a man is to wait till he weaves anecdotes into systems, he may be long in getting them and get but few.'

Dr Johnson to Boswell

McKellen's workaholic years from *The Lord of the Rings* on didn't stop being feverishly filled with roles. He said ruefully in 2007 that he had turned down highly paid small parts and that he'll do them when he's decrepit. But, as we have discovered, McKellen takes on a small part or walk-on role in a play, and it immediately becomes a leading role. Sometimes he confessed to being very tired and exhausted – and even claimed to be fed up with being such a public gay man, and wanting a quiet life. 'I'm going back into the closet. But I can't get back into the closet because it is absolutely jam-packed with other actors.'

He played the minor role of Sir Leigh Teabing the historian in the £40 million *Da Vinci Code* in 2006. Even involved in this he hit the headlines: 'Money, not Christianity, behind [Westminster] Abbey's rejection of *The Da Vinci Code*, says Sir Ian.' He was 'happy to believe Jesus was married to Mary Magdalene . . . I thought that would be absolute proof Jesus was not gay.' He believed every word while he was reading the book, but when he put it down he thought, 'What a load of potential codswallop.' His performance in the film was perfectly all right and passable, if not greatly memorable.

He was never one to turn the other cheek to a slighting reference or some mockery of his position – and yet had this mischievous ability to turn it round to his advantage. Perhaps the first instance of this goes back to his rival Richard Harris who commented, 'Sir Derek and Sir Ian, let's get their titles right, are technically brilliant like Omega watches. But underneath they are hollow, because their lives are shallow.' Ian had responded he was happy to be in Derek's company, as well as Kenneth Branagh's, all included as 'passionless'. Later, in 2000, he accused Harris of having failed an audition for Gandalf. 'Dumbledore was a poor second to Gandalf,' said Ian.

One day in 2013 a spat erupted with Damian Lewis. Lewis made a generic comment that he did not want to end up a 'fruity actor who is known for playing wizards'. While it might be said there were a number of these, Ian took it personally: 'No one need feel sorry for one,' and 'I wouldn't like to have been one of those actors who hit stardom quite early on and expected it to continue.' Lewis apologised. Ian seemed to enjoy this Schadenfreude display.

When he was approached by Ricky Gervais to appear in his programme *Extras*, which irreverently poked fun at fellow luminaries such as Ben Stiller and Kate Winslet by having them send themselves up, Ian came in for burlesque in the script Gervais sent him as the vain and self-important luvvie. ('How do I act so well? What I do is pretend to be the person I'm portraying in the film or play.') At first he objected to Gervais poking fun of him as gay and insufferably pompous, adding darkly this 'made for tricky territory', especially by the 'queenly insistence' he should be addressed as 'Sir Ian'. He grumbled on: this was 'wrong a little, as he was one of those knights who prefers not to use the title professionally', and Gervais had confused him with another Sir. He instanced another: Ben Kingsley, whose knighthood was displayed on posters of *Lucky Number Slevin*.

Gervais got back to Ian that he had not got the point of being sent up in the script. 'That's it, you see. My job is to make you

287

look crap so I can win the BAFTA.' McKellen relented, and took it in good part. Finally, his participation was applauded. One journalist commented on the end result: 'If there is an apogee of acceptable modern celebrity, he reached it in 2006 with his own self-parody, on Ricky Gervais' *Extras*.'

Small parts aplenty lined up to be played by him, which mainly he turned down. Stephen Frears reports that when he offered Ian the role of Sir Joseph Cantley, Jeremy Thorpe's judge in *A Very English Scandal* in 2018, he said no. He gave as his reason the fear that his performance might be compared unfavourably with Peter Cook's 1979 impersonation of Cantley when he addressed the jury: 'You are now to retire carefully to consider your verdict of not guilty.' Yet he made a palpable hit in 2019, appearing just in one scene with his aristocratic peacock Earl of Southampton, who visits the ageing Shakespeare played by Kenneth Branagh in *All Is True*. Extravagantly bewigged, he rebukes the poet of the sonnets dedicated to him for his retirement into Stratford domesticity and anonymity, and becoming just 'a small man', when he could enjoy wealth and worship for his success. He reproaches Shakespeare for his early infatuation (clearly not reciprocated) and ruefully admits he is 'straight' and married to Elizabeth, although his body language mischievously displays ambivalence over this.

He kept a close eye on his profession, worrying about its future. He complained in 2012 at the death of regional reps. For many actors, he said, 'There's a desert.' He held up his three years' experience of rep in Coventry and Ipswich as proof of how much better actors had it in the past. The system couldn't produce another actor like him, nor like Derek Jacobi, Mike Gambon or Judi Dench. Films were no good to give actors a grounding because they had no audience. At awards ceremonies you see recipients who can hardly make it to the centre of the stage, they are so nervous. 'I'm still getting better,' he adds. Libby Purves, the *Times* theatre critic, took exception to the Cassandra utterance. 'With due respect to grumpy Gandalf, rubbish.' She made the case for local theatres being now just as vivid and exciting as they were in the past, while opportunities for actors had increased and were more diverse.

He claimed he invented blogging long before it was invented – 'e-pods' he called them then. He is far from being a dinosaur harking back to the past. He embraces the future and he is an enthusiast for communicating on the internet. Millions and millions of people, Ian declared to an *Observer* journalist with self-deprecation – with 'bafflement' – visited his website and follow his tweets. 'There was a time when I was the third most visited website in the world.' The bafflement was quite genuine, as was the modesty, as he did not want or like to hear friends praise him, and as Judi Dench pointed out, he once left the room when those there started talking about him.

Like most of his generation, McKellen's admiration for Paul Scofield surpassed that for most other actors, although not without a tinge of rivalry. When a celebration at St Margaret's Church, Westminster, was proposed for Paul in 2009, a year after his death, Simon Callow approached McKellen, saying to him, 'You're head of the profession, you have to give the valedictory address.' But he declined, saying, 'I can't. I would look like a hypocrite.' Why? Why would it compromise him to say how great an actor Scofield was? On the other hand, I can understand why he said this: to allow no leakage from the construct, as Brian Cox believed McKellen had made of himself. Finally he did agree that he would read at the end of the service from St John's Gospel: 'In the beginning was the Word, and the Word was with God, and the Word was God,' while complaining to Canon Wright, who conducted the ceremony, 'What does this mean? It's all nonsense.' Among the many generous tributes to others on Ian's website, in his one on Paul and after expressing great admiration, he sums up, 'His acting intelligence was emotional and physical, not rational.' Nothing could be further from the truth, because Scofield's emotional and physical powers were forged and tempered by his supreme acting intelligence.

Gyles Brandreth's anecdotes about Ian nicely sum up both the mischievous and the generous, open-handed side of his character. Gyles recorded in his diary, he tells me, that when in April 2007 he hosted a Shakespeare quiz with star RSC actors for the end of year-long Shakespeare birthday celebrations in Stratford, he appointed Ian and Juliet Stevenson as 'captains'.

Ian had 'come dressed as a mad scientist – beady eyes, lab assistant's coat and the Macbeth tartan tie.' He was 'full of Lear: "Did it last night. It drains you. But then one night we just flew. It simply happened. The question is, once we're there, will I be able to act what I now feel?" He delivered for us in full measure.'

When Donald Sinden answered correctly that Anne Hathaway was eight years older than Shakespeare, Ian observed with a twinkle, 'Of course Donald had the advantage of knowing them both personally!'

When Brandreth appeared in *ZIPP*, a revue attempting to perform one hundred musicals in one hundred minutes as part of the Edinburgh fringe in 2001, Ian, reports Gyles, at the end 'generously led the standing ovation'. In their skit of *The Rocky Horror Show* Brandreth wore fishnet stockings and suspender belt. This had an unintended consequence. Next day Brandreth met Ian in the street and they had a coffee in the sunshine. 'He pushed his head towards mine and whispered. "You're wearing your suspenders and your stockings under your trousers, aren't you? I know you are."

'" I am", I said. "How did you guess?"

'"Because I'm wearing mine!"'

'He treated me (an enthusiastic amateur) as though I were Donald Wolfit. When my son wrote to him from Cambridge asking him to talk to him about Cambridge – he had no idea who he was – he said, "Come over" and my son was given a

morning and a marvellous interview. Later, partly as a consequence, my son is now an authority on rhetoric and though a
QC by day also teaches rhetoric at the RSC.'

At one of the reunions of the former cast of the *Love's Labour*'s
musical from Cambridge, at the house of the late Simon Relph
in Islington, Simon told me a story of how Ian and Derek were
trying out some kind of anti-ageing product or cream in his
photographic dark room. I put it to Ian at our meeting in The
Grapes. He remembered nothing – then laughed as he did.

'About twenty years ago I was given some make-up product
by a person who worked in films, a sort of cream and you put
it under your eyes, and in five minutes all your bags disappear.

'I don't remember showing it to Derek, but I showed it to
everyone, because it was absolutely magical and I would sometimes wear it if I was giving an interview and the bags would
vanish, it made you look like . . . slightly Asian, and eventually
it hurt the skin, so when my bottle ran out that was that – so I
may well have shown it to Derek.'

Ian was the subject of two *South Bank Show* films shot at
twenty-year intervals, and after the second a somewhat coy fan
contacted his website. 'Not only was last month's *South Bank
Show* a tantalising peep into Sir Ian's busy life but we got a
wonderful view of his rather nice bottom.' Explaining further
this comment Ian remarked, 'In the *South Bank Show* in 1984
there was a full-frontal shot as I showered during the National's
Coriolanus. I suppose the SBS thought it was time to see things
from a different perspective.'

Patrick Stewart has generally been flagged as Ian's close friend
from *X-Men* onwards, although they had not been close before.
The friendship was cemented with the sequel, *X-Men 2*, again
directed by Bryan Singer and filmed in Canada. Stewart celebrated his sixty-second birthday there, with Ian doing George
Formby's 'I'm leaning on a lamp post' as a party turn, while
Brian Cox, who had joined the cast to play William Stryker,

recited Burns's 'My Love is Like a Red, Red Rose'. *X-Men* went on, with McKellen and Stewart appearing in the series, but not in all of them, until the seventh in 2014 when in *X-Men: Days of Future Past* both appeared together again. By this time the franchise had grossed over two billion dollars. With Cathy Newman on Channel 4 News to mark the release of *Days of Future Past*, the McKellen–Stewart friendship, or 'bromance', as it was now dubbed, had become legendary, with even academic articles exploring the authenticity of the union. Both actors couldn't resist the chance to express views about immigration and have a dig at Nigel Farage and Ukip.

Ian has appeared on the Graham Norton chat show many times, and in one instance in 2013, when he was soon to officiate at Patrick Stewart's wedding, he made the audience respond with uproar and laughter when he declared bluntly, 'I'm going to marry Patrick.' It became a jokey headline talking point as 'McKellen marries Stewart.' As if to reinforce the tongue-in-cheek game, both friends mouth-to-mouth kissed on the red carpet at the premier of *Mr. Holmes* in May 2014.

Gay banter with sexual innuendo on chat shows had become almost obligatory. Presided over by dapple-whiskered Graham Norton, in a further show both knights appeared, with Hugh Jackman (who plays Logan/Wolverine in *X-Men*). 'Sir Patrick' – 'call me Beef-Stew' – revealed how moving it was for him that Ian now called him 'my brother'. McKellen told a tale of the Oscar ceremony when prior to it he was carrying a Pounamu, a New Zealand charm, visibly round his neck, and encountered Maggie Smith, who asked him what it was for. He imitated her cynical accent. He said it would bring him luck when the Oscars are announced. After, and when he hadn't won it, he met her again as he left: 'It didn't do you much good!!' – sending up Maggie Smith's voice. Again loud laughter greeted this self-put-down. As ever Ian's face creased, and he laughed and his body language exuded many-sided roguishness and charm.

His unforced, natural domination of the media or chat

shows has continued into his eightieth year, and he is always good value. On a visit to a Russian literary festival he plied his social activism in favour of gay tolerance in defiance of the anti-homosexual laws there, but then was arrested for smoking outside Koltsovo international airport, which was against the law. Fierce public debate followed locally as to whether, as a well-known foreign celebrity on a visit, he should be put on trial and fined.

In January 2018 he provoked a mixed reaction when in Oxford he commented on the sexual misconduct of celebrities and that 'some people get wrongly accused – there's that side as well.' He illustrated this with an example from the 1960s when the director of the theatre he was working in showed him photographs from women who were wanting jobs. Some had written 'DRR' at the bottom of their pictures – directors' rights respected. In other words, 'If you give me a job you can have sex with me.' He pointed out that it was madness. Yet the espousal of his cause meant much to many who suffered the long-lasting effect of being a victim: 'I get letters from preachers, school-teachers and businessmen who feel it is too late to tell the truth,' he avouched. 'A seventy-year-old said he was facing death but had told no one he was gay. I wrote back and said: "Well now you have told me, so it is not too late to start!"'

'He can wear what he likes,' wrote the *Sunday Telegraph*, rainbow-coloured bootlaces or gay ribbons on straw boaters, which can explode suddenly in an utterly unrestrained way and completely captivate in its two extremes – anger and riotous anarchic comedy of mannerism. Unlike Laurence Olivier, who kept to his mission of 'I want to make everyone in the audiences want to fuck me,' McKellen wants everyone to laugh with him, cuddle, and revere him. He bounces back, adroit and acute in the self-management of his image. He coasts along easily with persiflage, saying, 'Don't take any of this too seriously.' He shows such a rare status, able to be popular, credible, lauded and loved, yet plays suitor straight-faced, old or young. 'Rot them for a couple of rogues,' says Gainsborough on David Garrick and Samuel Foote. He might have been writing of Ian and Patrick. 'They have everyone's face but their own.' Ian would never stop: 'With the new technology you can look younger! Maybe Patrick and I can play Romeo and Juliet? It could be the end of cosmetic surgery – or the end of the need for it.'

By the time they played in *Waiting for Godot* in New York the McKellen–Stewart 'bromance' had become overplayed. On a fun day off touring the city they posed in Beckett tramp mode wearing shorts and bowler hats, holding hands, munching corn on the cob with Elmo, and on top of the Empire State Building. The photographers had a field day. 'The world needs more friends like these,' admirers posted on social media. There was more kissing at the awards ceremony of the British film magazine *Empire* in May 2017 when Patrick received the Empire Legend Award presented to him by Ian, who said of Patrick, 'He's one of my heroes. He's that actor of my generation people would like to be.' Ian did mollify the hyperbole somewhat by quoting Nietzsche: 'Success is an impostor. It conceals the flaw, the wound, the fundamental doubt at the core of the artist's being,' but added, 'I wanted to go down as the only actor in history to quote Nietzsche!'

33

It's a Mad, Mad World, My Masters

'Serendipity is my favourite word, both for the sound it has
and its meaning'

Ian McKellen

'Seventy-five? You don't look like an old man,' says Don Antonio in Eduardo de Filippo's *The Syndicate* (Minerva Theatre,
Chichester, 2011). By 2013 Ian was aware of growing older;
among people of his own age they talked of nothing else. How's
your back? And so-and-so's going blind . . . In 2006 Ian was
diagnosed with prostate cancer. 'You do gulp when you hear
the news. It's like when you go for an HIV test, you go "arghhh
is this the end of the road?" They say you have cancer of the
prostate, and then that you can have it zapped. You can have
it snipped but you are not a candidate for that. You are waitful
watching.'

He grinned broadly at the *Daily Mirror* man, with a glint
in his eye. 'You're going to write "Ian McKellen is decrepit.
He can't see, he can't hear, he can't pee, he's having his
teeth done."' He also confessed he had hearing aids (on the
NHS, which otherwise would have cost five or six thousand
pounds) and a cataract. But over the next six or seven years
the cancer did not get worse. 'When you have got it you mon-
itor it and you have to be careful it doesn't spread. But if it is
contained in the prostate it's no big deal . . . Many, many men
die . . . but it's one of the cancers that is totally treatable so I

have "waitful watching". I've not had any treatment.'

There was another scare when he discovered he had shadows on his lung that he believed were caused by his heavy smoking, which he gave up (for as long as he felt he did not desperately have to have a fag and then lit up again). He found subsequently the shadows were his nipples.

Doctors had initially prescribed the radiotherapy option for the prostate cancer. He told them, 'I have to do this panto-mime first.' And so he did. 'He's been wanting rehearsal after rehearsal late into the night,' commented a laconic wardrobe worker on Ian's engagement as Widow Twankey in the Old Vic pantomime – *Aladdin* – directed by Sean Mathias, in the winter of 2004 when Kevin Spacey was artistic director. 'He tries on dress after dress.'

When it opened we had a wonderful display of McKellen ad-libbing and endlessly stopping the show with laughter at topical jokes about David Blunkett, busty model Jordan, Jacobi, Peter Hall and the RSC's 'way of spouting Shakespeare'. Twankey became a plumpish, frumpish and of course Lancas-trian housewife with a complexion of leather and rouge. He sent Derek up as the marble-mouthed Shakespearean actor, saying at one point, when Aladdin rants with passion, 'What an honour working with you, Sir Derek!' According to Frances Barber (Wishy-Washy), Ian 'becomes Derek without saying a word, and you can easily guess who it is'. He joked the panto was 'longer than a Trevor Nunn production' and made a mock-agonised plea for 'no more Shakespeare directed by Hall'. Character-acting to the death, as if it would never go away, he brought pick-axe demolition to the whole still luminous seam of Cambridge theatre. What a riot of fun! 'Dame Ian is this show,' wrote Quentin Letts. 'He engulfs it in his voluminous skirts . . . Troublingly good legs he has, too. Widow Twankey, in Sir Ian's big, butch hands, is a lascivious man-eater and a bow-legged fashion disaster . . . One moment he is mincing (actually stomp-ing) about in something Yves St Laurent-ish, the next moment it is a Pucci frock that if ever televised would make cathode ray tubes explode.' Nicholas de Jongh, hardly much of a McKellen aficionado, proclaimed him 'The mother of all drag queens!'

After all this barnstorming the cancer cells took flight and retreated. On his next examination his doctor confirmed him 'completely cured!' As one of Ian's immortal performances it had to be unifying body and soul work.

Mathias was Ian's main, if not sole director, and whatever way one may view this (for example, that he was directing himself through Sean), it worked. Here, surely, we were back to the old actor-manager syndrome of leading the company, although there were first-class other performances. He played the sub-Pinter civil servant rogue in an undistinguished play called *The Cut* by Mark Ravenhill, displaying beautiful subtle gestures, but leaving critics unable to imagine why he was in it.

With a curious twist of logic McKellen seemed to have got it into his head that, 'If I was a star, it would be difficult to go off and do *Coronation Street*. So I guess Ian is not a star.' Now in ten episodes of *Coronation Street* he impersonated the eccentric novelist Mel Hutchwright whose bodice-ripper *Hard Grinding* is a favourite of the Weatherfield Book Club. He had a fantastic time in the ten weeks before Hutchwright was exposed as a con-man, and struck up a friendship with Antony Cotton who plays the witty and gay Sean Tully. Cotton in his little Fiat had been running Ian around in Manchester during the filming, and Ian invited Cotton to be his personal guest at Sir Elton John's lavish annual White Tie and Tiara Ball so the tittle-tattle factory, under the banner headline Lord of the Flings, went into overdrive with a new McKellen 'affair'.

That was about the sum of it! Cotton brought his mother to meet the star when he gave a final-day party, and in spite of the lurid headlines, it would seem discretion ruled. He just wanted a companion. He continued on uninterruptedly from one diverting role to another, gracing each and every one with complete dedication and unvarying excellence, as well as unbounded pleasure still to be working full-time. 'I think ten years more is probably all I've got as someone who can hop on a plane and remember the lines and not fall over.'

Meantime *The Lord of the Rings* was earning $3 billion at the box office and boosting tourism to New Zealand by 40 per cent. In 2008, three years after his *Corrie* appearance, *The Fellowship of the Ring* was voted 'The Greatest Movie of All Time,' well ahead of *Star Wars*, *Pretty Woman*, *The Godfather* and *Gladiator*. By the end of 2012 the prequel based on *The Hobbit* had turned from two projected films into three, with Jackson justifying this by saying Tolkien's 1937 novel was 'breathless', in which 'very major events are covered in two or three pages . . . Once you started to develop the scenes you wanted to do a little more character development.' High-level casting was the major concern, as they could not be given slight material, while McKellen, set to reprise Gandalf, defended Jackson, saying, 'Anyone who thinks Peter Jackson would fall for market forces, instead of artistic imperatives, just doesn't know him, doesn't know the body of his work.'

McKellen renewed his love affair with New Zealand in 2012 and in that year he earned £6.3 million after paying tax. He called his company Kirikir, a Maori word that means 'sand'. He was as crucial to the publicity, in spite of some negative feelings about being away from London, as he was pivotal to the plot. Ian Nathan saw him as supplying the continuity between the *Rings* trilogy and *The Hobbit*. He reassured fans and backers that the new trilogy would be good and bring gravitas to what might otherwise be dismissed as just a fantasy film. The studio rubbed their hands in glee, knowing they were going to make the money back.

The filming of the prequel, three films based on Tolkien's 1937 *The Hobbit* with additional material from appendices and postscripts to *The Lord of the Rings*, entered once more the ring of epic endeavour, uncertainty, hysterical skulduggery and in-fighting. The trilogy was *An Unexpected Journey*, due for release in December 2012, *The Desolation of Smaug*, to be released a year later, and *The Battle of the Five Armies*, expected in July 2014.

The Jackson team had wanted to film *The Hobbit* since 1995, even possibly their choice before *Lord of the Rings*, but the success of the latter turned planners and story-boards for a follow-up to sixty years before *The Fellowship of the Ring* starts. While McKellen toured his Lear (to bypass the finger-jabbing, the legal writs and studio manoeuvring, the wrangling between the Tolkien estate and MGM, United Artists, New Line Cinema), a plan crystallised to make two films in 2007. Development of scripts progressed in 2008. The fantasy cinéaste Guillermo del Toro was engaged to direct them in spite of his reservations about 'little guys and dragons, hairy feet, hobbits'. He became the prime mover and motivator of the project.

The overall arc of the storyline, assembled from disparate sources by a quartet of writers, including the Jacksons, del Toro, and Philippa Boyens, is initiated up front by Gandalf the Grey. He convinces Bilbo Baggins to recruit the thirteen dwarves in the quest primarily to find gold and reinstate Thorin Oakenshield to his rightful heritage as King, by reclaiming the lonely mountain from Smaug the dragon (voiced by Benedict Cumberbatch), who lives underneath Lake Tom and terrorises its people. The plot-line is clear and easy to follow, much more so than *The Lord of the Rings*, and highly satisfactory via well-paced suspense adventure, which over the three films climaxes (in Part Two) in the destruction of Smaug, by the bowman Bard (Luke Evans), and then the extended battle between dwarves, elves and orcs. It was nearly not filmed in New Zealand, but in Eastern Europe, for after the go-ahead was given for filming by New Line and Warner Bros, they refused to engage performers on union-negotiated agreements. The response of the International Federation of Actors was to proclaim a 'DO NOT WORK' order; where Ian's trade unionist's DNA was in all this, is not recorded.

Rallies organised in New Zealand protested that if the films were made elsewhere the country would lose up to $1.5 billion. Warner Bros withdrew the threat when the NZ government, headed by the outspoken John Key, passed laws to remove the right of workers to organise trade unions in the film production industry. Ian's hero Jeremy Corbyn would not have approved. Everyone came round in the end, with the unions (changing their minds) calling those who demonstrated 'patsies'.

Casting McKellen had been crucial, although beyond being the initiator, his Gandalf the Grey role, to begin with that of commander in chief, and later as supporter of Bard the Bowman, when he tries to convince Thorin and the elves not to fight each other, is not nearly so central to *The Hobbit* as it had been to *The Lord of the Rings*. He was an altogether more heroic and less spiritual wizard than Gandalf the Grey in *The Fellowship of the Ring*.

There was still something unusual to pick out when Gandalf is giving Galadriel (Cate Blanchett) a sly, understanding and complicit look – I had seen this before in Alec Guinness's performances. It is a look of recognition of who you are, but also of a fellow soul, of brotherhood (or sisterhood). In other words, you are just like us, you're one of us. This moment came when he arrives at the conference with Saruman and the beautiful Galadriel appears. She understands that something more profound is going on, that he is concealing something and has a secret. Ian, at this deep level, knows how to convey this perfectly and without words. It tells you much about Ian. About his power (and Gandalf's).

Apart from intimate, knowing looks, the vintage Gandalf on display showed all the well-honed customary and warrior qualities of Gandalf the White. There was not much of a poetic or spiritual nature, but endless warlike operations and commands of the military leader. There is virtually no philosophy in the suffering he undergoes in successive batterings and orc torture, until he is saved by Galadriel and Saruman the White

(Christopher Lee), nor does the outcome of the running battles depend upon his wizardry and spells.

The main relationship is that between Bilbo and Thorin. Gandalf is employed to comment, almost as a therapist, that evil as always will destroy itself. The scarcity of his appearance in *The Battle of the Five Armies* smacked a bit of tokenism, as if writers and director were at a loss as to what to do with him to give him a bigger say in the computer-generated adventure playground. Gandalf's quasi-infallibility in *The Lord of the Rings* gave him an ambiguity which had little place in the trilogy of *The Hobbit*, and he does not quite fit in the relentless action pace. His triumph, even moral triumphalism, pared down as in *The Lord of the Rings*, and sacrificed somewhat to the building-up of the characters and the choices they make, but best expressed in his statement, 'the old heart is strong, does not wither,' gave way to a more modern, novelistic, free-and-easy, even opportunistic, narrative.

Jackson's final statement applauded the spirit of complexity and defended his introduction of new characters such as Tauriel and Bard the Bowman. He caught something fundamental, something very complex, as Milan Kundera expressed in agreement, about the very nature of the novel and storytelling: 'The novel's spirit is the spirit of complexity. Every novel says to the reader: "Things are not as simple as you think." That is the novel's eternal truth, but it grows steadily harder to hear amid the din of easy, quick answers that come faster than the question and block it off. In the spirit of our time, it's either Anna or Karenin who is right and the ancient wisdom of Cervantes, telling us about the difficulty of knowing and the elusiveness of truth, seems cumbersome and useless.'

Some were highly sceptical of Ian's 'artistic imperatives', as Toby Young in the *Spectator* described them in *The Hobbit*: 'an Unexpected Journey in its one hundred and sixty-nine minutes'. Young quoted an American critic: 'It begins to feel like a Buddhist exercise in a deliberately inflicted death wish.' The cost of the trilogy was over $620 million dollars, $250 million more than *Pirates of the Caribbean: On Stranger Tides*, the most expensive single film of all time. A veteran *Telegraph* reviewer said, 'As a lover of cinema, Jackson's film bored me rigid; as a lover of Tolkien, it broke my heart.'

In November 2017 Graham Norton pulled Ian up sharply in his chat show with the disclosure that a new *Lord of the Rings* film was in the offing, made by Amazon. 'What do you mean, another Gandalf?' he reacted. 'I haven't said yes because I haven't been asked,' McKellen replied. 'But are you suggesting someone else is going to play him?' News was announced in February 2019 that writers were at work on a £1 billion pre-quel, for which Amazon beat Netflix to acquire the rights for £200 million, which was due to air in 2021.

How the trilogy would have turned out if del Toro had not been obliged for reasons of time to leave the directing to Jackson, is speculation, although many believe it would have been more of a fairy tale. The upshot was that the films bear the distinctive Jackson hallmark , are gripping and watchable, and especially moving in the vistas of great scenic beauty and flower-covered landscapes, thus providing relief from the relentless battles, carnage and special effects. Although much criticism has been levelled against them I cannot fault them for what they are: pure entertainment. The public flocked!

34

Small Men Locked in a Big Space

While Ian was positioning himself to take on Gandalf again for this gargantuan second slice of Tolkien, he set out to provide, as the publicists would call it, the 'theatrical event of 2009'. As with the earlier success of *Bent*, a new Sean Mathias idea carried him along to tackle *Waiting for Godot*. He was to be Estragon and he asked Derek Jacobi if he would play Vladimir. According to Derek's account, he had no wish to work with Mathias.

Ian has it differently as, after asking Jacobi to play in *Uncle Vanya*, 'We asked him to play in *Waiting for Godot* and he said yes, or didn't say no. Eventually he said, "I don't like the play." And if he'd told us that at the outset, we wouldn't have wasted such a lot of time. But it's always – people's reasons for not doing something – it's difficult to put into words. But, "it's not quite right", you say, or "I'm not feeling well" or "I've got another job," or "I don't like the play."'

Mathias then thought of Judi Dench as Vladimir, the more restrained and accordingly second fiddle, in other words the more passive of the pair. The Beckett estate refused. After this, either McKellen or Mathias came up with the idea of Patrick Stewart, who then with the slightly defective memory of both became 'first choice'. McKellen thought fans would like and recognise the relationship from Magneto and Professor Xavier in *X-Men*.

Peter Hall's original 1955 British production – which made Beckett's reputation – incurred Beckett's strong disapproval because it made *Godot* into music-hall burlesque. This angle, with Beckett long gone, was open game for McKellen, Mathias and Stewart. Beckett had wanted the play set 'on a country road' with just a tree and a mound for décor. Stephen Brimson Lewis, who designed the set, added rubble, a wall of broken brick and concrete and a half-shattered proscenium arch to pick up on the play's oblique references to the theatre itself, and Beckett's suggestion that the tramps are also clowns, second cousins to Chaplin, Laurel and Hardy. One of the ways McKellen and Stewart would tolerate their endless wait for the elusive Godot, they proposed, was by breaking into little dances, sometimes singly, sometimes together.

As for the other pair, Simon Callow played Pozzo as a red-faced, exotically moustachioed blend of showman, huntsman and eighteenth-century grandee, whose ferocious cruelty concealed insecurity, and eventually gave way to baffled pain – a complex character-reading of the role. And when it came to the casting of Lucky, Pozzo's hapless sidekick, Mathias phoned up Ronald Pickup and told him, 'All the good young actors are phoning me up to play Lucky, but I decided on an old one!' Pickup struggled, feeling he was not open enough in his approach to the role, and should not have learnt the lines before rehearsal. Ian seemed to him very unsure of the play at first and very vulnerable, as he went on digging to find the role. He and Ian would go outside from rehearsal as both were smokers. They read through and discussed the text for ten days.

When they opened, Pickup found his first entrance on the end of the rope dragged by Pozzo deflated by a loud crude crash, taking the place of the more real live off-stage sounds, which for him wrecked an entrance laugh. Ian and Patrick came out first on the opening night to take the curtain call, followed by Pickup and Callow. There was a row and Callow lost his temper, thinking this was not right for the four-hander play. But they soon made up, Ian explaining he only wanted to have the tramp duo take their bow first in the style of an old-time Variety act. As

Callow points out, the play poses a lot of problems as each of the four lonely characters live in different worlds.

Mathias went on to win the Critics' Circle of the Year Award for his direction. Mathias is, comments Callow, a puritan in the way he directs, and 'very down on anything showy or West-Endy'. Few could bring such variety to the business of being bored, was the general critical response. 'They're moving, they're witty, they're, well, excellent.' Benedict Nightingale found the appeal to popular taste had 'moved the comics . . . to the comic books, which was no bad thing,' and claimed it would go down in posterity as the *X-Men Godot*. For Michael Coveney it was 'trans Pennine shuttle of Boltonian McKellen and West Yorkshire Stewart'.

Not all critics praised it. The prestigious *Sunday Times* found Stewart awkward and miscast, and too sprightly as a sixty-year-old to McKellen's pitifully doddery eighty-eight. He had no gift for slapstick, while Callow did not fit into the meagre, nay-saying world of Beckett. Only Pickup, Christopher Hart thought, 'is wonderfully strange and affecting', adding that 'the biggest setback is the set'. The whole production was far too obvious despite McKellen's fine turn, and it misunderstood Beckett and was a 'slow-paced bore' for Ian.

Audiences responded rapturously everywhere they took it on a tour after the sell-out Theatre Royal Haymarket run, and in his diary, McKellen wrote that it was an absolutely joyous job. 'I'm the luckiest actor working.' He did mention that he had the impression that people thought it was a cheap version of the play and exaggerated the comic side at the expense of the intellectually challenging or emotionally affecting. And here perhaps Ian toppled over into disingenuity and projection, neg-lecting the first observation that friends will tell you what you want to hear:

'I put this to people who knew Beckett, and every one of them said, "No, he would have loved it."

'It's perfectly obvious to me that Beckett, as a child, had gone to see the sort of stand-up comics and duos that I loved when I was a kid.'

If Ian had met Beckett, he might have formed a different notion. Beckett told me when I interviewed him and met him for a drink in Paris in 1977, he had scant regard for his own work and in advance had said he would not talk about it.

In defence McKellen said they would attend to the passage about dead voices, as someone thought it had been reduced. 'We said to ourselves that there are dead voices in theatres, there are ghosts. And in fact, at one performance, Patrick saw a ghost on stage, who he thought had come up from the audience, wearing a long brown coat. He was just going to suggest to him that he get back in his seat, and he vanished.' Here is his wrapping-up in his diary: 'There are not many things in my life I can be absolutely proud of or certain I got right, but one of them is that I've got better as an actor.'

On tour, outside the theatre in Melbourne, he was squatting on the ground at the stage door in costume, enjoying a cigarette, cap on ground beside him, when someone passed and put money in his cap.

There was a second bite of the cherry, revived at the Haymarket again after the tour. This time again, according to Pickup, they offered the part to Jacobi, who refused a second time (he did not like the play). 'We're continually scratching our heads,' says Mathias, who replaced Patrick Stewart with Roger Rees. 'I have to let go of Patrick and let someone else in.' This was the Court of King Ian!

The original contract to put on *Godot* had been with Arnold Crook, the owner of the Haymarket, Duncan Weldon and the Haymarket Theatre. Mathias and McKellen broke this to put it on themselves in New York, along with Harold Pinter's *No Man's Land*. Weldon had had a clause in their contract to option *No Man's Land* for the sum of £5,000 to present the Pinter play in New York with *Godot*, which was ignored as the new management team went ahead on their own. In spite of its success the New York run was extremely costly; the sets had to be changed every night, while the lifestyles of the management living in New York were no less demanding. The production lost something in the region of $3 million, paid for out of the pockets of McKellen and Mathias, and a less than happy Stewart. Arnold Crook's principle was not to allow artists who have broken a contract with him to enter the Haymarket Theatre again, and legend has it that on one occasion McKellen was turned away from its doors. 'I thought we had a friendship . . . but it was a matter of money. I don't want to talk about it,' Crook commented.

Ian would never let anything stand in his way in his quest to prove that stage-acting provides the only proof of whether an actor can act greatly (as Shaffer had believed). His two Lear understudies never had even one chance to play the role. In 2018 when he pulled a calf muscle on his way to the Duke of York's Theatre for a Saturday matinee, sooner than let his understudy go on, he 'chatted on stage to the audience while they waited for their money back and I tried out a few new routines and some old ones – a bit of Gandalf and a couple of Shakespeare speeches.' He had, too, his permanent director-partner Mathias to back him up, if not actually take the initiative. Fortunately, as he generously admitted to himself, he has spared any partner close involvement by remaining on his own. It may not be complimentary to report this, but it was central to the McKellen mystery: he was a man of genius and could be – sometimes, but not invariably – as Shaw said, 'a sublime altruist in his disregard of himself, an atrocious egotist in his disregard of others'.

35

What Do We Do Now We're Happy?
Vicious Old Queens

'As lives, so loves oblique may well
Themselves in every angle greet:
But ours so truly Parallel,
Though infinite, can never meet.'

Andrew Marvell

The differences between McKellen and Jacobi, the two great classical actors of their Cambridge generation, will fascinate theatre historians in the future. Thea Sharrock, the director, summed them up:

> They are like chalk and cheese. Ian never has the hands-on attention and loving care that Derek has with a part, nor indeed does he have the technical perfection of an actor that Derek has . . . [He] is a much more formal type and tends to hold forth when you meet him first . . . Ian is not someone who is immediately on your wavelength. I have a sense that Ian is much more of an improviser, he will experiment and change fluently his performance in unexpected ways. Derek on the other hand has to have everything perfectly prepared beforehand, so everything he does is solid and securely worked out. He is the perfect craftsman.

In 2012 they appeared together in a sitcom series, *Vicious*.

If in Ian is the DNA of the Nonconformist campaigner and the touring actor, in Derek is the DNA of the Prussian shoe-maker craftsman and the Versailles aristocrat imprisoned for his Protestant beliefs. McKellen said of Derek and himself:

The trouble is we are too alike, we are the same age, we have exactly the same background – we're the same sort of person, and whether we are both being gay has anything to do with it, I don't know, but if you look at our careers we have played an awful lot of the same parts. Both [have] had successes on Broadway. If our names were more similar I think people would be constantly confusing us. Initially he played Edward the Second at Cambridge, which got him going, and then I played Edward the Second professionally, which is what got me going. We've both done Vanya, both done Richard the Second, both done Hamlet then King Lear . . .

Jacobi almost counter-commented:

We have always been close but never intimate. I admired him as an actor, first as Shallow which was marvellous, and I always saw him as a character actor, saw him not as himself but as someone else. Not confident as a face (blond and blue-eyed) he was handsome in his way, but not a great looker, and I was never a great looker either. At Cambridge he wasn't that outgoing, a little introverted, his own man. I find him very funny, he has great humour, a great companion. He was much closer to Trevor Nunn, who was more his contemporary.

They have never fallen out, though they sometimes perhaps like to wind each other up. Ian once bought a T-shirt with Derek's image as Macbeth in a tea-shop in Stratford and put it on to tease Derek who had not exactly been a riotous success.

'I think we're both', said Ian, 'allowed to send each other up as we both know what we're up to.'

When Derek praised him as Twankey, Ian replied: 'What about the Ugly Sisters?' Neither could imagine the other not working.

At one time, staying with Derek and his partner Richard in France, Ian was sent off to pick some sunflowers before the expected arrival of Derek and Richard's guests. Frances Barber, ever faithful to both, was there too. Ian had to climb through a fence to get the flowers. Derek was nervous of what the local farmer would say. He initially helped Ian, but when he turned back to him in the fields with an armful of flowers Derek had disappeared. 'Well, fair enough, he did have to live there, and would have to deal with an irate farmer if he came along. I'm sure Frankie [Barber] blew that up into a huge tale of comic caricature and proportions. Frankie would caricature Derek as being very, very nervous, and me as carefree and showing off. Probably there's a touch of truth in that I suppose. I'm much more of a self-publicist than Derek.'

He and Derek came tantalisingly close to acting together in a Peter Shaffer play about Tchaikovsky, according to Allison Pearson. Jacobi loved the idea, which Shaffer told him about over lunch in New York where Jacobi was appearing as Lear. Ian fell in with the idea, ready, as he had done *Amadeus,* to take the play on trust. 'Four Cambridge lads,' he murmured approvingly to me. Derek was to play Tchaikovsky, and Ian his brother Modest; he was enthusiastic about what a wonderful story it was, and had written the first two acts, but had a problem with the third. He wouldn't exactly tell Derek what that problem was, but his great revelation was about the mystery of the composer, namely his death in 1893 from cholera and how he caught it.

Now the two main ideas were either, first, that he knew cholera was raging in the city at that time, and deliberately drank a glass of water, knowing it would kill him – so it was suicide. Or, he drank it by accident, without knowing it would kill him. But, according to Alexander Poznansky, one of the biographers, this was just a cover-up by Modest, who when he wrote his brother's life concealed the gay side to maintain the romantic image. Shaffer told Derek, 'I've got another solution to the mystery of the death, and this other solution is that Tchaikovsky and his brother, both being gay, both being quite promiscuous, particularly the brother . . .'

Peter's solution – according to Derek it was 'very Shaffer' – was in a scene where he showers with a boy he has picked up and while they are in the shower he is kissing the boy, in fact he is licking the boy's shoulder. That's how the water gets into his system, and he gets the cholera – 'So it's a sexual thing . . . A perfect idea, very visual, emotional, it's a wonderful image and not necessarily against the known facts.'

Derek then asked Shaffer, 'Which is the best part, Modest or Tchaikovsky?'

Shaffer replied, 'Well, as far as parts go, probably Modest is.'

'Oh well, Ian will play that, Ian will want to play that!'

Modest was Oscar Wildeish, recalls Derek, much more worldly, more unpleasant certainly, but also 'out', flamboyant – he was obviously gay, in contrast to Tchaikovsky who concealed it and married a woman. Shaffer never finished the play. Jacobi was convinced it was in a drawer somewhere in New York. He also told Jacobi at lunch in New York – Shaffer was eighty-four and very frail – that he was working on something else, also a play, working very slowly and not sure when he would finish it. The play had a title: '*PS*'.

It never happened. Another near-miss of working together occurred when Ian approached Derek to play another part with him. This was for the 1992 production of *Uncle Vanya* at the Cottesloe Theatre, in the view of some admirers the most moving performance Ian has given. On Mathias's suggestion, Ian asked Derek to join it, offering the part of his choice, Vanya or Astrov. 'We had it all set up. He said, "Vanya", so I said all right, "I'll play Astrov" and he withdrew, I can't remember why.'

One day when I was round at Derek's house in Belsize Park, sipping coffee and admiring his priceless collection of Staffordshire pottery, I asked what was on the cards next. He replied that Ian and he had been sent a script for a television sitcom called *Vicious Old Queens*, written by Mark Ravenhill (of *Shopping and Fucking*) and Gary Janetti, the San Francisco screenwriter. Derek hadn't responded well to the script but said he had felt a bit miffed he had not appeared in *Coronation Street*, although Bella, his much-loved dog, had. He said, with tongue in cheek, he was so envious of Ian appearing: 'Maybe my character could appear as Emily Bishop's lodger while he's away doing a local gig . . .'

The pair hummed and hawed over this new script, but ultimately Derek was convinced by Ian, who said they should work together to make the scripts better. So they agreed, with misgivings, and started rehearsing it for ITV with Frances de la Tour also picked to star. The series was heralded by weeks of hype approving the appearance of the 'thespian heroes in the first ever sitcom about cohabiting gay men', and ultimately aired not with its original title, *Vicious Old Queens*, but simply *Vicious*.

Stuart and Freddie are a gay couple who, after fifty years together, find that their mutual affection is matched only by their mutual contempt. They wile away hours exchanging barbs or scowling at one another from either end of their sofa, like gargoyles in cardigans. Freddie (the McKellen role) is a retired actor from Wigan whose career had peaked at killing a prostitute on *Coronation Street*. Stuart (Jacobi) is a former Leytonstone bartender. He still has not got around to admitting his sexuality to his mother. Together in a drab central London living room they duel in cartoonish camp, and are rather unpleasant company, for viewers as much as the handful of visitors who drop in. Foremost among these is the imperious Frances de la Tour. Neither her fellow cast members, nor the live television studio audience who cackled with laughter throughout, appeared to have noticed that the world had moved on since Leonard Rossiter and *Rising Damp*. As Violet, she was required to make eyes at Ash (Iwan Rheon), a young man who had moved into the flat upstairs, and 'repeatedly trot out a feeble gag about whether Zac Efron was a person or a geographic location' (according to the *Sunday Mirror*). There was the odd glimpse of how *Vicious* might have amounted to something sharper, as when, for example, McKellen turned to Jacobi and says, as one ageing man to another, 'I don't know which would be preferable at this point, if you woke up dead, or I did.' Jacobi leaves the sliver of a pause before hissing back, 'I know which I'd prefer.'

Even so, 5.7 million people watched. Nearly every opinion was contemptuous of the first six episodes. I was in the audience during several recordings. The interplay between cast, de la Tour, Ian and Derek, improvised and unexpected, between or during retakes, was infinitely funnier and more spontaneous than the clanking of the lines. The cascade of guffaws from the gay elderly couples in the audience, whipped up into a frenzy by the gag man who took over at every break in recording to tell lewd jokes, was embarrassing. The gag man picked on members of the audience to reveal some titillating indiscretion or risqué admission about themselves.

These first episodes were followed by six more, when the scripts did improve to some extent, and there kicked in a much-repeated phenomenon of culture and entertainment. The public's first reaction had almost completely written off the show, but American audiences lapped it up. Money talks. Gradually the camp extravagance became a kind of acceptably carpet-slippered, if not also reassuringly soothing, pap food. Public perception switched to good, simply because the acting wore down adverse response, and the popular personalities of the performers had taken over. When they were in South Bank studios recording live, 'The people of my generation who were in the [studio] audience were ever so chuffed to see me,' said Frances de la Tour, putting her hand modestly on her breast. 'I got an entrance round!' she told John Walsh of the *Independent*.

Ian was in his element, twisting quite banal lines to sound like comic manna from heaven. He quite outshone his old friend who was trapped in two-dimensional camp without any real or substantial character to play. It was a contrast to Derek's rich and rounded portrait as Anne Reid's endless wooer in the BBC serial *Last Tango in Halifax*, screened at the same time. It showed how Ian could play any old rubbish and make it outlandish and riveting, but Derek, the master craftsman, had to find a real character emotionally and physically, to bring out the best. This was not to say he wasn't an equal foil to McKellen's extravagance, but it was only too obvious in the performance, poorly directed as it was, how thin his material was.

By the middle of 2015 *Vicious* had become a hit, thanks to (in the eyes of the *Sun*) the 'realistic portrayal' of Freddie and Stuart. Homosexuality was a part of everybody's lives, as McKellen has striven for. Freddie and Stuart could legally marry. And if they did, it would be a potent symbol of a journey, or symbol of progress made. So pronounced Janetti, chatting up the audience, although Ian had been a little more circumspect. 'Our purpose,' he said, 'is to make people chuckle and giggle.' There was now the impending marriage towards the end of the second series of Jacobi and McKellen, and in the rising and repetitive hype to celebrate, Ian confessed to having had a crush on his friend (at Cambridge) while Derek said he was oblivious to it. 'I had absolutely no idea . . . he kept so much to himself.' The story, reinvented as new, did the rounds yet again.

People were, Ian conceded, rather disparaging about *Vicious* at first, 'but we were gargantuan and over the top . . . we were playing to the studio.' Playing to the studio as well as to the world at large, on the set, which consisted of just a huge double bed, Derek and Ian, not exactly in romantic nudity, but in appropriate and colourful night attire, consummated their earlier partnership to the standing ovation and cheers of a triumphant studio audience, which rose to its feet to applaud. 'There is even a new series in the offing in 2019,' says Derek, although it transpired that everyone had had enough. Marvell's parallel lines had come together and been fused at last.

36

Corporate Caretaking

'You cannot escape the drudgery of comparing yourself
to your peers'

Unknown

Ian always repeated that he had two Oscar nominations, but
sometimes this morphed into 'two Oscars', once at least in the
Daily Telegraph. He paired up with Patrick Stewart, who is now
his second acting other half, or one might say default spouse,
for a revival of Pinter's *No Man's Land*. Ian claimed that the
first production of this play, written specifically as a vehicle for
Ralph Richardson and John Gielgud, could never be bettered.
The pair were reluctantly drawn into it when he and Stewart
had a read-through of the script with Mathias in New York and
persuaded themselves, rather easily it seemed. As more theatre
of the unsaid, it was a natural progression or sequel to *Waiting
for Godot*.

There was another read-through in London, albeit a more
fluid one. Evgeny Lebedev, the Moscow-born owner of four
London newspapers including the *Evening Standard* and the *Independent*, who holds British citizenship and attended Holland
Park comprehensive and Mill Hill, had by now McKellen
and Mathias in his wide social circle, and he was keen to be
included in this project. Evgeny is a perfectionist with enter-
prises in journalism and the arts. This had brought him into
the McKellen and Nicholas Hytner world. He had loved the

theatre from an early age, and with his wide-ranging talents, which included playing the cello, had met up with Mathias who was introducing the 'inscrutable Hackney playwright Pinter' to Lebedev.

Their read-through as an exercise fairly quickly, in his words, 'morphed from rehearsal to drinking game'. In Lebedev's account, 'Matching the characters, drink for drink, is not the easiest of tasks, particularly when you're the alcoholic Hirst to Sean's poet Spooner. Hirst, it cannot be denied, knows how to drink, but he does so most improperly, starting off with whisky, then moving on to vodka, then champagne and finally beer.'

It opened at Wyndham's Theatre in the West End in late 2016 after having run on Broadway with *Godot* and toured the UK. The pair's two minders, Briggs and Foster, were played by Owen Teale and Damien Molony. *No Man's Land* takes place in Hirst's Hampstead mansion, where Foster and Briggs, in Hirst's employ, alternate abuse and serving the pair while they drink. Hirst (Stewart) bickers and banters with Spooner (McKellen). Ian joked about the chair-bound nature of the role after Stewart played Professor X in *X-Men*: 'Patrick is great at sedentary roles.'

Following on the rather careful, politically correct vocabulary of *Vicious*, sanitised for the American TV audience, *No Man's Land* is by contrast loaded with Pinter's most vituperative and dark vocabulary.

This whole production and the actors' performances, after its sell-out run at the Cort Theatre in New York, were among the most fêted that the pair has ever given, with Paul Taylor in the *Independent* calling it 'the funniest account of the play I have seen'. The audience roared. They captured the times and the *Times*. Where is it all going? The answer could well be *No Man's Land*.

They are the Dud and Pete of their era, the duo scoring wittily off each other, pursuing non-sequiturs and shocking diversions, possibly in the 1960s and 1970s Cambridge Foot-lights tradition – 'At times the writing borders on sketch-show silliness,' noted Dominic Cavendish in the *Telegraph* – but taken over and pushed to its extreme by Pinter, the master of threat and inconsequential menace. He knew when to stab the au-dience, vulnerable and exposed by a laughter-provoking line, effectively with his own brand of psychological loneliness and bullying.

Both this and its sister play *Godot* – 'profoundly and essential-ly bourgeois', Jean-Paul Sartre called *Godot* – had ended up in McKellen's hands attaining the status of high culture as great crowd-pleasers. Decadence, despair and cynical back-biting comfort well-heeled audiences sitting in expensive seats as long as they can laugh and dispel serious reflection by being taken 'out of their minds'. It was just the right time for Sean Mathias's transposition of the play into the post-fact or 'fake news' era, when it was assumed the nexus with reality had gone, and we were plunged into a roller-coaster of imperiousness and terrified bewilderment (Stewart as Hirst), and the hilariously tragi-comic Spooner (McKellen). 'I was sped along by gales of laughter' was the general verdict, especially for the expletives 'cunt!' and 'fuck' – an ironic underscoring of what Spooner says: 'All we have left is the English language.'

For Spooner, McKellen used every possible trick in his py-rotechnics of business, playing him as a raffishly determined gay man of his era. There was little balance, no equal weight between Spooner and Hirst, although I found Stewart was per-fectly competent and steady. When Spooner makes a game of drinking champagne – 'I am drinking champagne' – McKellen stretched this out to eternity, swilling it round his throat, tasting, then swallowing it. My seat was in the middle of the front row. As Ian's practice is to single out members of the audience on to whom to fix his gaze, I sank as low as possible and turned my head away twice so that he wouldn't notice me. McKellen was unashamedly playing the audience for laughs. In the matinee performance at Wyndham's to which I went, the two biggest (nervous?) laughs came when Foster says, 'I'm not a cunt,' and secondly when Briggs says, 'What the fuck are you talking about . . . he's a . . . fucking shit cake baker.'

'I haven't ever been loved; from this I draw my strength,' was the line I remembered most. It was perhaps slightly sloppy persiflage, an extended laugh-a-minute sketch performed by celebrity actors, a recycled vehicle for bravura and pyrotechnical display of fragmented thought, vapid and numinous inconsequentiality. The ghosts of Sophocles and Aeschylus would turn in their amphitheatre graves at Pinter's darkness, his relativism and, above all, his situationism. But maybe the actors were not happy too, and it was an 'off day'. To be live, as in 'live theatre', can mean unpredictable. This example of cultural populism seemed too often to undermine the Pinter message, while much of the menace went missing in the overlit set. Susannah Clapp called the production 'lacklustre' in the *Observer*.

Evgeny Lebedev and Sean Mathias had drunk on at their initial reading as they matched Spooner and Hirst in drink for drink, although, as Lebedev wittily pointed out, out-Pintering Pinter in going from whisky, vodka, champagne, then to beer. 'It goes completely against the old Russian wisdom about never reducing your alcohol percentage as the night goes on. But still, I think Welshman Sean was more drunk than me at the end.'

I am all for 'old Russian wisdom'.

Lebedev, Mathias and McKellen had 'a natural', even Pinteresque 'synergy', which came together in yet another lasting venture. Sean suggested in 2011 the trio buy The Grapes. When Mathias, who was living with his spouse Paul de Lange, had told Ian two years before his plan to move back to the home he owned next to Ian, McKellen had apparently responded: 'That's wonderful. Would you like to buy a pub as well?' Mathias, ruefully noting that Ian would get the pub into any conversation he could, reported that he could see Paul thinking, 'I would love to run that pub,' and felt like a 'trapped little fox' between them. De Lange, a qualified hotelier, took on the running of it. Lebedev became part-owner. Ian declared that he'd never been much of a pub-goer, even after shows at Stratford: 'Not part of my life. I'm not a pub-goer at all. No! I don't find any joy in just sitting there drinking.' He did enjoy doing the Monday-night pub quiz, remarking with usual self-deprecation, 'No, I am absolutely appalling! Thank God I am in a team of people. I went in to do the quiz last night and I forgot to book myself a table. Had to retire to my house and order fish and chips from the pub and bring it home. Couldn't get into my own pub!' At Christmas he is guaranteed a seat because he is the quiz master and sets the questions.

He was now the height of fashion in public, always wearing something different and noticeable, whether it was the rainbow-coloured bootlaces, matching the ribbon on his straw boater as he stretches out his legs, or the complicated boots themselves, skinny jeans, a tightish shirt, and bright herringbone jacket (three sizes too small, as fashion demands). Into this he has now evolved or flowered from the duffel-coated homely Northerner of Cambridge days.

But did the final Pinter, the final Lear to come, mean the line was being drawn under the Cambridge or Oxbridge dominance of the stage and films since Peter Hall first directed *Waiting for Godot?* Perhaps Hall's death in September 2017 was really the end of an era of that Marlowe Society–Gielgud–Olivier domi-nation of the classical stage with a whole different set of values from those of McKellen's final acting years.

Ian played a cognitively deductive and impressively tender Sherlock Holmes in a new film in 2014. His Sherlock is aged ninety-four and flashbacking to his sixties to reassemble mem-ories. It certainly set up Freudian overtones when Ian was searchingly questioned once more by Appleyard. Ian told him he was looking at some photographs – they were of his young parents – and thinking, 'She would never see me grow up, and neither of them knew she'd [his mother] got breast cancer, they'd no idea what the future was, and they looked so happy and beautiful. I have an emotional response to it. I've got some letters from my father to my stepmother, and I don't think I will be able to read them.'

He was asked finally about his legacy as a campaigner for gay rights. 'I've always been a bit shy,' he responded, 'and I've always supposed that what appealed to me about acting was that I could stand up in public and draw attention to myself and not feel shy, because I was protected by the fact that I knew what the next line was.' There had been some dispute about this childhood shyness. Cousin Margaret had said he was, in fact, a show-off. 'But does it matter now that she says I was a little show-off, and I think that I was shy?'

Would remembrance, as with Freud, now be 'a professional necessity'? By the age of seventy-eight, he once again pronounced on how impossible he had found the idea of writing a memoir. He had been stumped by the task of understanding his beginning, he told Louis Wise of the *Sunday Times*, and that he got so upset thinking about those two young parents of his who must have seen the war coming.

'I can't ask them about it. I would like to be their witness, and I can't be, and I thought, "I'm not going to be able to get through this book," and I gave up. I was getting too emotionally upset that I hadn't been a good enough child, because I'd not shown enough interest in them.'

Is accessing deep emotion the hardest thing for him? asked his interlocutor.

'Yes, it is. It's a big failing, that.'

Cambridge's influence was still vibrantly potent, with McKellen coming back to his greatest-ever stage performance as Lear, first at the small Minerva Theatre, Chichester, in 2017, then in its transfer to the Duke of York's in 2018. And so we return to our beginnings, to the Cambridge ADC and its formative seating to Nunn's Courtyard, and we come full circle in this final undertaking.

37

Gandalf Doesn't Do Weddings – Neither Does Lear

'Naked I was sent back – for a brief time, until my task is done. And naked I lay upon the mountain-top. The tower behind was crumbled into dust, the window gone; the ruined stair was choked with burned and broken stone. I was alone, forgotten, without escape upon the hard horn of the world. There I lay staring upward, while the stars wheeled over . . .'

Tolkien, *Lord of the Rings*

Patrick Stewart and Ian had become such good friends that in 2013 McKellen officiated at a church ceremony at Stewart's wedding to his third wife, the singer and songwriter Sunny Ozell. (He has two children by his first wife, Sheila Falconer. His second wife was the TV and film producer Wendy Neuss.) Since that wedding McKellen has had other requests to marry people. 'I was offered one and a half million dollars to marry a famous couple in California, which I would perhaps have considered doing but I had to go dressed as Gandalf. So I said, "I am sorry, Gandalf doesn't do weddings."' This was Sean Parker, Silicon Village's $2.4 billionaire, first president of Facebook.

In 2017 the second temptation to play Lear could no longer be resisted. Unfinished business again. Friends suggested he have another go. The previous production rankled – so much that when it opened he not very tactfully rang Nunn, asking him, 'Have you seen the Chichester production?' 'Fuck. No,' answered Nunn. 'I'm not going to see it – or in London.'

'I hope you understand I wanted to do it in a small theatre.'

One critic, Patrick Marmion, early in the run, was not too happy: 'So persuasive is the whiskery grandfather of the British stage that he seemed to me to be struggling with his lines, creating the sort of anxiety that comes with being around old people who you fear might fall over. It's not at all comfortable to watch, and when Sir Ian's Lear pauses or hovers in his lines, you get the uneasy sense of a mind adrift.' Here it would seem there was a sense of Lear 'occupying a parallel universe', the defining feature less of a determination to disrobe and more the pathos of a lonely, frightened old man slipping into the oblivion of dementia.

There have been in the past seven years three Lears at Chichester. Jonathan Munby's staging on a red-carpeted circular open stage onto which characters empty out of fortress doors, reinforced by explosions of *musique concrète* sound, had a fluidity of style and integrity of effect that never wavered, but sometimes overstepped the mark. For example, the elevation of disgraced Kent in a cage yanked high above the stage was frankly absurd, while the abattoir setting for the hovel/ruin with pigs' heads and carcasses' – 'Let us anatomise Regan to find what breeds around her heart' – which doubles for Gloucester's blinding scene, jarred too graphically. Artaud's Theatre of Cruelty warred against the fine abstract evocation of Edgar and Gloucester on Dover's Cliffs, when the red disc floor turned to barren chalk.

McKellen's second bite at the Lear apple was in strong contrast to the more rhetorical and far less successful Trevor Nunn production ten years before. This had pulled every kind of lever to elevate it to the heroic Olivier level. The reading was more patently a tragedy of wrath and revenge over the infamy of self-esteem with 'showy' (Ian's word) displays and bravura theatricality, but now we could even dismiss the 'waving of Gandalf's wand' as part of the sexual rhetoric. This time it became, in the parallel stories of Lear and Gloucester, a tragedy of declining years and old age, in which their folly lies in the evil they bring upon themselves, and they learn, or become sufficiently aware of, to regret and atone for it.

I had not thought from the first few moments that it was going to turn out so. For in the opening scene, overlooked by McKellen's bemedalled and trim-bearded portrait, such as you would find of monarchs in Buckingham Palace, Lear entered alone, walked downstage to front stage, and eyeballing the audience from left to right seemed to be throwing down the gauntlet with, 'I am Ian McKellen playing you, my audience.' The scene's tableau that followed by comparison shrank to actors on a stage playing their objective roles in *King Lear*. The deposition scene when Lear gives away his kingdom is always a tricky one and was confused here by Goneril standing in front of Lear at the table while he made much play of cutting up a map of Britain with scissors. The large map segments, although meant symbolically, were at odds with Lear's later insistence of fifty, then twenty-five retainers, as he battled with Regan and Goneril. The anger was muted. McKellen played the almost stereotypical gruff old man character with a high voice filtered through whiskers. It did not have the sudden, inciting flare-up to set alight the chaos of passion Lear unleashes. But subsequently, when Lear is moved into and through his wheel of fire, the self-inflicted humiliation, with at first little if no soul-exposure or affecting vulnerability, it did grow into a great acting performance with every detail from the outside thought out and well-placed. Ian brought beautiful blow-by-blow detail to every word, gesture, inclination and movement as he told us about Lear's mental decline. This was his masterclass in versatility and range of effect, but quite often in the performance I felt I was watching one well-interpreted and calculated effect following another, rather than actually being taken inside and shown it, so the suspension of disbelief did not quite work.

Even so, the conversational level at which the whole of

Munby's production was pitched succeeded in bringing clarity and lucidity to the three hours and forty minutes, coaxing thoughtful rumination and modern association from every scene. One especial example was the 'girlie' affection between Regan and Goneril, the rapturous hissing and cheek-smacking kisses almost to the very last moment when they are killing each other, which pointed to our contemporary hollowness of love and affection through social media. The way Regan stripped herself in sexual display, as well as her hysterical delight over Gloucester's blinding, struck me as another telling stab at our double standards. I stopped short of applauding the casting of Sinéad Cusack as Kent, 'an achingly trendy bit of gender-blind casting', as one critic called it, which added nothing except political correctness. Kent's lines and description in the eyes of others contradict it. The way she embraced Cordelia was inappropriate 'sisterhood' stuff, her vocal disguise as an Irish scallywag frankly absurd. Still, this removal of the outer husk of Kent's maleness did not wholly detract from Cusack's (and Kent's) tender expression of love and loyalty, which she managed well, without the contrasting gruffness. The 'gender bending' was not a total disfigurement. '[It's] all right for people who do not know the play to fulfil the woman quota,' said Ronald Pickup.

Overall, this achievement of Ian's over the play's exhausting length was colossal and at the age of seventy-eight, hardly matched by any living actor. It put the theatre, the stage actor, at the front of acting excellence, as he or she should be. It was supreme, and while I would claim the same of Jacobi's Lear in terms of a different interpretive mastery of the love and redemption at the centre of this play, and its universal theme of spiritual forgiveness, Ian's equal, more secular reading of this demanding text achieved a very different power.

These actors, in their sere and yellow leaf, were equal firsts. Both came just as near to contradicting Charles Lamb's criticism that 'The Lear of Sh. [*sic*] cannot be acted' as is possible.

'The greatness of Lear is not in corporal dimension,' Lamb had written, 'but in intellectual; the explosions of his passing are terrible as a volcano, they are storms turning up and disclosing to the bottom that sea, his mind with all its vast riches. It is his mind which is laid bare.'

McKellen's performance disclosed to the very depth Lear's mind, showing how that mind 'was laid bare'. McKellen brought together disparate if not contradictory elements in himself and his acting, to which often he had surrendered, and even extended, to overcome those shadow ghosts of unfinished family business.

Specifically, in the gesture he made of turning round Cordelia's body in the final moments before he expires, he enfolded and embraced her with a new confidence and freedom, and with a complete, unconditional love he could not give her before – because of his pride and ego, and his insistence on being obeyed. In this unifying performance he had with subtlety, delicacy and enviable control laid bare his own mind, to give us a reading with which the audience identified. My fear, on his first entrance, of histrionic intimidation of the audience, melted in favour of submission, in the deftly chosen intimate space of the Minerva, to an inspired exploration of, in Lamb's words, the 'vast riches' of Lear's intellectual greatness. And so the two sides of Ian McKellen were healed nightly in this extraordinary way. He was unabashed at the success, posting on Twitter the *Standard*'s rapturous praise: 'Ian McKellen's intelligent performance is a triumph' – repeating his dismissal of 'Trevor Nunn's vehemently operatic production for the RSC'.

'Intelligent' was the key word. 'Strikingly conversational', the paper's critic Henry Hitchings called it. I heard later that in the middle of the play when he was off-stage McKellen took a forty-five-minute nap. And every night he took a motorcycle taxi to the Duke of York's Theatre, where it had transferred from Chichester for a hundred days in the West End.

*

'Do you want to know my secret?' asked the world-famous Indian seer and philosopher Krishnamurti before a packed audience. 'This is my secret.' He then answered the question: 'I don't mind what happens.' Could this be true of McKellen? This ultimate 'surrender' to compassion had also something very unexpected about it yet had always been there on the horizon. The climax of his acting life had been reached and triumphantly passed. There needed to be no regret, for nothing remained unachieved. There would be no looking back.

Finale

'How come Ian always manages to send a card or flowers or just be there?'

Trevor Nunn

Tuesday 1 September 2018, 5.30 p.m.

I knock on the dark green door next to Ian's. It opens and Deborah Owen, wife of David Owen, asks me in. David and Deborah, a distinguished literary agent whose clients have numbered Delia Smith, Jeffrey Archer and Amos Oz, are warm and welcoming. David takes me to the expansive window of the Owens' now knocked-through two houses overlooking the Thames. The tide is almost in, the lifelike figure of the Antony Gormley sculpture imposingly stands in the eighteen-foot tidal Thames, purchased by Ian, and testimony to his community spirit. It took three years to go through the official channels to get clearance to put it up, and the police specified it should not be covered with the tide above the waist, as it might mistakenly be reported as someone in difficulties in the water calling for help. On the head a gull perches. David Owen tells me that once this beautiful terrace was to be knocked down and 'developed' but saved by the owners. It is an extraordinary corner of Limehouse, and the Owens enthusiastically tell me as Ian's next-door neighbours how he champions and nurtures it.

A curious coincidence once again drawing together Ian

and Jacobi is that Francis Bacon, the painter, once owned and lived at Number 40 on this street. In John Maybury's *Love is the Devil*, Jacobi filmed in a studio recreation of Number 40 his portrayal of Bacon, in which Daniel Craig played his sado-masochistic lover George Dyer. In the 1990s while filming in New Zealand Ian had extensive developments made to his property, and there was a lot of noise that affected Deborah Owen's home-based agency. 'He was wonderful, so considerate a neighbour,' says Deborah, for when away filming he sent flowers to her once a month with apologies for the racket caused. The Owens call his embrace and preservation of the neighbourhood generous, and he contributes to local Isle of Dogs and Canada Wharf performance events as sponsor or participant. He is never too busy or puffed up to join in. Deborah calls this rare. He has a devoted PA, Louise Harding, and he puts up friends or if they are painters allows their work to be exhibited.

When I left McKellen that day in 2006, even then I never realised the extent to which he stood alone and apart from that extraordinary mafia of Cambridge figures who came to dominate the entertainment and media world, or the degree to which, at least with fame and celebrity, he towered head and shoulders above the rest. I can think of few if any of this generation who commanded such attention; witness this surprise headline in the *Daily Mail* of 9 February 2018: 'Sexual fluidity is the future, says Ian McKellen' – a subject that sparked serious debate. Could one ever imagine Olivier or any leading actor in the last century pronouncing on such an issue?

In the decade and more since 2006, I have become drawn into determining what sets Ian apart from everyone else, and what has made him into such a world-wide presence, both as an actor and an activist for gay rights. As he passes the milestone of eighty, he is in a category quite on his own, as he has been a different kind of achiever from those distinguished actor knights or dames with worthy stage and screen credits, or those titled or untitled tireless campaigners for social justice, who sit on the back benches or carry shadow cabinet ministers' briefs. He was an inspirational figure across generations. Is this because he combines in one person what most would think of as two separate lives and ambitions? Is it chance or design?

Ingrid Bergman, with whom McKellen once clashed at a dinner party, said the key to happiness was good health and a poor memory. As he heads from four-score years towards many more, the remarkable drive is there intact, and there is no intention of retiring. 'Theatre is for now,' he rightly said, like life, while young actors today haven't heard of Laurence Olivier. He did have an eye, but here surely a mischievous one, on taking his final bow. 'If it happens now, "Oh b—"' He invoked a friend whose hand he held while he died, and who said, 'I don't want to miss anything.' This sentiment, too, haunted the lonely independent artist. So for the final curtain there was a running order for the Memorial Service in a large theatre, with his own words, 'I'm sorry to be missing this show' – so we'd better hold a rehearsal now. 'I'm in favour of death. I'm in favour of a line drawn. I feel there is a purpose to it.'

Now has come my final moment in the traditional manner in attempting to sum up McKellen, the man and actor. The audience pulling power has never flagged. Just staging his one-man show, *Tolkien, Shakespeare, Others and You* in late 2017, in the 200-seater Park Theatre to raise funds, generated a quarter of a million for this unsubsidised theatre. It would be a mixture of high art, anecdotes drawing in the audience, and the by now predictable holding forth on politics and gay sexuality, the recurrent theme of his life. He wanted to go on working to the very end, and after ending *King Lear* in 2018 he took to the road again in his eightieth year with his one-man show, blazing a trail of glory and delighting audiences in eighty different venues and places. This redefinition of the birthday bash saw him appearing not only in main city centres of the UK, but back to Wigan Little Theatre and Bolton to celebrate his birthday in May 2019. Sean Mathias sprang a surprise dinner party for 150 people at Bolton School the evening before the performance in the Town Hall. *Tolkien, Shakespeare, Others and You* has extended its run to the end of 2019, opening in September at the Harold Pinter Theatre in the West End. 'This isn't a farewell tour – I'm saying hello again!' he said before he set out. He compared it to the old days of music-hall artistes flitting from booking to booking. A good part of the tour would be 'particular to the place . . . remembering things (such as acting opposite Margaret Drabble at the Arts, Cambridge). Not only would it keep him on his toes, but it would prove 'quite emotional'.

This coincides with a Warner Brothers feature, *The Good Liar*, in which he plays Roy Courtnay, an octogenarian conman with an espionage backstory, and shades of Iago's 'honesty'. Courtnay looks up Betty McLeish (Helen Mirren), a seemingly unsuspecting widow, to devour her and her fortune, but bites off more than he can chew.

But, after all, to sum up the professional side of his life, he has said, 'I'm only an actor. I'm not a writer. I'm not going to leave any legacy . . . All I've ever done is learn the lines and say them.' He has said others were better than he was, and he had spent his life disguising these limitations – overtly emotional scenes, when a character breaks down, cries, or has a speech about his deepest feelings. He freely admitted he didn't have much experience of expressing deep, complicated emotions for the benefit of somebody else. 'That's not how I've gone about my [private] life. So when a character does that I suppose sometimes you come up against a block and say, "I can't imagine what that's like." And then you start using other little triggers and ways of stirring it all up.' In not claiming too much for himself, he would share the famous dictum of Ralph Richardson, another great actor: 'Actors are the jockeys of literature. Others supply the horses and we simply make them run.' And again in this statement made in 2019: 'Derek and I and Patrick are all the same person really. We've all played the same parts. And all of us were at the New York Pride when we were Grand Marshals a couple of years ago, so our public and private lives have overlapped a bit.'

Yet as an actor that, as Hazlitt wrote, 'we only have for a few moments', his strong sense of rivalry and competition with other great actors has continued to the very end, in particular with Olivier. Retiring was simply not an option.

But what of my belief, encompassing both his acting genius and his social activism, that he is a significant phenomenon of our age?

Close friends like Jacobi have mentioned his determination to ensure his legacy lives on. Was he seeking a kind of immortality in the late flowering of a cause, his notable contribution to social change, when he insisted that his CH (Companion of Honour), awarded by the Queen in 2008, should be for services to society as well as for the arts? Other friends aver that while he has turned down a peerage, his ambition was quasi-immortality, which meant a state funeral in Westminster Abbey, and burial next to Garrick and Irving in front of the plaque to Shakespeare. Perhaps they would also be playing a recording of him reading *Henry V*, as happened at Olivier's funeral. But this doesn't fit at all with my different reading of McKellen the man, and his innate modesty.

Perhaps as a child in the zeitgeist of the fifties and sixties and Colin Wilson's landmark book *The Outsider*, one key note is that he still likes the feeling of being an outsider, and notably because of his sexual orientation. This was how Brian Cox, along the same lines, had seen him as 'a construct. He nailed it [the construct] down and encased it in lead.' Cox wondered if he ever really wanted to know himself, as if there was something he was in fear of discovering, and was just not interested. As Cox also said, he was the first 'secretly to question his own worth'. As such he was very isolated. But this was at the core of his being and a necessary part of his greatness as an actor: impenetrability.

Joy Leslie Gibson saw him back in 1985, taking an image from seventeenth-century England torn by religious and political strife, as 'a Cavalier at heart. But that he has had a Roundhead upbringing.' She called attention not only to this divide in him, but also to 'his essential Englishness', but wondered 'if he would be considered intelligent in the outside world'. She answered that while she is struck by the vividness of phrase and the immediate communication of emotion or thought, when considered more carefully, 'the thought is not carried through', and the effect is 'more of a clever undergraduate than a true thinker'.

Paradox perhaps ultimately is something that can never be wholly plucked out, yet it goes to the heart of the McKellen mystery. A man of extreme secular views, a Corbynista dockland gay socialist with no belief in an afterlife or attachment to Old Testament fundamental beliefs, or even in an underlying difference between good and evil (and especially 'Nature' as found and often defined in Shakespeare), the extraordinary paradox stood, and will stand. Apart from the simple answer that he is an actor, this paradox played a central role which brought him tens of millions and worldwide fame, moulded in the traditional and strongly devout Roman Catholicism of J. R. R. Tolkien. 'A lot of people who came to see *King Lear* [in 2017 and '18] were drawn by Tolkien rather than Shakespeare,' he told the *Evening Standard* in November 2018.

Where had the spiritual imperatives, instilled in early years by Margery and Denis, gone in all this jockeying for place among celebrity actors and artists? Descending deeper into the man, as I must try finally to do, one thing for sure can be said: his love of pleasure is open and undeniably visible. From an early age he has gone after what he most desired without conflict over it or self-recrimination. He has provoked and gratified extreme desirability, respect and admiration in others, and done this both in life and in art, yet maintained deep reserve. Mathias was accurate about him when he said, 'He's the most extraordinarily private person. Very secretive.' He gave himself pleasure in many areas, and in so doing brought huge and abundant pleasure to everyone else. He freed himself gradually from self-denial and self-obstruction with permission to have all that life and art had to offer. He has ended up, successfully, creating himself as almost a universal brand and certainly a phenomenon. In a similar way, when he came to enjoy the pleasure of social power, he showed he had that power to share with others. Yet he only ever answered to himself and his personal god or instincts.

'When my contemporaries were having babies, I didn't feel anything but pity for them. People are always complaining about being parents and children seem to be nothing but a problem. If I'd had children, I couldn't have behaved as selfishly as I have.' How could he know? When he was last tackled on this sensitive issue, namely that acting is transient, and being exclusively gay meant he would be without issue, he was quick to backtrack on the reference to children. Appleyard, here his interviewer again, mentioned the philosopher Roger Scruton's argument that homosexuals have less right to a stake in society since their 'barrenness', by which he meant lack of children, made them so, but Ian contradicted this, saying he was not depressed by his lack of children, although to his questioner he betrayed loneliness and a yearning for continuity. Apart from the simple answer that he was an actor, and this went to the heart of his mystery, 'But the secret has been my own life, and if I had been at ease with this . . . I don't think you necessarily do that by putting more human beings in it.' At another time he has claimed he would be 'an awful father', and adds, as most people are, of course.

This should be placed perhaps against what he said about his mother dying when he was twelve: 'I can remember nothing but love . . . The memory I have is of a person who felt fulfilled by her life, by looking after me and my sister and running the home.' There was his father Denis and their failure to connect.

As far as the defining moment in his life – his coming out – goes, it is interesting to hear him on the subject of 'Michael's Letter to Mama' from Armistead Maupin's novel *More Tales from the City*. 'It is,' he says, 'so, so well argued . . . It's very much the letter that Armistead wrote to his mother when he came out, and it's so beautifully argued.' 'Argued' is the operative word here. Argument in matters of the heart never brings final redemption from pain.

> At the end of the show, having read it, I give it to someone in the audience. I say: 'You just pass it along until it reaches somebody who knows somebody who would benefit from reading this letter.' A number of people have used it as a model for coming out themselves, so that's always very moving.

He continues: 'And of course, it was a letter I didn't myself ever write. That's how deeply I was in the closet. That bloody door is so hard to open.

'You don't want to be in there. A closet in English is a cupboard. And cupboards are dusty places. You keep skeletons in them. You can't live in a cupboard. It's a very good image for what it feels like. You're enclosed, the whole of the world is outside. All you've got to do is open the door and walk out.'

He and Denis had battened down their emotions when Margery died. Forty-six years later, when Princess Diana died, Ian realised that Prince Harry was the same age that he had been in 1951. 'My joining in that communal experience of grief was very much a personal thing related to my mother. I think a lot of people had myriad reasons why they were so affected by her death.' Yet even this had to be acknowledged publicly, in the one-man show *Knight Out*. He went as far as identifying with

Prince Harry over his mother's death, encouraging children to go to funerals and express grief over the death of a loved one. Going naked as the best disguise had become a habit, as was so evident from the abundance of recent articles, interviews and so on in the press and on television.

And so we are drawn into his choppy waters of unease, uncomfortable conflict, and continuing uncertainty, while the manner – 'verbose, and a touch grandiloquent, tinged with self-doubt', as Appleyard noted – shows him sometimes more tortured and disturbed by these issues than his 'born again' buoyancy would suggest.

If he ever had written his memoirs, Ian said he would ask, 'Why did I become an actor?' This is a variation of the question Sam Mendes said he always posed to actors: 'Who was I doing it for?' Perhaps in Ian's case the answer could be similar to Jacobi's 'My mother and father' – perhaps subtly metamorphosed into 'The shadows of my mother and my father'. There had been an obstacle in finishing the business with his parents, and here glorious art took its place. There is a flash of inspiration in his realisation when playing Widow Twankey, as he was shaking his legs on the Old Vic stage, that he was his dead sister Jean.

Was there not also a lifelong Don Juan element in this life, like Mozart defying his father who appears as the Commendatore figure in *Don Giovanni* – and the bottled-up, yet avowed homosexuality, an integral part of him, similar to Mozart's waggish rebellion and amorous foulmouthed-ness? Elton John was quoted in December 2017 that his father wanted him to be something else than what he was. 'I've spent my life trying to prove to my father that I was a success. He has been dead years and I'm still trying to prove the point. It stays with you. I tried to outrun my darkest secret, that I couldn't love myself. I thought I didn't deserve to be loved, cared for.' Does the shadow of his dead father still stalk Ian with what he imagined would have been the reaction to his being gay?

To pluck the heart out of the mystery we have peeled away

as many layers of the onion as we could. But, as with an onion, what is at the centre? An actor taking on many roles, including those of himself?

One thing for sure we can say: McKellen wholly inhabited the actor's role in his own time and continues to do so. Sharing his longevity and knowing him well since they met in 1958, John Tydeman, reading this account and feeling for him the greatest love and admiration, wrote at the bottom of the last page, 'A protean chameleon caught in a kaleidoscope tube. Just a mere boy full of questions who really didn't want to grow up.' A true Enfant du Paradis, a child of paradise. McKellen remains an extraordinary if not the extraordinary figure of our age, its perfect mirror, like Judi Dench, whom he partnered in *Macbeth*.

Before I leave his neighbours' house in September 2018, I head out onto the terrace to have a look at the Gormley sculpture again, and Ian's luxurious plants and staircase next door. As I stand there the presence of the figure partly covered by the tide commands awe and sends shivers up my spine. Gormley is justly celebrated for his Crosby Beach, Liverpool, statues. The incoming and outgoing tide is a specific attraction to him. 'You are encouraged to linger a bit longer by the tide coming in.' He has said of these human forms based on his own body that they are an attempt to materialise the place at the other side of appearance where we all live.

Acknowledgements

'The general and rapid narratives of history, which involve a thousand fortunes in the business of a day . . . afford few lessons applicable to private life,' wrote Dr Johnson. This biography is not intended as an exhaustive account of Ian McKellen's career. The 'business' of Sir Ian McKellen's life in the wide sense meant here are his film and theatre roles, numbering over several hundred. Some of these have more detailed coverage than mine in Joy Leslie Gibson's 1985 biography, published by Weidenfeld & Nicolson, Mark Barratt's 2005 unauthorised biography, published by Virgin, and David Weston's *Covering McKellen*, published by Oberon. I would refer the reader to these, and to Sir Ian McKellen's own record of his life and acting, his website at www.mckellen.com, for further reading.

I acknowledge with warmest thanks the generous help given to me by Times Newspapers and Associated Newspapers, namely John Witherow, editor of *The Times*, and Ted Verity, editor of the *Mail on Sunday*, who authorised my exploration of their truly impressive archive materials on McKellen. The size of these, especially those of the *Mail* and *Mail on Sunday* in Derry Street, possibly exceeds that of any contemporary stage performer and I was not in any way expecting to find as much as I did. The Associated Newspaper library has not only hundreds of carefully folded paper cuts from all major publications in their hallowed buff envelopes before they moved on to database memory in 2005, but over eight thousand entries for McKellen just from major press publications since that time. I must specially thank Su Blanch of the *Mail on Sunday*'s features desk, and Jonathan Bain and others of the library; also my gratitude goes out to Steve Baker, Ian Brunskill and Marc Cutler of the *Times* archive situated in Bromley-by-Bow; Victoria Ewart for undertaking research, and my special debt is owed to Samantha Hill for valorously puzzling over my handwriting, and typing successive drafts. Alan Samson, the publisher, has given me massive support, as has Peter Cox, my manager and agent, and editor, Celia Hayley. I thank also Natalie Dawkins, for her help with the illustrations, and the meticulous copy-editing of John English.

To acknowledge each and every person who has contributed by talking to me about Ian McKellen over the years would run to pages. Of the scores of those who have helped me in amassing my items, quotes and accounts, many are no longer with us, and some have no wish to be named. All have my unbounded thanks and love, as indeed have my wife and family for their support. I must add that all the opinions, theories, comments and suppositions are entirely my own, and if I have made any mistakes of fact, or in quotation, every effort will be made to rectify these in future editions.

Index

Ian McKellen is IM throughout.

Abraham, F. Murray 141
Acting Shakespeare (one-man-show)
    148–9, 154, 208
Actors' Company 92–100
AIDS/HIV 154–5, 179, 180, 187,
    206
Aladdin (pantomime) 296, 337
The Alchemist (play) 142
Alfred the Great (film) 71
Alfreds, Mike 147
Ali, Muhammad 111, 143
All Is True (film) 288
Amadeus (play) 138–40
Amateur Dramatic Club (ADC),
    Cambridge 35–6, 37–8, 40
Ambassadors Theatre, London
    127
An Unexpected Journey (Hobbit film)
    298–9
Anderson, Terry 155
Anderton, James 202
Annan, Noel 46, 157
Annis, Francesca 107
Ansorge, Peter 87
Appleyard, Bryan 187, 242, 255,
    335, 336
Apt Pupil (film) 221–3, 227
Arden, John 62
Arlidge, Antony 5
Armstrong's Last Goodnight (play) 62
Arts Society, London 175–6
Arts Theatre, Cambridge 6, 40,
    71
Arts Theatre, London 43
Ashcroft, Peggy 29, 30, 35, 101,
    172
Atkins, Eileen 92
Auden, W. H. 237
Avenue theatre company 128

Bacon, Francis 330
Bakshi, Ralph 261
The Ballad of Little Jo (film) 212
Banks, Geoffrey 45, 65–6
Banks, Liz 66
Baptists 14–15
Barber, Frances 272, 277, 279,
    280, 296, 310
Barnes, Clive 98–9
Barratt, Mark 45, 57, 66, 99, 216,
    259
Barton, Anne 104, 151

Barton, John
  at Cambridge 35, 37–8
  and IM 51, 52
  Playing Shakespeare 196
  at RSC 77, 101–3, 108, 111
  The Battle of the Five Armies (Hobbit film) 299, 301
Beale, Simon Russell 163
Bean, Sean 144
Beckett, Samuel 85, 303–4, 305–6
  Endgame 30
Belgrade Theatre, Coventry 49–52
Bell, Colin 42
Bell, Tom 133, 186
Benigni, Roberto 225
Bening, Annette 212
Bennett, Jill 66, 67–8, 127, 128
Bent (play) 130–4, 185–7, 193
Bergman, Ingrid 126, 331
Berkoff, Steven 57–8, 206
Berry, Cecily 102
Billen, Andrew 224
Billie (Sean Mathias' mother) 125
Billington, Michael
  on *King Lear* 279
  on *Macbeth* 115, 118
  on *Othello* 175
  on *Richard II* 73
  on *The Three Arrows* 99
  on *'Tis Pity She's a Whore* 80
Bird, John 37
Black Comedy (play) 70
Blair, Tony 218–20
Blakiston, Caroline 93
Blanchett, Cate 300
Bodleian Library, Oxford 267

Bogarde, Dirk 249
Bolton Grand Theatre 30
Bolton Little Theatre 45
Bolton School 23, 25, 28–9
  The Boltonian (school magazine) 29
Bond, Gary 75, 80–2
Boulevard Theatre, London 128
Bowie, David 156, 242
Boyens, Philippa 258
Bragg, Melvyn 147, 166
Brahms, Caryl 103, 126
Branagh, Kenneth 103, 114, 147, 165, 287, 288
Brandreth, Gyles 290
Brantley, Ben 161, 163, 279–80
Bratman, David 250–1
Brett, Jeremy 61, 80, 81, 82
British Empire 13, 281
Brook, Faith 86, 87
Brook, Peter 30, 89, 198
Brook Theatre, Soham 39
Burnley, Lancashire 11–12
Burrell, Michael 39, 45, 175, 197
Bury, John 144
Bush Theatre, London 128

Caine, Michael 189
Cairncross, James 86
Callow, Simon
  activist 204
  Amadeus 139–40
  Being an Actor 135
  'coming out' 157, 161
  and IM 223, 289
  on *Richard III* 213
  on Shakespeare 192

Waiting for Godot 304–5
Calvert, Phyllis 59
'Cambridge mafia' 35, 37, 137–8
Cambridge Mummers (acting society) 35
Cambridge Theatre, London 89, 91
Cambridge University 33, 35–6
Cameron, David 182
Carey, George 205
Carpenter, Humphrey 237–8, 239, 248
Cashman, Michael 160, 182–3, 185, 209
Cavendish, Dominic 318
Chamberlain, Neville 13, 14
Charleson, Ian 154, 179
Château Castellaras, Provence 260–1
Chekhov, Anton 92, 98, 142–3, 147
The Cherry Orchard (play) 147–8
Chetwyn, Robert 51, 84, 85–6, 130, 185, 186
Citizens Theatre, Glasgow 126, 146
civil rights movement 232
Clapp, Susannah 319
Clark, Kenneth 278
Clause 28 156–7, 160–1, 178, 182, 203, 206–7
Clifford, Richard 150, 183, 310
Clunes, Alec 30
Cochrane, Elspeth
  background 50–1
  and Guthrie 55
  and IM 59, 62, 67, 87

and Olivier 63
retirement 186
Codron, Michael 59
Cold Comfort Farm (film) 221
Collins, Michelle 183
Congregationalists 14–15
Connery, Sean 240–1
conscientious objectors 13–14
Cook, David 167–8
Cook, Peter 288
'Cool Britannia' 218–19
Corbyn, Jeremy 220, 300
Coriolanus (play) 143–6
Coronation Street (ITV) 297
Cort Theatre, New York 317
Cottesloe (Dorfman) Theatre 147
Cottingham, Paul 182–3
Cotton, Antony 297
Cottrell, Richard
  and the Actors' Company 92, 93
  director 72, 76, 94
  on IM 38–9
  National Service 43
  on *Richard II* 73
  on *Richard III* 213
  translator 147
Couëlle, Jacques 260
Courtyard Theatre, Stratford 272, 277
Coveney, Michael 85, 105, 187, 269, 305
Coward, Noël 61, 249
Cowardice (play) 127
Cox, Brian
  on Bent 134
  on Hall 138

Cox, Brian—*(contd)*
  on IM 144, 253, 289, 333
  King Lear 193
  Richard III 194–5, 198
  X-Men 231, 291–2
Craig, Daniel 330
Crawford, Michael 56
Cresson, Edith 208
Crick, Francis 33
Criterion Theatre, London 185
The Critic (play) 147
Crook, Arnold 306, 307
Crowley, Bob 194
Crucible Theatre, Sheffield 92
Cumberbatch, Benedict 299
Cumming, Alan 231
Curry, Julian 86
Cusack, Sinéad 326
The Cut (play) 297
Cuthell, Nick 254–6

Da Vinci Code (film) 286
Dalai Lama 72, 74
Daltry, Jill 41
Dance of Death (play) 228, 262–3
Day-Lewis, Daniel 242
Day, Richard Digby 56–7
de Jongh, Nicholas 204–5, 297
de la Tour, Frances 263, 312–14
de Lange, Paul 319–20
de Vito, Danny 212
del Toro, Guillermo 299, 302
Dench, Judi
  and IM 289, 338
  Lady MacBeth 110, 113–14, 118
  Much Ado About Nothing 97

Nightingale on 117
  praise for 114, 115
  The Promise 69–70, 99
  Romeo and Juliet 30
  Waiting for Godot 303
The Desolation of Smaug (Hobbit film) 299
Dexter, John 137, 138–9
Diamond, Marian 93
Diana, Princess 336
Dickens, Charles 150
Dirty Duck (pub), Stratford 278
Doble, Lawrence 66–7
Doctor Faustus (play) 103–5
Dolan, Monica 280, 282–3
Donmar Theatre, London 284
Donovan, Jason 207
Doran, Greg 117–18
Downey Jr, Robert 212
Dowson, Ann 41
Drabble, Margaret 43, 45, 126, 218–19, 332
Drummond, John 5, 124
du Maurier, Gerald 65
The Duchess of Malfi (play) 146
Duke of York's Theatre, London 59, 307, 322, 327
Dunlop, Frank 58
Dyer, George 330

Eccleston, Christopher 185
Eddison, Robert 92, 93, 94, 95, 97, 98
Edward II (play) 75
Eliot, T. S. 4, 96
Elizabeth II, Queen 273
Ellis, Robin 93

Elsworth, Michael 244
Evans, Frank 101
Evans, Luke 299
Evans, Tennial 93
Everett, Rupert 118–19
Ewing, Maria 140
Extras (BBC) 287
Eyre, Richard 193–6
   at Cambridge 36–7
   Charleson's funeral 154
   director 212
   on IM 216, 226, 262, 271
   National Theatre 35
   Richard III 123–4, 202
Eyre, Ronald 97, 103

Fairbairn, Sir Nicholas 208
Fanfan la Tulipe (film) 260
The Fellowship of the Ring (film) 261, 263
Ferguson, Euan 264
Finney, Albert 51, 57, 61, 70, 138, 190
Fleetwood, Susan 86
Fletcher, Jacqueline 144
Footlights, Cambridge 35
Forbes, Bryan 112
Ford, John 96
Forster, E. M. 33
Forster, Margaret 218
Fortune, John 38, 40
Fortune Theatre 66, 69
Fox, Angela 53, 190
Foxxe, David 274
Frank, David 222
Frears, Stephen 36, 167–9, 288
Freud, Sigmund 281–2

Frost, David 38, 169
Fry, Stephen 28, 49, 206

Gale, George 187
Gambon, Michael 227
Garai, Romola 277, 283
Gardner, Ava 166
Garrick Theatre, London 187
Gay and Lesbian Pride March 178, 332
gay rights cause 160–1
Gervais, Ricky 287–8
Gibson, Joy Leslie 77, 114, 145–6, 172, 333–4
Gielgud, John
   and IM 74
   King Lear 28
   Macbeth 112
   memory problems 138
   No Man's Land 316
   Richard III 212
   smoker 254
   theatre roles 30
   What the Butler Saw 84
   and writers 85
Giles, David 96
Gill, Peter 142
Gilpin, Jean 104
Gods and Monsters (film) 223–4, 227, 229
The Good Liar (film) 332
Gormley, Antony 4, 329, 338
Grace, Nickolas 51–2, 86, 87
Grandage, Michael 274, 284
The Grapes (pub) 128, 150, 151, 256, 319–20
Greer, Germaine 276, 278

Guinness, Alec
film roles 242, 249, 300
Hamlet 88
and Housman 7–8
and IM 74
religious beliefs 179–80
Richard II 72, 73
Guthrie, Tyrone (Tony) 53–6, 58, 73, 107

Hall, Peter
and *Amadeus* 140
background 34–5
death 320
diaries 116
on directing 75
Hamlet 83
on IM 100, 162–3, 226
IM on 141–2
on *King Lear* 274
National Theatre 137–9, 146
Waiting for Godot 303–4
Wars of the Roses 101
Hamlet (play) 9, 85–6
Hammond, Roger 124, 134, 269
Hancock, Sheila 153, 154
Hands, Terry 102, 147
Hank Cinq (musical) 94
Hardiman, Terence (Terry) 40, 43, 44
Harding, Louise 330
Hardman, Paul 72
Hardwick, Edward 128
Harris, Richard 240, 242, 287
Harry, Prince 336
Hart, Christopher 305
Hawthorne, Nigel 184, 212

Hazlitt, William 332
Hemmings, David 71
Henn, Tom 34
Henry Miller's Theatre, New York 70
Hewison, Robert 157, 196
Hicks, Greg 144
Hilary, Jennifer 59
Hill, Susan, People 14, 29
Hitchings, Henry 327
HIV/AIDS 154–5, 179, 180, 187, 206
The Hobbit films 243, 298–301
Hobson, Harold
on *Edward II* 76
on *Hamlet* 87–8
on IM 77, 97, 105
IM on 175
influence 40
on *Love's Labours* (musical) 43–4
on *Much Ado About Nothing* 62
religious beliefs 74
on *A Scent of Flowers* 59
Hoffman, Dustin 4
Hogg, Ian 115
Hoggart, Richard, *The Uses of Literacy* 274
Holden, Anthony 141
Holm, Ian 241, 245–6, 261
homosexuality 157–9, 177–9
illegality of 46
Orton and 84–5
in plays 77, 130–3
in society 314, 335
Hopkins, Anthony 61, 138, 241
Housman, A. E. 8
Howe, John 242

Hurt, John 167, 169, 170
Hussein, Waris 41
Hyde, Jonathan 283

Ian McKellen on Stage – With Tolkien, Shakespeare, Others and You (one-man-show) 331–2
Infidelities (play) 128
International Federation of Actors 299

Jackman, Hugh 229
Jackson, Fran 242, 243, 258, 259
Jackson, Glenda 102, 270, 271
Jackson, Peter 241–7, 249–52, 257–9, 263, 266–7, 301
Jacobi, Derek
  at Cambridge 40–4
  and Coward 61
  and Dexter 137, 138
  Harris on 287
  I, Claudius 167
  and IM 150, 203–4, 284, 291, 296, 308–12
  IM on 183
  King Lear 272, 273–4, 282, 284–5, 326
  Love is the Devil 330
  As Luck Would Have It 7, 8
  and Olivier 189–90, 190–1
  and parents 337
  and playwrights 85
  in rep 50
  sexuality 28, 46
  and stalker 175
  theatre roles 62, 71, 75, 77, 112, 303, 306

Vicious 312–15
James, Emrys 105
Janetti, Gary 312
Jarman, Derek 202–3, 206
Jenkins, Roy 206
John, Elton 156, 297, 337
Johnson, Dr Samuel 8
Jonson, Ben 142

Kay, Richard 46
Kendal, Felicity 93, 95, 97
Kennedy, John F. 111
Kerr, Walter 140
Key, John 266, 300
Kidd, John 75
King Lear (play) 193, 199, 268, 271–4, 276–85, 321–7
King's Rhapsody 22
Kingsley, Ben 287
Kinnear, Roy 146
A Knight Out in Los Angeles (one-man-show) 336
Kott, Jan 72
Krishnamurti 328
Kulukundis, Eddie 87, 94
Kundera, Milan 301
Kushner, Tony 129
Kyle, Barry 108

Lahr, John 155, 188, 268–9, 277, 280
Lamb, Charles 326–7
Lambert, J. W. 115
Lancashire 16
Last Tango in Halifax (BBC) 314
Laughton, Charles 225
Laurenson, James 79

Lawrence, D. H. 165–6

Leavis, F. R. 33, 102

Lebedev, Evgeny 256, 316–17, 319–20

Lee, Christopher 241, 249–50, 261, 301

Lee-Potter, Lynda 207

Leigh, Vivien 30

Leighton, Margaret 112

Letts, Quentin 296

Levin, Bernard 117

Lewenstein, Oscar 84

Lewis, Damian 287

Lewis, Peter 70

Lewis, Roger 196, 214

Lewis, Stephen Brimson 304

Lighthouse (charity) 154–5, 156

A Lily in Little India (play) 66, 126

Loach, Ken 168

Locke, Joseph 30–1

Loncraine, Richard 211

London Lighthouse 154–5, 156, 180

Long, Matthew 93

The Lord of the Rings films 228–9, 240–54, 257–67, 298–301

Love is the Devil (film) 330

Love's Labours (musical) 43–4, 291

Lowe, Frank (Victorian uncle) 17

lunacy 84–5

Lyceum Theatre, Edinburgh 208

Lyric, Hammersmith 43–4

Lyttelton Theatre, London 143, 212

Macbeth (play) 110–18

Macdonald, Marianne 207

MacDonald, William 100

McEnroe, John 143

'McKellen 18' 203

McKellen, Alice, 'Mother Mac' (née Murray) (grandmother) 15

McKellen, Denis Murray (father) 12–17

  career 24

  character 18–19

  death and funeral 59–61

  and IM 26, 185, 239

  and Mesnes Park 18, 23

  photos of 321

  theatre trips 30, 59

McKellen family 11–17, 19, 48

McKellen, Gladys (stepmother) 31–2, 48, 59–60, 160, 268–9

McKellen, Ian Murray

  acting at Cambridge 37–44

  'acting badly' 86–7

  activist 156–9, 177–80, 205, 209, 220, 271, 292, 293, 321, 332

  behaviour of fans 175

  birth 11, 15

  blue plaques 15

  book deal 8–9

  at Cambridge 5, 6, 32–3, 49

  character 97–8, 215–16

  childhood 13, 17, 20–3, 31

  childhood theatre visits 22, 28

  on children 270–1, 335

  'coming out' 135, 136, 156–9, 164–5, 177, 181–2, 335

  on 'community' 31

  'a day in the life of' (Doble)

66–8

debating societies 29–30, 43

documentaries on 18, 229

early films 70–1

education 20–1, 23, 25, 27

and father 26, 88–9, 185, 239

on *Hamlet* 88

head boy 27

on heterosexual marriage 183–4

homes 3–4, 12, 15, 17–18, 24, 65

honours 133, 175, 178, 202–4, 220, 229, 255, 333

illnesses 20, 295–6

and journalists 8–9, 22, 26, 167, 187, 207, 288, 293

legacy 333

marriage officiant 323

mother's death 25–6, 31, 70, 335

'Northernness' trait 18

nude appearances 276–9, 278–82

Oscar campaigns 224–6, 255, 264, 265–6, 292

'paradox' 334

pets 31

relationships 45, 48–9, 65, 81, 123–30, 134–6, 254–6

and religion 25–6, 208–9

in rep 49–52, 53–8, 226

school plays 28–9

screen tests 70

sexual drive 79–80

sexuality 21, 22, 28

Shakespeare passion 4, 33, 34, 71–2, 115, 148–51, 211

theatre awards 61, 116, 135, 140–1

vegetarian 5

Visiting Professor (Oxford) 181

wanting to be 'an actor' 28

website 289

and worthy causes 154–5, 331

McKellen, Jean (sister)

amateur actress 17, 28

childhood 12, 13

death 267–8, 337

and IM's sexuality 48

McKellen, Margery Lois (née Sutcliffe) (mother) 11–18, 21–3

'ghost of' 26–7

illness and death 24, 25, 237

photos of 321

McKellen, William Henry (grandfather) 14, 15

Mackintosh, Ian 76

McShane, Ian 69

McTeer, Janet 217

Major, John 202, 205–6

Manchester 160

Manchester Free Trade Hall 15

Manchester Opera House 22, 28

Mannion, Anne 128

Marathon Man (film) 4

Margaret (cousin) 321

Margaret, Princess 264

Marlowe, Christopher 77, 104

Marlowe Society, Cambridge 6, 35, 39

Marmion, Patrick 324

Marquand, Richard 77

Mason, James 242

Mason, Margery 93–4, 95, 96, 276
Masters, Anthony 127
Mathias, Sean 123–30, 134–6
  awards 305
  director 185, 216–17, 262, 296, 297
  The Grapes (pub) 256, 319–20
  and IM 155, 225, 266, 274–5, 283, 334
  influence on IM 153
  and Lebedev 316–17, 319
  No Man's Land 316, 318
  Waiting for Godot 303–7
Maupin, Armistead 155–6, 335
Mellor, Kenneth 96
Melly, George 158
Mendes, Sam 284, 337
Mesnes Park, Wigan 17–18, 21, 23
Middlemass, Frank 99–100
Miles, Christopher 165
Miles, Sarah 165, 169
Miller, Jonathan 163, 192
Milton, John 179
Minerva Theatre, Chichester 295, 321
Mirren, Helen 169, 262, 332
Mission: Impossible 2 (film) 241
Mitchison, Amanda 227–8
Molony, Damien 317
Montagu of Beaulieu, Edward, Lord 46
Moody, Bill 144
Moore, Harry T. 165
More Tales from the City (Maupin) 335–6
Morgan, Father Francis 238–9, 240
Morgan, Wendy 146
Morley, Sheridan 107
Mortensen, Viggo 242
Mr. Holmes (film) 320
Much Ado About Nothing (play) 61–2
Munby, Jonathan 324
Murdoch, Iris 95
music hall 30

Nathan, Ian 298
National Service 5, 14
National Theatre 141–8
  directors of 35
  and IM 61, 99, 100, 199
  Napoli Milionaria 205
National Youth Theatre 123
Neville, John 52, 54, 58, 74
New Labour 218–119
New Line Cinema 267, 299
New London Theatre 282
Newman, Cathy 292
Nightingale, Benedict
  on Acting Shakespeare 149
  on Coriolanus 145
  on IM 57, 106, 263
  on King Lear 283–4
  on Macbeth 113, 117, 173
  on Othello 175
  on Richard III 194, 197–8
  on Uncle Vanya 217
  on Waiting for Godot 305
No Man's Land (play) 306, 316–19
Noble, Adrian 112, 173–4
Nolte, Nick 224
Norton, Edward 225
Norton, Graham 292, 302

Novello, Ivor 21–2
Nunn, Jacob 173
Nunn, Trevor
  Barber on 277
  at Cambridge 37–8
  Hamlet 84
  and IM 52, 99, 124, 193–4, 271
  King Lear 272, 274, 277, 279, 324
  marriages 172
  Othello 171–5
  at RSC 102, 105–6, 108, 110–13, 115–17

Oasis 218–19
O'Brien, Edna 7
O'Connor, Garry
  actor 6, 77
  book subjects 7–8
  director 43
  education 27
  on Hall 137
  and IM 3–10, 150–1
  on IM 174, 330–1
  on *King Lear* 326
  on *Othello* 172–5
  on *'Tis Pity She's a Whore* (play) 96
Old Vic, London 147, 296
Olivier, Laurence
  character 190–1
  film roles 242
  Hall on 162
  and IM 28, 191–2, 213–14
  King Lear 273
  Macbeth 117
  memorial and legacy 189–90

  as Othello 62
  and playwrights 85
  Richard III 192, 211
  theatre roles 30, 54–5, 63, 137, 147
  Titus Andronicus 37
  weight-lifting 67
Olivier, Richard 128
Olivier, Tarquin 191, 198
Olivier Theatre, London 144
Orton, Joe 84–5
Orwell, George 13, 16, 18, 284
Othello (play) 171–5
Other Place (theatre), Stratford 111, 113, 116, 171, 173–4
O'Toole, Peter 88, 101, 112
Otway, Thomas 142
The Outsider (Wilson) 333
Owen, David 206–7, 329–30
Owen, Deborah 329–30
Owen, Michael 81

pacifism 13–14
Pacino, Al 212
Page, Anthony 127
Paisley, Ian 208
Paquin, Anna 229
Park Theatre, London 331
Parker, Sean 323
Parri, Stifyn 160
Parris, Matthew 162, 213, 253
Parry, Susan 30
Pearson, Allison 310
Peck, Bob 115
Pennington, Michael 142
People (Hill) 14, 29
Peter, John 98, 147

Petherbridge, Edward 91–3
and IM 146
on the part of Iago 171
and Stride 62
theatre roles 95, 108
'Tis Pity She's a Whore 97
Pettifer, Julian 5
Picart, Caroline 222
Pickup, Ronald 61, 304, 305, 306, 326
Pinter, Harold 164, 318
Pirsig, Robert M., Zen and the Art of Motorcycle Maintenance 180
Plater, Alan 165
Playing the Part (documentary) 229
Pleasance, Donald 170
Plowright, Joan 128, 190
Plummer, Christopher 240
Popov, Duško 260
Porter, Eric 217
Portillo, Michael 207
Powell, Colin 265
A Prayer for Wings (play) 128
Priest of Love (film) 165–6
The Promise (play) 69–70, 99
Prospect (touring company) 71, 75, 80, 112
Proud, Elizabeth 44
Prowse, Philip 146–7
'PS' (unfinished Shaffer play) 310–11
Pulleyne, Tim 167
Purves, Libby 288–9

Quayle, Anthony 190
Queen's Theatre, London 84

Quilley, Denis 112

Ramsay, Peggy 84, 85
Ravenhill, Mark 312
Raymond, Paul 128
Reagan, Ronald 200–1, 270
The Real Inspector Hound (play) 147
Redgrave, Corin 38
Redgrave, Michael 249
Redmond, Moira 93
Rees, Roger 306
Reid, Anne 314
Reid, Sheila 93
Relph, Simon 40, 291
repertory, provincial 49–52
The Return of the King (film) 264, 266
Rheon, Iwan 313
Rhys-Davies, John 261
Rich, Frank 200
Richard II (play) 71–4, 77
Richard III (film) 210–15
Richard III (play) 189–200, 202
Richardson, Ralph
Hall on 162
Macbeth 112
No Man's Land 316
Othello 54–5
quote from 332
Richard II 72
What the Butler Saw 84–5
Rigg, Diana 112
Roberts, Glenys 32–3, 37
Robertson, Toby 84
artistic director 71, 73, 75–7
Hamlet 86–90
on IM 162

and Jacobi 282
Robeson, Paul 172
Robinson, Tom 160
Romeo and Juliet (play) 106
Romijn, Rebecca 232
Rosencrantz and Guildenstern Are Dead (play) 92
Rowe-Beddoe, David 5
Royal Court Theatre, London 185
Royal Shakespeare Company (RSC) 35, 84, 97, 101, 102, 278
Ruling the Roost (play) 94, 97
Rushdie, Salman 250
Ryall, David 62
Rylance, Mark 151
Rylands, George 'Dadie' 35, 76, 77, 106

Sackur, Stephen 161
Scandal (film) 169–70
The Scarlet Pimpernel (TV) 126
A Scent of Flowers (play) 59–60
Scofield, Paul 138–141
    IM on 241
    King Lear 272
    memorial service 289–90
    posture 176
    writers and 85
Scott Thomas, Kristin 212
Scruton, Roger 335
The Seagull (play) 227–8, 271–2
Second World War 13–14, 21
Seldon, Anthony 205
Sexual Offences (Amendment) Acts 68, 182, 207
Seymour, Jane 126

Shaffer, Peter 65, 70, 79, 139–40, 310–11
Shah, Kiran 245
Shakers (play) 228
Shakespeare, William 32, 71, 106–7, 129
Sharkey, James 186
Sharrock, Thea 308
Shaw, George Bernard 110, 209
Shed 21, Wellington 259
Shepherd, Jack 93, 97
Sher, Antony
    Beside Myside 216
    'coming out' 161
    and Doran 117–18
    on IM 63, 192, 203–4
    on *Macbeth* 112
    Uncle Vanya 216–17
Sheridan, Richard Brinsley 147
Sherman, Martin 130, 134, 188
Shulman, Milton 128, 143
Simmons, Jean 28
Sinden, Donald 290
Singer, Bryan 221–3, 230, 231
Smith, Maggie 61, 67, 189, 212, 292
Society of Friends of Richard III 214
South Bank Show (ITV) 147, 166, 291
Spacey, Kevin 296
Spall, Timothy 108, 242
Speed, Doris 28
Spence, Christopher 154, 180
Spencer, Charles 279
Spiegel, Sam 164
Stephens, Robert 61

Stevens, Ronnie 93
Stevenson, Juliet 290
Stewart, Patrick
  marriages 323
  No Man's Land 316–18
  Richard III 212
  Waiting for Godot 294, 303–7
  X-Men 229, 231–3, 291–2
Stonewall movement 178, 182, 208, 209, 225, 271
Stoppard, Tom 92–3, 147
Streep, Meryl 212, 265
Stride, John 30, 61, 62
Stringer, Graham 160
Stubbs, Imogen 172, 173, 279
Suchet, David 170
Sutcliffe, Dorothy (aunt) 16
Sutcliffe, Grandpa 14, 16
Suzman, Janet 127, 166
Sweeting, Elizabeth 71
Swift, Clive 5, 37, 40–1, 43, 44
The Syndicate (play) 295

Tatchell, Peter 160, 177, 182, 209
Taylor, Brian (Brodie) 45, 48–9, 56–7, 65–6, 80, 81
Taylor, Doris 49
Taylor, Paul 317
Teale, Owen 317
Tennant, Anne 281
Thatcher, Margaret 133, 202
The Tomb of his Ancestor (BBC series) 70
theatre critics
  accolades 68
  American 199–200, 301–2
  on *Bent* 134

Critics' Circle 175
Daily Mirror 278
  on *Hamlet* 89
  Sunday Times 195, 305
  The Times 56, 62
Théâtre de l'Odéon, Paris 202
Theatre Royal Haymarket, London 84, 305–7
Third Ear (Radio 3) 157–9
The Three Arrows (play) 95–6, 99
Three Point Six studios, New Zealand 257
Tinker, Jack 127, 128
'Tis Pity She's a Whore (play) 80, 94–5, 96–7
Titus Andronicus 37
Tolkien, Christopher 267
Tolkien, Edith (née Bratt) 240, 251
Tolkien Estate 267
Tolkien, J. R. R. 209, 237–40, 248, 250–2, 298, 334
Tolkien, Mabel 238–9
Tolkien, Priscilla 267
Tolkien, Shakespeare, Others and You (one-man-show) 331
Too True to be Good (play) 110
Tordoff, John 93
Townsend, Stuart 242
Trewin, J. C. 89–90, 142
Trump, Donald 270
Turner, Bridget 50
Turner, Graham 178–9
Tusa, John 5, 41
The Two Towers (film) 246–7
Tydeman, John
  at Cambridge 5, 37
  director 51

on IM 73, 172, 219, 337
Tyler, Liv 241, 251, 254
Tynan, Kenneth 40, 88, 112, 137

Uncle Vanya (play) 192, 216, 311
The Uses of Literacy (Hoggart) 274
Ustinov, Peter 56

variety stage 30
Varne, Rosemary 175
Venice Preserv'd (play) 142
A Very English Scandal (BBC/Amazon) 288
Vicious (ITV) 184, 308, 312–15

Waiting for Godot (play) 294, 303–6
Walsh, John 314
Walter (TV film) 167–9
Walter and June (TV film) 169
Walters, Hugh 41
Wardle, Irving 25, 73, 76–7, 105, 143
Warner Bros 299–300
Warner, David 83
Warner, Deborah 193
Watson, Jesse 66
Watson, Sylvia 84
The Way of the World (play) 98
Webster, Paul 245
Weinstein, Harvey 264
Weldon, Duncan 127, 167, 306
Wellington Knitting Club 260
West, Timothy 75
West Yorkshire Playhouse, Leeds 226
Weston, David 272, 278, 280, 283
Whale, James (director) 223–4

Whalley, Joanne 170
What the Butler Saw (play) 84–5
White, Willard 171–3, 176
Whitelaw, William 207
Who Do You Think You Are? (BBC) 17, 240
Wigan Grammar School 20, 23
Wigan, Lancashire 15, 17–18, 20
Wigan Little Theatre 18, 332
Wigan Wesleyan school 20–1, 23
Wild Honey (play) 142–3, 148
Williams, Clifford 191
Williamson, Audrey 74
Willman, Noël 95
Wilson, Angus 162
Wilson, Colin, The Outsider 333
Winchester, Philip 280
Winner, Michael 139
The Winter's Tale (play) 108
Wise, Louis 321
Woddis, Carole 156
Wogan, Terry 159
Wolfit, Donald 87, 88, 290
Woo, John 241
The Wood Demon (play) 98, 99
Wood, Elijah 241, 246
Words, Words, Words (anthology) 148
Worsthorne, Peregrine 157–9
Worth, Irene 144
Wrede, Casper 190
Wymark, Patrick 86
Wyndham's Theatre, London 317
Wyngarde, Peter 65

X-Men films 228–233, 291–2

York, Michael 71
Young, B. A. 117
Young, Lailan 215–6
Young, Toby 301

Zeffirelli, Franco 61–2
*Zen and the Art of Motorcycle Mainte-
    nance* (Pirsig) 180